ANGEL PROMISES
REMEMBERING KAREN LEE

KATHERIN B. FITZPATRICK

ANGEL PROMISES

REMEMBERING KAREN LEE

KATHERIN B.
FITZPATRICK

© 2010 by Katherin B. FitzPatrick All rights reserved.

2nd Printing 2014.

Trusted Books is an imprint of Deep River Books. The views expressed or implied in this work are those of the author. To learn more about Deep River Books, go online to www.DeepRiverBooks.com.

No part of this publication may be reproduced, stored in a retrieval system or transmitted in any way by any means—electronic, mechanical, photocopy, recording or otherwise—without the prior permission of the Publisher, except as provided by USA copyright law.

Unless otherwise noted, all Scriptures are taken from the King James Version of the Bible.

Scripture references marked AMPLIFIED BIBLE TRANSLATION are taken from the Amplified(r) Bible,
Copyright © 1954, 1958, 1962, 1964, 1965, 1987 by The Lockman Foundation—Used by permission.

Scripture references marked LIVING BIBLE TRANSLATION are taken from The Living Bible, © 1971 owned by assignment by Illinois Regional Bank N.A. (as trustee).
Used by permission of Tyndale House Publishers, Inc., Wheaton, Illinois 60189. All rights reserved.

Soft Cover:
ISBN 13: 978-1-63269-174-3

Library of Congress Catalog Card Number: 2007901121

DEDICATION

Dedicated to the memory of Karen Lee FitzPatrick 1982-2001. Karen died while fighting the Thirtymile Fire with her twenty-one man crew from the U.S. Forest Service on July 10, 2001, near Winthrop, Washington. At that time, Karen Lee was believed to be the youngest female career firefighter ever killed in the line of duty in America.

Karen was full of smiles, laughter, and was an inspiration to all who knew her. She grew up hearing many of the poems that I, her mother had written when I was young. Karen went on to write poems herself during her junior and senior years in high school.

Also included are poems and expressions sent to us in remembrance of Karen and the three firefighter comrades who died next to her.

Anyone who is interested may continue to read about Karen Lee FitzPatrick at the Fallen Firefighters of America website: www.lastalarm.net. This website lists Karen and the others who died at the Thirtymile Fire by date (7-10-01) and WA Cascades, as well as "Warmly Remembered." Also updated general information can be seen at: http://www.karenleefitzpatrick.com/

Karen Lee FitzPatrick

From little child...

To a youth with great achievements,

To a dynamic young woman of God

At only 18 years old…who inspired many.

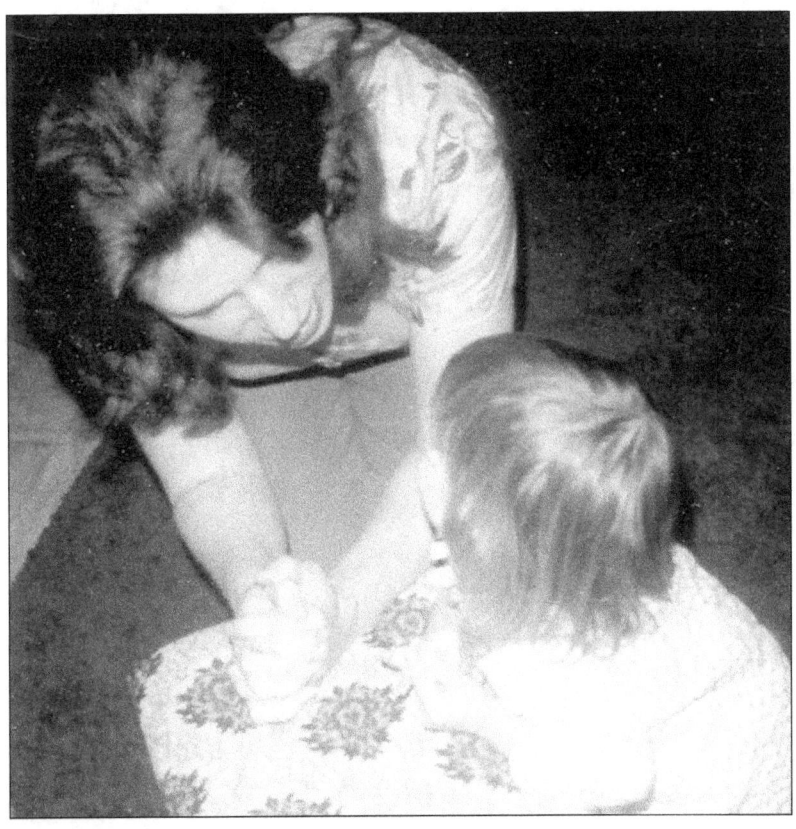

It was a great privilege to know you!

Love, Mom

LETTER FROM THE PRESIDENT

THE WHITE HOUSE
WASHINGTON

July 18, 2001

Mr. and Mrs. John FitzPatrick
7903 Poplar View Way
Yakima, Washington 98908

Dear Kathie and John:

Laura and I were greatly saddened to learn about the loss of Karen. We know your hearts must ache.

Those who willingly risk their lives to ensure the safety of our communities are true heroes. As you reflect on Karen's life and accomplishments, I hope you are comforted knowing that Karen's devotion to duty will long be remembered.

Laura and I send our heartfelt sympathy. We hope your sorrow will be eased by the love of your family and friends.

God bless you.

Sincerely,

George W. Bush

Table of Contents

COME LOOK AT BABY KAREN	XV
ANGEL PROMISES	XVII
Open the Door...	XX
INTRODUCTION	XXI
DROPS OF KISSES	1
Aaron: An Inspiration	5
After Sunday...	10
After Sunday	13
Passing	19
Crimson Lips	21
February Full Moon on Friday Night	25
The Wanted Companion	32
Basketball Games Not the Same	35
More than Just Espresso	37
The Need Inside	41
LILIES GROW IN DIFFICULT PLACES	43
An Essay by Karen Lee FitzPatrick...	43
KAREN'S CHRISTMAS TEA	51
Karen's Christmas Tea	52
Song for Karen	57
KAREN LEE'S 18TH BIRTHDAY	61
KATHIE'S YOUTH POEM COLLECTION	63
Gentle Sweet Secret	63
Experiences of Life	65
Willow Tree	66
White Candle...	67
Darkened Veil	68
Through Children's Eyes	69
I Am Small	70
A Song	71
Old Friend	72
Tears...	72
A Child and a Kitten	73
My Child	74
Youth	74
Young Dreams	75
My Eyes	76
Oh, Christmas Tree	76
The Humble Spider	78
Help Him Across	80
The Saga of Virgil and Nathan	81
Walls of Silence...	84
Trust	85
Home Fire	86
Old House	87

Love Is…	88
Even a Rose	90
Only Love Can	91
Dreams…	91
It's Christmas…	92
Interpretation of Colors:	93
To Be Cherished	95
On Happiness	95
Freedom	96
Solitude	97
Truth	97
Wealth	98
The Butterfly	98
Flower Story	101
The Green, Green Sea	103
Attitude	105
Rocking Chair	105
Innocence	106
Men Who Love	107
Material Gain	108
Life	108
Nap in the Park	109
Nelly the Bell	111
The Blind Duck	113
Unity…One Heart	115
A Wise Proverb	116
One Tiny Raindrop	116
The Little Grey Mouse	117
Wisdom	119
Four Clay Jugs	120
Leadership…	122
Outward Appearance	122
Strength	123
Weakness	123
Questions	124
Children	124
Children	125
Every Child	126
A Friend	126
Future	128
Prayer of life	129
Touch	130
Friendship	131
The Mind	132
Peace	132
Spirituality	133
Eternity	133
Coming Out	134
Never Again So Close	136
"Never Again So Close"	137
I Caught a Glimpse of Karen One Day	139
Message of the Sea	141

SISTERS: A PHOTO ALBUM ... 143
- Christmas Time, 1999 ... 148
- There Is Another Sister ... 149
- Sisters Forever ... 150

KAREN, THE BEAR CHASER ... 151

"SHERMIE" ... 155

ANGEL STUFF ... 159
- Karen's Angel Blanket ... 160
- The Guardian Angel Thing ... 162
- Window of Destiny ... 164
- Thoughts from Paula Hagemeyer ... 165

THE SIGN IN THE CLOUD ... 169
- The Thirtymile Fire Cloud ... 169
- The Sign in the Cloud...Karen's Legacy ... 171
- The Firefighter Boots ... 174
- She Knew ... 177

COPING WITH GRIEF ... 179
- The Mysterious Angel ... 180
- Thinking About Psalms 91 ... 183
- "Surrounded by Swirling Flames" ... 184
- "Ye are the light of the world..." ... 186
- The Rose, the Rose, the ROSE ... 188
- The Roses on the Walk ... 189
- The Rose Beyond the Wall ... 190
- The White Padded Mailer with the Single Red Rose on It ... 192
- It Was Her Appointed Time. She Knew It, but It Was OK ... 193
- Going Home ... 195

THE THIRTYMILE FIRESTORM ... 197
- Conversation with Matt Rutman ... 197
- The Forces Gather ... 199
- Firetraining—June 2001 ... 202
- "For two years Karen FitzPatrick has been waiting to fight fires..." ... 203
- Images from the Fire ... 204
- Obituary: Karen L. FitzPatrick ... 211

HEROES REMEMBERED ... 215
- Some of the Monuments ... 215
- The National Memorial Site in Winthrop, WA ... 218
- The Monument at the Naches Ranger Station ... 219
- Karen's Bronze Face at Night ... 225
- The Four in the Okanogan ... 230
- A Beautiful Expression ... 234
- August 1997: Winthrop, Washington... the Only Other Time Karen Had Been There ... 246

THE "ESSENCE OF KAREN" ... 251

JUST HEARTWARMING ... 253
- Karen Loved a Dog Named Cici ... 253
- The Parades ... 257
- Karen: The Hairstyles ... 261
- Striking a Pose for the Camera ... 263
- Mother's Days and Birthdays; Never Again Quite the Same ... 266
- The Red Dresses ... 268
- Karen: "The Athletic One" ... 269

The Coat	*273*
Watch Out World! It's Photography Class	*274*

ASSORTED POEMS, LETTERS, AND MEMORIES 279
The Day the Angels Cried 281
To the Parents of Fallen Firefighters 284
Goodbye to My Childhood Friend and Cousin, 7/11/01 286
A Letter from the Gottlieb's, ... 289
Karen Lee FitzPatrick 293
To All Parents 298
From Karen and Jessica's English Teacher, Dan Peters 299
Memories and Letters 301
Karen Lee… 302
Karen: In the Clouds? 303

KAREN STREET—HER AMAZING ROOM 305
Karen Street 306
Her Walls Speak 309
A Favorite Poster of Karen's, "Faith Is." 313

WARMLY REMEMBERED 317
You're Invited to Visit the Fallen Firefighter's of America Website: www.lastalarm.net 317
Lastalarm.net: Karen L. Fitzpatrick Recent Postings: 318

LETTERS 333

MORE ABOUT KAREN 339
Notes from J.I.V.E—"Jesus Is Very Important in Everything!" 339
Is The Worst Thing that Can Happen to You to Die? 341
The Last Prom, the Last Flame. 343
Graduation Night, June 8, 2001 353
Senior Wills 356
Getting Smacked Hard with a Strong Sense of Destiny 357
I Wish I Had Known Karen Better 359
A Few More Comments from Karen 359
Karen's Thoughts on the Death Penalty: A High School Assignment. 361
Karen's Comments on Health: A Homework Assignment 364
Three Things in a Brown Bag Speech 369
Karen FitzPatrick: "Why I Want to Be a Firefighter" 371

KAREN'S JOURNAL NOTES 375
Letters from and to Amber… 396
Nearing the Time of the Fire… 400

ABOUT THE AUTHOR 403

COME LOOK AT BABY KAREN

"Girls! Yvonne, Jaina...come look at Baby Karen," I said, calling out in a quiet whisper, as she was sleeping in her crib. The girls joined me, peering up over the rim of her crib with childhood curiosity. Older sister Yvonne picked up Jaina, only four, for a peek. Karilee (her baby name) had her pink angel blanket wrapped about her with other baby blankets underneath.

"Look at her eyeballs," I said. Karen was only a few days old. The curve of her eye and cornea stood out slightly under her closed eyelids as they darted about quickly, as if she was watching activities in her sleep. Then Karilee smiled and *laughed*, as if she was amidst delightful experiences.

"She's dreaming," Yvonne, who was eight, whispered. Jaina, looking on, just busted out in a little smile and a snicker as they watched, peering over the rim of her crib. We watched her for a while. It was an unusual phenomena. "OK, girls, let's have you play downstairs right now, OK?" Baby Karen adventured on in dreamland.

Later, when I took Karen in for her two week check-up, I mentioned it to our doctor. "Impossible," was his response. "She has no memory bank, no experiences have yet been recorded in the brain. Must be gas."

Gas? I speculated and dreamed further. How was this baby seeing visions of the future? "Is she hearing 'Angel Promises' whispered in her ear?" I asked her curious sisters. Yvonne and Jaina just giggled at the thought. They decided they liked that explanation best. I decided I did too.

ANGEL PROMISES

*By Katherin Blackwood
FitzPatrick
(A poem written about Karen Lee
when she was a few days old.)*

Little new baby resting sweetly…
She is calm and at rest so
Completely,
Not knowing about
Danger, wars
Or evil,
Famine, greed or nasty people.
The world is a brand new place,
A blank page in which to trace
A brand new life.
Her little head rests upon my
Shoulder,
So soft and warm.
Her face reflects a smile
From some far off distant place.
I wonder, pausing for a while,
Where comes this smile
Upon a face only a few days old?
It cannot be…
I am told.

ANGEL PROMISES

But her sleeping eyes move
As if in a dream.
It seems as if she's hearing
Angel Promises,
And watching all the good times
She will have one day,
Running through green fields,
Gathering flowers,
Merry-go-round rides and
Fun by the hours,
Building sand castles at the beach,
Growing tall and learning to reach
For her place in the sun.
Do they tell her she's the one
We'll always love?
Those voices from above,
When they whisper
Angel Promises
In her ear?

July 10, 2001: Karen Lee FitzPatrick is a vibrant and alive young woman of 18, excited about life and the future.

July 11, 2001: The American flag flies over the nation's capitol at half-mast to mourn her death, along with three of her firefighter comrades, at 5:30 P.M. on July 10 at the Thirtymile Fire. The American flag was flown over the nation's capitol consecutively each day in memory of each of the young fallen firefighters the week following the tragedy.

Karen FitzPatrick, June 2001, the Rookie Firefighter, Courtesy of KAPP-TV, Yakima, WA. Karen walked through a regional TV news story describing the graduation of the newest USFS rookie firefighters. "Three fires were lit on purpose by the Forest Service up at Gold Creek on Highway 410. Then we had to go put them out. It was our final test," Karen told them.

Open the Door…

View the heart of a young
Woman who knew God intimately…
Yet she had an internal time clock,
And she also knew
She would not live far past
Her teen years.

INTRODUCTION

By Katherin B. FitzPatrick

If you have ever had doubts about whether God is real and, if He is, whether or not He leaves signposts along the way in the normal events of life for us to recognize and learn from; or further yet, is destiny—future events only completely known by God alone—somehow mysteriously already cast in stone? Is there something called "divine providence," and is it real?

For answers, I invite you to walk into the heart and life of Karen Lee FitzPatrick, who, at the age of only 18, was the youngest of four firefighters to perish while fighting the infamous Thirtymile Fire on July 10, 2001, in the Chewuch River Canyon near the small mountain town of Winthrop, Washington, only a few miles from the Canadian border in the North Cascades. There you will see the results of a bright, living example of Christ vibrantly alive in a close relationship with human life as He intended and as it was described by Jesus in John 14-15. I call these "the relationship chapters." There, in the words of Jesus, He tells each of us how to have a personal relationship with Him right now that will be strong enough for us to walk through every trial and difficulty in this life, then last forever in the next. In Psalms 66:10, the Bible says God will refine us with fire, or "You purifieth us with fire," much as a silversmith or goldsmith refines the precious metal. It is said that the goldsmith continues to lift impurities off the liquid, heated gold until he can see his own reflection in it. This is what God desires to do with each human life.

Everyone who knew Karen Lee also knew she had a rare "God connection," and that she had the ability to be both a spiritual inspiration and fountain of life to others. She was wise far beyond her years, and her friends included not just teen peers but many adults as well. Her life was well lived in an exemplary way on every level, and her death was no accident in the scheme of time on earth. She met with an appointed time as described in the Bible in passages such as Hebrews 9:27 and Ecclesiastes 3:2.

We live on a planet that is torn by war, tension, and natural disasters and in a society of individuals who are often determined to do things in life their own way, without God. But life is often harsh, and our hearts are often shipwrecked as we continue to proudly build our handmade rafts of sticks and twine that we are determined to sail the seas of life with, only to discover we were not prepared to face the huge waves and tsunamis of real life. Only God can prepare us and strengthen us His way and in His time. In God's divine, extravagant love, He wants to give us an ocean liner! How can we refuse?

I suppose the argument for the reality of the existence of God and His desire to interact lovingly with us throughout this earthly life and then carry us on to continue that relationship forever in the next will be a debate that will continue until the end of time as we know it. Curiously enough, once one meets up with the living Christ, that experience suddenly clears up all doubts and all issues, much like Saul of Tarsus on the Damascus road. But how do most of us arrive there? Jeremiah 29:13 says, "If you seek me diligently with your whole heart, you will find me." This is truly God's address. Karen did seek diligently, and she did find Him. She then deposited those living seeds into many around her whom she knew and loved. Probably most remarkable of all, after her passing, we have watched those living seeds flourish and bring many into the knowledge of God in a deep and living way, even though Karen no longer walks this life. In that sense, Karen Lee FitzPatrick does indeed live on, both here and forever!

Drops of Kisses

A Poem Collection by Karen Lee FitzPatrick

Welcome to Karen's private teen world! This is Karen's poetry from her junior and senior years of high school at West Valley High School in Yakima, Washington.

"These are poems I experienced," she said. Karen was very fond of her English teacher, Dan Peters, and wrote in the front of her poetry collection, "Thanks for direction, Peters."

Karen poured her life out to others, to music, and to her writings. Many of the teens in her high school already knew about "Karen's 'heart-attack' poems." Her poems deeply expressed who she was inside. Here they are:

When one door
Of happiness closes,
Another opens,
But so often we look so long
At the closed door
That we do not see
The one which has been
Opened for us.

—Helen Keller

DROPS OF KISSES

DEDICATED TO MY FAMILY AND CLOSEST FRIENDS:
JESSICA, LACY, JENNIFER, HEATHER, AND AARON:

"A friend can tell you things you
don't want to tell yourself."

—FRANCES WARD WELLER

> "Crimson was the dress I wore…
> Crimson was my lipstick…
> Crimson was the break in my heart…"
>
> —Drops of Kisses poem collection by KLF

Aaron: An Inspiration

The Band is called to attention
But that doesn't stop my eyes
From glancing to the side
Only to study his divine appearance
Standing a few inches taller
His back slightly arched
Shoulders back
His eyes a bit higher than the horizon
Horn to the press box—
A statue of pride and glory
Has taken the form of my friend
For only what is a brief moment
His concentration, pride and benevolence
Shine forth rays that only I seem to admire.

Recalling back in time
The first day I saw him
I knew there was something especially different
But what?
Little did I know how well we would mesh
Would he even notice that?
Only time will tell of it.

I remember that day as many others:
The afternoon was hot
And the band room filled with new faces.

Ah, our fellow "Freshmeat"
Then, Mr. Walter, with the drum majors
Lined us up to only begin learning the halftime show
This takes time, devotion and cooperation.

As I prepare to deal with
The same old thing as every year
I notice a positive presence near.
I look up to take my chair in the trumpet section
Then, I see him sitting next to my place
Which belongs next to him.
From then on I found myself
Secretly studying his every move.
His unique individuality in character stood out
Discipline, commitment and total respect of authority.
Little by little I appear into his life.
To what extent? I cannot tell
But only as a trumpet player
Standing next to him in the show
Not nearly as good a player as he though
But he is forgiving.
Figuring positions with him
From move to move
I enjoy the company of his instruction
And look forward to the season
A season of sweet memories
With this new friend I've found.

Weeks passed speedily as do the days
Yet I felt as though
The trimester of band was prolonged.
"Hey Aaron, wait up man!"
He's out the door
Immediately following commands
While others linger about in the room.
Through the parking lot we walk
The morning early
The air is chilling
My heart is racing.

His friends call him Jamo.
They say he lacks people skills
But I sure don't think so
Just needs a little more experience, that's all.
Nothing seems to get him down
Even when he is surprisingly lost
In drum major tryouts
He took it as a Stotan
And in his heart, as God's will
I spent the day with him at Cavalcade
And the band scores were not
High enough to place.
Disappointed as I was,
I got down on my personal performance
Without resistance, he shared with me
His positive views which seemed

To neutralize with my naturally negative thoughts.
Before long, he had me feeling more confident
In our performance as a whole

I talked with him about many things;
Many mornings on the way
through the parking lot
Down to the football field
I would catch myself at times
Looking at everything we talked about
Through the eyes of an admirer,
Trying to contemplate the future perhaps
But I know he had no inclination of my observations.

I do not know, and appreciate,
The way he looks at me among others.
Not as most guys do with only one thing in mind,
But in purity, innocence and respect.
His heart has never been broken
By what we call love,
But has been reserved for a truer purpose.
A rare find I have found
A friend who sees the best there is in me
Without the eyes of a normal man
But through the eyes only given by God.

Drops of Kisses

Left: Karen, shown here as drum major for the West Valley Panther Marching Band in the ninth grade, 1998. Here she is leading the band at the annual Apple Blossom Parade in Wenachee. Her band received one of the top awards.

Right: Karen, getting ready to leave and go out on one of the many parades with her friend Aaron and other classmates from the high school marching band. Karen was also a drum major for the West Valley Junior High Panther Band, and led many parades, including the yearly Apple Blossom Parade in Wenatchee, WA.

After Sunday...

Today is my Lord's day.
When I wake up,
I see the sun shining brighter
Than other days.

I've learned through the years
To keep this day holy,
And set apart for the Lord.

To be free from cares
And distresses from
The week before

To teach me to set apart more of
A place in my life for Him.
Then do I come to hear what I need

And before, I prepare my heart
For the Word of the Lord to enter in soon
Soon? Perhaps in God's timing…

After Sunday

By Karen Lee FitzPatrick

Today is my Lord's day,
When I wake up
I see the sun shining brighter
Than on other days
I've learned through the years,
To keep this day holy
And set apart for the Lord
To be free from cares
And distresses from the week before—
To teach me to set apart more of Him.
Then do I come to hear what I need
And before, I prepare my heart
For the Word of the Lord to enter in soon.
Soon? Perhaps in God's timing
Not mine, but to trust
Is what I'm learning to do.

To a warehouse I go to
Meet with my godly family.
We share the day together
And pray for each other's needs
According to God's Word that was given.
I sit and listen to the Words
Of Life from the Bible.
My heart is cut and

The Words go in deep.
They do their job if
Only I'll do mine.
This is when I pray to my
Savior for strength He
Promised to furnish me—.
Since he sees my every
Thought and motive,
What can I hide from Him
Whose eyes flame like fire?
Yes, he sees it all—
The more the Word
Exposes my life,
The more I see the truth about me.

"Oh Lord, please save me
From myself I pray,
And what the world expects me to be!
Let your will be mine and give me
A heart to run in your ways."
I must trust in what I pray—
For it's only biblical.
After morning service
I sit and contemplate the Words
That earlier penetrate—
While sitting to eat lunch
With the others.

They speak of encouraging things
From living, experiencing,
God's Words and commands

Tom speaks of our lesson
Even while we eat,
Just for us to interact or
Contribute to what's being preached.
The afternoon service includes communion.
In remembering the death
And resurrection of our Lord Jesus Christ
Tears enter our eyes for the
Love He showed at Calvary
Such love constrains me to give my all
And follow His call.

My thoughts race as I contemplate on the
Words that contain the power to save my soul.
My life is no match for the Word of God
That cuts me to shreds—
But only that I might be healed.
I don't obey all that I hear
Nor do I live according to what I ought.
My heart is distressed only
To be lifted by His love
To walk in the light that I have been given
Then shall more be added.

The prayer chair is up.
Anyone who has a need
They want us all to agree on in prayer
They just tell us.
Aleishia sits and asks for prayer
In her marriage—
Her husband isn't a Christian
And he lacks giving her the affection.
Kathy sits next after we pray for Aleishia.
Holding the tissue box,
She cries over the lost condition
Of her family…
We pray for God to draw
Their hearts to himself to be saved.

Many concerns are mentioned;
Tears are shed;
Lives are changed little by little
Every time we meet.
God works in hearts
And minds of those to will to do
What so few Christians actually attain:
A personal relationship with the Savior.
The world would be drawn to—
Out of their dark lives racked in misery
And emptiness as a result of
Sin we were born with
Into Life Eternal.

Jesus came to bring us
Piercing Words; once again
Intrude the darkest parts of my heart
When hearing of the empowerment
The apostles received from God in Acts.
We study what the Bible says about
Receiving the Holy Spirit.
How can the Christian live
The life without the Lifegiver?
For what is flesh is flesh
And what is spirit is spirit.
I hear of Saul martyring Christians
Then God chooses him,
And gives him the Spirit;
His name changes to Paul
Then goes to the temple
And proclaims Jesus as the Christ.
Now look at who's being
Sought to be martyred
Boy, how God works.
When seeing powerful stories
God gave us about the first Christians
I see how far we've strayed from relying
On God to give us life to live the life
We're called to live

He said He'll give us His spirit as a helper,
Advocate, and comforter in life's trials.
I kneel to pray in my room
By my bed—
The day is done
Where is my heart and life
In all of what I've heard.
Honest before Him who
Will grant my petitions
Only to receive mercy to
Overcome judgment.

"Glorify your power through
My weakness,
Fill me with yourself so I won't
Fill my need with foolishness.
Then I would be miserable like the rest.
Keep me from the things I shouldn't do
And soften my heart to know the difference.
Thank you for listening and giving
Me a chance to change
And eventually inherit Eternal Life
In Jesus Name, Amen."

PASSING

By Karen Lee FitzPatrick

Lately I have become accustomed to
Waking up exhausted
Going to bed exhausted
And every other day is Sunday
As I ask myself—
"Wasn't I just here?"
And the week passes as five minutes.

Precious time rushes by

And now, each day I drive
I look for resolutions to my problems
To only find that prayer is a main reliance
And to trust in my convictions
Hold faith firm.

I hopefully wait upon the Lord

And then I will know what is true in me
As I live to obey His Words
And pray for my weaknesses.
There can be new energy brought
And hope for each new morning
As I spend what moments I have left…

Angel Promises

Karen, in the crimson dress she spoke of in her poem on the same night, minutes before she met her prom date in the "White Room." To the left, on the chandelier, is hanging her favorite ornament, an angel in a white netted gown. One year she took it off the Christmas tree and hung it there so she could look at it year round. It's still there.

CRIMSON LIPS

By Karen Lee FitzPatrick

Crimson was the dress I wore;
Crimson was my lipstick;
Crimson was the break in my heart

You appeared as tall, handsome,
Easygoing yet sincere
A guy I hardly knew to recognize
But certainly you were not far from
Entering my world.
Unexpectedly you came
And decided to show the feelings
You had for me.
The secret touch of your hand in mine
Changed my world that day
But was that the best you could've done.
Now, recalling back the situation
It had been set up to fail from the beginning.

Our start together was awkward.
How you entered my heart
Was through my most personal door.
I tried to receive you more as
A guy-friend
And not as an intruder.
This was a battle I fought inside.

Homecoming, two weeks away
Go ahead, ask me;
I'm surprised you had the guts to do it
At lunch when all my friends already knew.
Excited as I was,
I was scared of the unknown in you;
I felt you didn't belong in my world
Not now and maybe never—.
The battle continued…
That night took forever to come
And would so quickly slip by
And yes, the night I couldn't forget
Maybe, even if I tried.

You were my first date to a dance.
The night was nearly at nine.
After dinner at the Black Angus
The fairgrounds held the dance
"Secret Garden."
On entering through the golden gates
You held me close on your arm.
I felt so proud to walk by your side
Greeting friends with surprised faces
Dancing, dancing, dancing
At times with you, slow and close.
How could I forget the smell of your cologne?

Drops of Kisses

As the song "Lady in Red" plays
I believe you felt that song down deep
"Lady in Red" dancing with me…
I hardly know, this beauty by my side
And I won't forget, "the way you looked tonight."
Lights faded and the music dimmed
As we finished dancing to that last song
My dream was almost over.

After watching a movie
At a house full of friends
The clock struck three—
It had been Sunday for three hours.
We left along with the other couples
Saying "Goodbye,
It was fun, and I'll see you Monday."

Before long you were parked
At the bottom of my driveway
Helping me out of your red truck.
You inquired of my still crimson lips
As you took me for a long, sweet kiss.
I hadn't felt that way in years
My heart sank within
Knowing that when this kiss ends
And the night is over

Everything will go back to the way it was
To before, where you would exit out
My heart's door
Because nothing would become of us.
The attraction to crimson lips
Was only a mere game.

This is a photo of her window sill with photos including her with the boy the night of the prom. Cont. same photo: [Karen's room: window prom portraits, center Karen in crimson dress with her date...the photo is fuzzy on purpose to cover the identity of the boy]

February Full Moon on Friday Night

By Karen Lee FitzPatrick

The victory over Sunnyside
Was won that night,
As West Valley cheered
Friends hugged, jumped
And laughed in pride and happiness.
The game was over,
Yet the night was still young.

What will it be?
Will we go to Red Robin,
Or possibly a friend's house?
"Follow Me!" a friend yells,
"Yeah, party at Jenn's"
I yell back.

Seven friends make
Their way into three cars,
Following a baby blue Beamer
As we speed out of the parking lot
Down Zier and straight west
Out to county roads.

Only two cars arrive at
The familiar house.
On approaching the front door

We were greeted by
Her excited yet scared dogs.
As I stood looking down
At the wet cement.
"He likes you, Karen."
Said a tall, handsome friend.
The others stood laughing
As we started through the door.

Photos of junior high memories
In a scrapbook
We're being remembered by each
As we all waited for the third
Car to arrive with the ice cream.
Bright headlights shine through
Her bedroom window.
"They're here with the ice cream!"
One said as we all
Go out to the kitchen
Where we joined the others who had arrived.

Gathering glass Sunday ice cream cups
And spoons, we exited outside
Into the full clear moonlight
And into the cold; frigid air
Could be felt as we went through a gate
And into the pool house.

Drops of Kisses

Blankets were shared among
The two couches, and ice cream
Was distributed as I got pursued
To the ground by a pro-wrestler
Which I turned into a tickle fight.
Since I don't know how
to defend myself or wrestle,
The lights were turned out
As we situate to watch
The movie, *Odd Couple II*.
I lay on the floor in front of Jenn.
One couch has only one person lying on it.
While the other has four—
The Tall, handsome, sincere friend,
Next to a new JV star,
On the girl's varsity,
Sharing a blanket with the soon to be
Drum major,
Which can't seem to sit so comfortably
Next to the pro-wrestler.

We're all cozy while we watch
The hilarious movie about two
Opposite best friends
Having the worst day of their lives.

Yet I notice something familiar
Happening between the first two,
Mentioned on the couch.
Small attractions turn into
The wrong start of a relationship.
"Like back in the days of Homecoming,"
I thought to myself.

One o'clock Saturday morning
We stroll out and get into our cars.
I'm taking home the future drum major,
And dropping by my tall handsome yet sincere friend
At the high school to get his truck
Because it's running low on gas.
Finally, I'm on my way home
Which happens to be on his way home.
I approach the final left turn off his way,
When I notice his truck parked on the street
To the right as I turn around
To see if I can help.
"Thanks for stopping," he says,
"But I'll call for my parents with the cell phone
And they'll bring some gas to fill up my truck
Since I only live a few minutes away."
"All right," I reply.
I get in my car and drive up Lincoln
When I realize—
I must go back and talk to him.

Drops of Kisses

I park along the curb
In front of his truck
And got out of my car
As he did the same.
Intuition from hurtful mistakes
Made in the past
Flooded my mind.
"I won't allow that past
To repeat itself to one
Of my friends—
I took a deep breath
And hoped for the best

His face looked different
Under the moonlight as
I approached him
He chilled wearing a T-shirt
In the frigid night air
As we both stood beneath
A street light.
"Look, your truck didn't
Run out of gas for no reason.
I need to talk to you about something.
You were getting close to her on
The couch tonight, weren't you?"
"Yes, I was," he said.
"Do you intend to do something
With what you've started with her?"

He paused, "Actually, I do"
"I'm just recalling back to Homecoming
For a moment, I know it was just one night and we—
"We got caught up in the moment,"
He interrupted, "Yes." I agreed,
Then went on, "I wondered if it was
Just going to stop there and it did
And I was hurt.
But it was best that way.
Don't get me wrong…I just don't want
To see my friend get hurt by you getting
Close, only to leave."
I paused to look at him in his shadowed eyes—
"We're all becoming such good friends,
I don't want to see anyone get hurt
By something as little as this.
You understand, right?"
"Yes, of course," he said, smiling.
I was glad to see that.

Aiming to leave before
His parents arrived,
I said goodbye and headed out
As I turned up my road
His parents turned down onto his

I felt good.
I said what I needed to say.

Drops of Kisses

The Wanted Companion

By Karen L. FitzPatrick

A girl he thinks so highly of
Simply breaks his heart
By deliberately leaving.
He pouts and sulks
Until he catches another's attention
Then, cheerfully like a child
She plays games on him
As he slowly reserves his past hurts
Only to temporarily appear happy
When inside his heart he only feels
The hole growing deeper
While a close friend
Watches and waits
At a distance
To lend a helping hand,

Watching, wondering, waiting,
Watching
Will he ever be mine?
I pray God will send him into my life
For some purpose
But only if it's for the better.
These thoughts predominate in my head
When talking to a friend who shares
With me the same feelings I have

Drops of Kisses

For my special friend
I move on by thinking—
"We'll see whom he eventually chooses."
But for now
I just enjoy our friendship—
Something she doesn't have.
Watching over the earth like a hawk
Sinful hearts are many
And righteous devotion was lacking—
Men, created to be God's friends
Until pride crept in as sly as a snake
To ruin God's plan number one.
Life continued on between God and man.
Sin, being the gulf separating the two,
Was only covered by the
Blood of sacrificed lambs and goats
In an annual ceremony done by priests.
God longed to be closer to his people
And set them free from mere traditions.
Jesus was the Christ sent as God's Son
To die as the ultimate sacrifice
Taking away the sin of those who would believe.
Rising from the dead
He led a train of vanquished foes
Signifying his victory over Satan's powers.

Now, then and always
God has planted eternity
In men's hearts and minds
Which nothing under the sun
But God alone can satisfy.
Without God,
What do you do with that place in your heart?
Do you really need him or her?
The question lies within the deepest layer
As the soul's most desperate, craving need—
The satisfaction of God's love.

If anything,
There's a place in God's heart for His people
When He tells them as their Creator and Redeemer
"Fear not, I have ransomed you
By paying a price instead of leaving you captive—
I have called you by my name,
And you are Mine."

BASKETBALL GAMES NOT THE SAME

By Karen Lee FitzPatrick

Your absence has
Made a difference—
Without your comments
Of observations to me,
I don't see or feel
The game the same way…

Four hours sitting
On the inside of a bus seat
Listen to our old
Classic '80s favorites
Through tiny speakers
Duck taped to the seat edges.

Breathless tunnels
Interrupt deep conversations
While hunched down in the seat
To hear a whisper.

Our first basketball game at State
Was that night at Mercer in Seattle
To play the undefeated Bellevue.
We arrived and set up the band
Behind the hoop right off the court.
The action was just feet away.

The band cheered louder than the crowd.
I turned to my side
To expect you to be there
Plugging your ears sarcastically
As we girls scream for "Ram" victory
But beside me sat an empty chair
I swore was yours
The place where you always sit
During a game—
Next to me.

You sit there and talk to me
When you're frustrated at the game
And I could swear in your mind
You're out there playing with the team
And subconsciously talking
To them out loud
Then to me saying,
"Oh man! Why'd they pass it there!
She was open right by the basket
"Do ya see what I mean?"
"Oh yes," I reply
"Are you talking to me?"
Jeremy asks after
Returning to his seat—
"Ah no, I was just talking to myself"
I replay as he turns back
To watch the game.

Talking to myself,
"I wish you were here"
You belong here.

More than Just Espresso

By Karen Lee FitzPatrick

Sliding the window open
I greet the customer with a smile.
"Hi, what could I get for you?"
Was the question I began
Asking many people back in May.
"Let's make it a 16-oz, sugar free
Iced nonfat vanilla latte
Two straws please!"
Yikes! Where's a pen and paper.
The phone rings as I answer,
"Valerie's Espresso"
It's Leslie just checking on
How business has been.
"Fast in the mornings
Slow in the afternoon," I say.
"Get low on anything
Just write it on the board."

More shot glasses to wash
Refill the steamers with milk
Punch cards to be found
In an overstuffed Rolodex
Cash register tape falls off again
Steam rises from the hot espresso grounds
Which need to be dumped
Put flavors back in their places
Fruity flavors on top of a white shelf
Coffee flavors on the bottom or side
Out to the shed for more Half-&-Half.
Clean up slight spills that occur during the rush.
Collect dirty rags to go to Clorox water.
Sit down to read.
Stand up to sing.
I wait for the next customer.
Drinks aren't the only things
Some people come for.
But perhaps it was I who gave
Them someone to talk to
Young, old, rich, poor, friendly, awkward—
They pulled up to the window.
I take their orders
And prepare their drinks.

Many concerns about
Work and family are mentioned:
"I've been so busy lately—

Drops of Kisses

If I take the job offer,
I'll have to move to Florida!"
"I'm staying single for the rest of my life;
The worst mistake I made
Was getting married at seventeen,
To a twenty-six-year-old!"
"I'm just visiting from Seattle for the weekend
30 days left on probation man!"
"The only thing to do is leave my husband."
"My dad kicked us out and
I'm trying to find a job.
His new girl friend doesn't like us."
As I try to listen the best I can
Over steaming milk
Blending granitas
And spraying whipped cream,
I still hear them
And when it's slow
We talk awhile.

It's more to them than just the drink.
Conversation blends into deeper shades
Revealing the motives of the heart.
Passed down opinions
Or stubborn ways of thinking
Blocks resolution from taking place
As I slip in words of life and encouragement
Quickened to my memory

From past Bible readings;
They can either take them or leave them
But this is where the rubber
meets the road.
And they could be healed
If they would just look into
What God says about their situation
Divorce, abandonment, anxiety, bitterness, addiction—
The Savior is just a prayer away from changing lives!

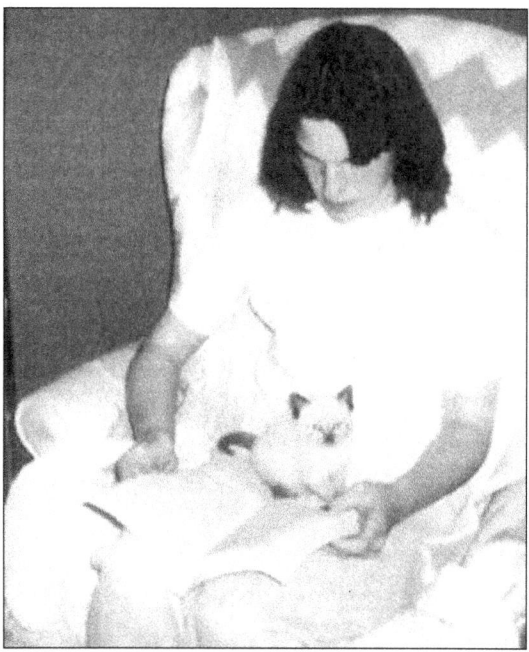

Karen, deep in thought, "drinking in" the Word of God. She grew to love reading the Bible daily. It was a well of life to her that she passed on to others.

The Need Inside

By Karen Lee FitzPatrick

Men of the earth
Look to themselves
Then look to the skies
Not knowing where
The Truth lies.

Trying to make their
Handy work better than
Nature's secret life
They compete with
God to suffice.

Though the answer
Doesn't lie there,
Their hearts remain bare.
Though the human tries
To master his own aim
Jesus Christ is the one
Who came
To set us free from
Our sin and will
And to give us direction
That guides us still.

Since many do not
Believe this Word
They try making others
Their Lord.

Afraid to deny themselves
And take up faith
The heart waits to wake.

They wander like needy souls
And only want to be made whole
With a reaching heart
To motivate their steps
They could submit their way
To the Truth God sent.

To trust in all He said
Is where the soul is truly fed.

Karen Lee FitzPatrick was born in Martinez, California, on December 27, 1982. After living in Benicia, California, for seven years, she moved with her family from California to Yakima, Washington, and attended West Valley Schools. Currently, she is a junior at West Valley High School where she experienced the poems written in this book. Karen continues to trust the Lord for direction in her future. This also includes finding that special someone whom she can't seem to wait for.

Lilies Grow in Difficult Places

An Essay by Karen Lee FitzPatrick...

Her personal journey toward a deep walk with God

"Give attention to this! Behold, a sower went out to sow. And as he was sowing, some seed fell along the path, and the birds came and ate it up. Other seed fell on ground full of rocks, where it had not much soil; and at once it sprang up, because it had no depth of soil; And when the sun came up, it was scorched, and because it had not taken root, it withered away. Other seed fell among thorn plants, and the thistles grew and pressed together and utterly choked and suffocated it, and it yielded no grain. And other seed fell into good soil and brought forth grain, growing up and increasing, and yielding up to thirty times as much, and sixty times as much, and even a hundred times as much as had been sown. And Jesus said, 'He who has ears to hear, let him be hearing (and let him consider, and comprehend)'" (**Mark 4:3-9**). **Amplified Bible Translation**

It was October of 1995 when we began meeting in the home with new friends for church—three o'clock to six o'clock around a large oak dinning table on Sunday afternoons for between-service meetings. These folks were all new to my family and me. We had met the preacher, Tom H., at a New Year's Eve potluck hosted by old-time gospel singers and friends who were part of the family of God. Most of them had connections or former relationships with the Gaithers, who were famous singers. The meeting was held in the Carter's new home. Steve Carter knew Tom from working on the Tieton Irrigation District with him. Kathy Hawkins and her children knew Tom when he visited her church to teach. The Wilsons were simply best friends with the Carters all along. We all attended different churches. The Carters and Wilsons were Nazarenes, my family was Pentecostal, Kathy was a former Catholic, then Presbyterian. Tom was a born again Christian. That's all he had to be in order to preach.

Soon enough, Sunday afternoons became too short. New revelations in the Word of God wrought through preaching drew our hearts and our interests in. We agreed to meet Sunday morning to evening in the home of the Carter's for church. Potlucks were served at our afternoon lunch break. Some of the best food I've ever eaten consisted of barbecued salmon or steelhead freshly caught by Tom, who is a great fisherman.

> *And Jesus said to them, 'Come after Me and be My disciples, and I will make you to become fishers of men'* (MARK 1:17). AMPLIFIED BIBLE TRANSLATION

After a year and a half of meeting in the home and getting to know each other as closest friends in the Lord, a brief Bible study and prayer meeting was held on Tuesday nights at my house. Many hurts, troubles, and concerns were lifted off hearts as they prayed according to their own personal knowledge of where they were in their spiritual lives. Clarity. Did we somehow feel blind to reality or what could distort spiritual reality? I think we all were there at one point or another.

> *We know that God does not listen to sinners; but if anyone is God fearing and a worshiper of Him and does His will, He listens to him* (JOHN 9:31). AMPLIFIED BIBLE TRANSLATION

Seven notebooks full of Sunday Bible lessons had been collected and looked back over. Seasons came and went, along with changing emotions and moral conflicts. Some friends came to hear the Word preached, others left for a while and then, in God's time, returned. "Other churches just don't have it," Steve and his wife Dee replied after spending a year visiting other churches. Their hearts had been cut, but God knows how to heal.

> *For the Word that God speaks is alive and full of power; it is sharper than any two-edged sword, penetrating to the dividing line of the breath of life and the immortal spirit, and of the deepest parts of our nature, exposing and analyzing and judging the very thoughts and purposes of the heart* (HEBREWS 4:12) AMPLIFIED BIBLE TRANSLATION

A few, if not all, of my fellow brethren in Christ, could say that the truth truly does hurt. What truth? The truth about ourselves as it relates to our sins that the Bible pointed out to us. Most of us had just been religious, uncommitted, nominal Christians who lived with no victory or direction in our lives, as many do. This became evident in the form of frustration. Not being able to live up to the standard of God's teachings showed us we had no power from above working for and with us all this time.

> *Jesus said to Nicodemus, I assure you most solemnly I tell you, unless a person is born again (anew, from above), he cannot ever see or experience the kingdom of God* (JOHN 3:5). AMPLIFIED BIBLE TRANSLATION

Our Sunday meetings were moved to the rented basement of the Allied Arts building in Gilbert Park. A living room is just too small. During this time, I wrote a poem included in my book *Drops of Kisses*, titled "After Sunday." It expressed how my heart felt when I was most sensitive and longing to become born again. Other poems were simply recesses of this inward struggle. I was not alone, but shared them with the others I met with. Inside, I felt so alone I thought that even God didn't really feel my pain. Stress. I had no complete relief or comfort. Though I willed what was right, I had no way to carry it out. I hadn't let God's power abide within my heart, the center of my actions.

> *The teaching of the wise is a fountain of life, that one may avoid the snares of death. Good understanding wins favor, but the way of the transgressor is hard; like the barren, dry soil or the impassable swamp.* (PROVERBS 13:14-15). AMPLIFIED BIBLE TRANSLATION

Others became born again and shared their testimonies on Sunday. This happened throughout a period of seven months. They told about how God truly convicted them of their sin; they repented, and by faith they received forgiveness of their sins. It sounds easy, perhaps, but it took me months to do. Those months were the hardest of my life. June 20, 2000, was my new birthday. God sure knew how to turn my world upside down for the better! I realized that I had been a transgressor and my way had been hard. Then I finally came to my end—the end of me leading my way in life, and I came through being entangled in a snare that only God could have delivered me from. God's power is designed to deliver humans from mortal failure. Though I wasn't deep, deep into sin, I got a taste of the life I could have led myself into. Misery and judgment, I'd rather have Jesus.

> *The basis of the judgment lies in this: the Light had come into the world, and people have loved the darkness rather than and more than the Light, for their works were evil. For every wrongdoer hates and detests the Light, and will not come out into the Light but shrinks from it, lest his works, activities, and conduct be exposed and reproved. But he who practices truth and does what is right, comes out into the Light; so that his works may be plainly shown to be what they are, wrought with God and prompted with God's help in dependence upon Him.*
> (JOHN 3:19-21). AMPLIFIED BIBLE TRANSLATION

His name was Mark B. I most recently began seeing him at the end of last May. I met him at my work on a Tuesday afternoon when I consented to work for my friend Kristi. I should have said no. But here I was, with little dating experience and confidence. Something about his "bad boy" type made me like him even more. He smoked, drank, quit doing other drugs, and was a vagabond. He knew how the world worked and just after recently graduating from high school had been traveling around America on a sales crew (originally from Montana). How could I trust him? He would be in town for two weeks and both weekends he'd like to spend with me. Coming back to my work, he'd ask me out. "I'd like to take you out to dinner and a movie. What do you say?" Sure, why not. I needed some kind of adventure. I hadn't been on a date for more than months.

Maybe my loneliness and his homesickness is what drew us closer. Our last good-bye was a little much and longer than I had expected. He then left Yakima to drive to Seattle and said he'd call me. I knew he wasn't what I needed. I felt wrong inside for liking him the way I did. He brought out everything in me that I hated. Or maybe that was God's doing. My sin was being exposed, and it left me feeling insecure and sick of myself for allowing this to happen. That's what I get for trying to find that crazy missing part in my heart through a relationship.

> "Long pursued by sin and Satan, weary, sad, I longed for rest;
> Then I found this heavenly shelter, opened in my Savior's breast."

Mark called me the following Monday. I knew deep inside, and couldn't convince myself otherwise, that I needed to break off our relationship. If I didn't, he'd come back to live in Yakima just to be with me. But I'd only continue dating if I was serious about marriage. He wasn't even close to my personal preference—not even a Christian. (Where do you find them? God, tell me.) His eighteenth birthday was approaching, June 20th. He wanted to come and spend the day with me. I said, "Mark, no, I can't. I can't do this anymore."

I didn't expect him to understand or try to fix any mistakes. I simply said no and continued to say no. After getting off the phone with him, I knelt beside my bed. I had to pray. "Jesus, come into my heart and be my Savior. I can't live a good life without you!" I finally felt the end of myself give it up to God. I knew from that moment on He received me just as I was. I was forgiven, and I will never forget what happened to me that day.

> "Peace which passeth understanding, joy the world can never give;
> Now in Jesus I am finding, in his smiles of love I live.
> Now I'm resting, sweetly resting in that cleft once made for me.
> Jesus, blessed Rock of Ages, I will hide myself in Thee."
> —"Sweetly Resting," W. Warren Bently,
> 19th Century The Nazarene Hymnal

And He said, The kingdom of God is like a man who scatters seed upon the ground, and then continues sleeping and rising night and day while the seed sprouts and grows and he knows not how. The earth produces by itself. First the blade, then the ear, then the full grain in the ear. But when the grain is ripe and permits, immediately he sends forth the reapers and puts in the sickle, because the harvest stands ready (MARK 4:26-29). AMPLIFIED BIBLE TRANSLATION

Today, my brothers and sisters in the Lord are happier than ever to be part of the family of God. I gave my testimony to them the following Sunday. I happily told them how I came to the realization of my true need for Jesus Christ to be my Savior. He's real and lives inside me now. I'm so glad I went through even a bad relationship to get there. It was worth every step of the way. Now that my friends from church and I are all born again and finally willing for God's will to be done in our lives, it makes it easier to understand the words from the Bible that are preached to us on Sunday—and also to do them. We are all yet young in the Lord and are in need of growth that comes from God and strength to stand. "We are weak, but He is strong." The demand for holiness is a necessity for the Bride of Christ that He will be returning for. Jesus Christ deserves and will take nothing less than the best.

> *And she said, I am only a little rose or autumn crocus of the plain of Sharon, or a humble lily of the valleys that grows in deep and difficult places. But He replied, Like the lily among the thorns, so are you, my love, among the daughters* (SONG OF SONGS 2:1-2). AMPLIFIED BIBLE TRANSLATION

Karen Lee, God's Official, Yet Rather Unofficial, Evangelist and Ambassador.

Karen turned up in the oddest and most unexpected places to do the Lord's bidding and speaking.

She had a gift that all evangelists dream of and pray for—unmerited favor with those who heard her or who were in earshot of her. In a restless day and age of the present-day society, generally unfriendly to the gospel, where it is no longer lawful to even display the Ten Commandments in public places, Karen moved freely to speak and sing about God wherever she went, including her high school campus. She did oral book reports on the book of Genesis and on the Book of Acts. A member of the Honor Society, Karen spoke freely about knowing Christ personally as the most important thing the human mind and spirit could achieve. No one dared stop her. The teachers loved her, and often wished more students were more like Karen in kindness, love, and consideration. While on duty at Valerie's Espresso downtown as a Barista, she kept her Bible handy and spoke to every weary, downtrodden soul who would listen so he or she could be lifted up from depression and hopelessness. Her friend Roberto likes to remember a cold December day. "I'll never forget the day she chased down the bag lady on Yakima Avenue. She had been waiting for her to show up again so she could give her food and presents."

Karen had three housecleaning accounts up on Meadowcrest Drive. They were large homes, some over 5,000 square feet. Each family thought of her as a daughter, and often invited her to stay for dinner. She often shared her faith to their open ears and hearts. "She was so full of joy, just singing away about Jesus while she was working," one of the Moms remarked. "And she didn't just clean for a certain length of time. She worked until my house was clean and the work was finished."

On a trip back east to upstate New York to visit family in 1998, Karen attended a church service in which the pastor was delivering a sermon filled with a "little too much humor and jokes." This angered Karen as she perceived that the people needed to hear the gospel message straight up and feel the presence of God in the service or they would have been cheated. In Karen's personal journal she describes marching down militantly to the front of the church at the end of the service and challenging this pastor face-to-face about his casual jesting. "You call that preaching? You have insulted God himself to his face and robbed these people of the truth they need to hear!" I don't think this full-grown man will ever forget the fiery encounter with this 16-year-old woman of God—all size six of her. The blazing eyes of Karen Lee are not easy to forget.

It seemed that when she spoke of the Lord from her own personal experience, the ones listening were enveloped by something like a cloud of reality and favor to receive the truth of what she was saying. She's gone now, but you can experience the same as you read her personal writings. Be sure to feel and notice it. She is still present, and so is the Spirit of the Lord who is from Age to Age and forever present with those diligently seeking Him!

KAREN'S CHRISTMAS TEA

Hugs and remembrances: Friends gather for annual Christmas tea.

> "*The story made the front page of the regional newspaper, and on the local 6 PM news…so we felt like we were sharing smiles with many.*"
>
> —Kathie

Karen's Christmas Tea

Karen had a tradition. Over the past four years she had gotten together with a few of her closest girlfriends, usually on December 23, to exchange presents from "the bag" and to share some of her favorite baked goodies. Karen often baked special cheesecakes, such as cranberry cheesecake, chocolate and cappuccino cheesecake, and other goodies for Christmas gifts for her friends, neighbors, and teachers.

After her death on July 10, it seemed unbearable to face Christmas without Karen's bright smile, laugh, warm presence, and her goodies! Instead of moping around, her sister Jaina and some of her friends and I decided we would replicate Karen's Christmas Tea the best we could and remember her warmly and fondly.

Trying to cook and bake like Karen was a challenge. Jaina loved the idea at first, but then the reality of trying to reproduce some of Karen's baked favorites hit home.

"Mom, I will never be able to figure out those Swedish ribbon cakes," she wailed. "And I can't find the recipe anywhere! And that million dollar shortbread chocolate thing—we're not trying to make that are we?" I came to the rescue and did most of the baking—with Jaina's help. So where do you think she learned most of it?

I donned Karen's favorite apron that had her name printed across the top and gladly walked into the role for the day. The group grew to about 35 friends—teen peers, guy-friends, and moms—who were close to Karen. Even her friend Roberto who used to stop in often at Valerie's Espresso where Karen worked for almost two years after school was there. Roberto left the street life behind and had been inspired by Karen to turn his life around and get into college to improve his life.

"No one has ever been able to inspire him to do that!" his mom, Donna, smiled warmly. Jonathan Gottlieb, one of the sons of Randie and Steve Gottlieb, one of Karen's house cleaning accounts, read a wonderful poem he wrote entitled "Song for Karen." The local ABC TV affiliate's cameras were present to take in all the luscious scenes of the goodies, decorations, and quick sound bites from Karen's friends who were having a very nice time remembering her.

On the six o'clock news that evening, the announcer who opened the story about "Karen's Christmas Tea" said, "Well, there were a lot more smiles than tears remembering Karen FitzPatrick at Karen's Christmas Tea this afternoon." Indeed, there were smiles, and at the end of the year when the regional news did a montage of stories over the past year, the Christmas tea was the last story to nicely crown it off! It was a very nice feeling for all!

Karen's childhood toys came all dressed up for the occasion.

> sometimes
>
> when one person is missing,
>
> the whole world seems
>
> depopulated.
>
> (lamartine)

Karen,
Things are not the same without you! I remember you nearly every day, and you will always hold a special place in my heart. Remembering you this Christmas season has made my heart soft, but it gives me great joy & comfort to know where you are. See you soon! —Jessie

Randie Gottlieb shares warm memories of Karen.

Jonathan reads "Song for Karen" for the guests.

Song for Karen

By Jonathan Gottlieb

Beautiful on the outside, as well as on the in,
An angel walking on the earth, her name is Karen.
To be joyful and caring, her spirit now free,
She was known as Karen, Karen Lee.

We know that her life passed by too quick,
Our hearts are full of strife; her passing makes us sick.
But we know that she now thrives, in a
kingdom close to God,
Karen Lee FitzPatrick now resides—in Heaven.

As a true Christian, a true lover of Christ,
With selfless devotion, and sacrifice.
Putting words into motion, changing lives,
Looking at Creation, through open eyes.

Even though I only knew her for a short while,
I can honestly say, that there was never a day,
That I ever saw her without a smile on her face.
There was many a time when she sat at our table,
Offering grace, thankful for all that life had to give.

Our friend Karen is gone before our eyes,
The way she went took us by surprise.
Her life went by too fast, but she always thought of others,
Even to the last…
We'll miss her caring attitude, and her loving smile,
Don't be sad, you'll see her in a while.

Christmas tea guests listen to memories and poetry readings.

Christmas tea—some of the "Karen" treats.

Karen Lee's silver service and tray complete with little presents. This time there are memory photos and a beautiful white angel in the centerpiece.

KAREN'S CHRISTMAS TEA

Cookies and treats set up on the familiar table by the balcony on a wintry day in December.

A "Karen cheesecake" in the making.

Karen's mom, Kathie, with Lacy, Jessica and Cheryl, the originators of the tea.

Karen's Christmas Tea, the following year, 2002: Lacy Chambers, Jessica Dean, and Cheryl Purcell. By the year 2004, members of the close-knit group had scattered from the area to college or married and moved out of state.

Karen Lee's 18th Birthday

December 27, 2000, was a monumental event that included family, friends, a special dinner she did not cook, fresh flowers on the dinner table, presents, and smiles galore! What warmth and gladness to brighten a cold winter's night only two days after Christmas.

Karen wore a special ring on her finger—a present from the family—a blue topaz ring in 14 karat gold that she absolutely adored. The greatest feeling of all was that Karen was just fine after a serious car

accident December 8, 2000 that could have crippled her or taken her life. Her car was "totaled out," but she walked away without a scratch! A miracle. This was the greatest Christmas present of all that year!

Teen poet, Kathie Blackwood FitzPatrick, at age 15 years old with her horse, Rex.

Kathie's Youth Poem Collection

Karen's mom, Kathie, had also been a teen poet. Here is some of the poetry from her world as a teenager, young woman, and mother who liked to read children's books and poetry to her children, Yvonne, Jaina, and "Baby Karen," or "BK."

Most of this poetry was written between the ages of 15-18 years old, and a few as late as in the twenties.

Gentle Sweet Secret

By Kathie Blackwood

Lovely stream by the grassy shore
I love to sit and watch you as I have
Before
On many a lunch hour's noon,
Letting your cooling waters swoon,
And ripple through my mind
Erasing every kind of fear
These hectic times can bring.
In the city cash registers ring,
As bustling people rush in the
Streets
Looking for something to eat
On many a lunch hour's noon.
I wonder if the food they eat

Can ease their troubled minds?
If they could only come here,
Maybe they could find
The same peace that erases all time
On many a lunch hour's noon.

The summer days here have grown
Dim.
The air is cool and the gentle
Wind
Has loosed the falling leaves.
Our friendship will be ceased,
And parted for a season.
Pulling my coat tight around me,
I wonder, and I reason,
Hoping I can wear the memory
Of this place in my mind
For another year.
For even though the world may
Unwind,
Your gentle sweet waters will only
Know peace.
Oh, if only you could teach
Your gentle sweet secret
To all who pass this way.

Experiences of Life

By Kathie Blackwood

The experiences of life
Are so like a patchwork quilt
That makes its pattern in my mind
One of a kind
So unique there can never be
Another.
Every morning of life
I find there is one more piece
To sew on to another
So firmly with the silken threads
Of memories and dreams
Forever to form the beauteous colors
And patterns
Of the world inside myself
That no one will ever see.
The only thing I can hope to be
Is that someday I may be found worthy
To share the warmth if it
That time has woven so carefully
With those I love
And those who try to love me
But especially those
Whom life has chosen
To do neither.

WILLOW TREE

By Kathie Blackwood

Hidden inside a willow tree
Is all the world there needs to be
For me and my lovely dreams.
The world outside looks in at me
Through green and lacy limbs,
That bend and touch the dry warm grass
Spread on the ground before me.
For there is the only place on earth
I can be content
For a time,
Forgetting my worldly cares.
I cast them away like willow sticks
That quickly disappear
Beyond the lacy veil.

Kathie FitzPatrick at 18 years of age.

White Candle...

By Kathie Blackwood

Peace, tranquility, serenity:
For these things we all are
Yearning
Like a long, white candle
Burning
All the way to the end,
And then poofs out in the dark.
Oh, to be held instead in a
Hand clenched tight
By those who have stumbled
And lost their sight

Traveling through this night
We know;
Who their way they cannot find.
Then we wonder why we're blind
When there are no candles of
Any kind
Left to lead us on,
Because, you see,
They are all burning peacefully.

Darkened Veil

By Kathie Blackwood

Ignorance feels good for a
Time.
But it's like walking through
A forest without a lamp
To see.
If the lion's don't get you,
Neither the cold or damp,
Or the vines that sting,
Or the briers that sting,
Or pits that go unseen,
Covered by the darkened veil;
And horizons seem so far…
If you ever come out on the other side,
You'll never know where you are.

"This painting, which I painted in 1972, demonstrates the fantasy faces in the flowers. When you try to count them, you will get a different number every time. Only I know how many faces are really in the flowers. My daughter Yvonne posed as the young girl in this painting when she was five."

Through Children's Eyes

By Kathie Blackwood

The mind of a child
Is a wonderful thing.
Their spirit sings
With such energy and freedom.
They see simple truths so easily
As it seems to eagerly greet them,
Like little faces in the flowers
That we have grown too old
To see.

"Kari-Lee," age four.

I AM SMALL

By Kathie Blackwood FitzPatrick

I am small.
The world is all so new to me.
I hear that men still long to be free
From spiritual darkness and slavery.
I hear that the world does not have long
To Live
You are going through natural resources
Like a sieve,
With hardly a forest still to be found.
I hope there is some beauty
Still around
When I am old enough to see.
Leave some of the earth
For me.
For I am small.

A Song

By Kathie FitzPatrick

I have been around almost forever.
But I do not live on the wind,
Or the hills.
I live somewhere in the heart
Of each man.
When words fail,
I speak.
I overcome tremendous obstacles.
I scale high and terrible walls
That exist hidden deep within
The human soul.
Wars have been fought over
My message.
But peace springs forth
From my lips.
For I speak the truth to the human
spirit.
I am a song.

Old Friend

By Katherin Blackwood

Old Friend…
How I long to see your face.
No one can ever seem to replace
Your warmth and understanding.
Oh how cruel life sometimes is
To separate such friends as us.
Worlds apart, miles apart;
The differences seem to never end
As I ponder them over so silently.
I keep a picture of you tucked away
In the jewel box of my mind,
A place where I know I can always find
My treasure,
Your shining face.
It always waits for me there.

Tears…

Those precious jewels that flow
From the heart
That help our minds
To grow wiser.
—KBF

A Child and a Kitten

By Kathie Blackwood

A child and a kitten play
In the wind
On a day of flowers and May.
The kitty loves her.
And she loves her kitty.
It seems to be that way
With girls so little and fair,
With dreams so rare;
That run everywhere,
And play in the noonday sun.
Fur so soft on a cheek like down,
And a cheek so young and pretty.
She may gaze in the eyes of the kitty she loves,
And the eyes gazing back are the same,
So pure in wanting love.
This child will grow to a woman
One day
Like that wonderful day of
Flowers and May,
But love will come in another way.
Will she be the same as the little
Girl then?
As a child and a kitten who played
In the wind?

My Child

By Kathie Blackwood

"Oh, my child, how may I
Understand thee?"
These words ring out in the
Heart of a child
Long without love or trust.
Like a fortune vast endowed
Us here on Earth,
Children can be a blessing
Or a curse
Depending on how we spend
Our love.
Somehow, love never fails,
Even beyond understanding.
A child was never made by reason.

Youth

By Katherin Blackwood FitzPatrick

Youth comes at a time when
It's hardest to enjoy it.
The world is all so new
We cannot digest the joys
Of being what we are.
Oh, for the understanding

That comes with age
At a time when we need it most;
For the sorrows of the young
Are many
But the joy of the old
Everlasting
Once gained.
Soon a weary traveler learns
To ask the way.

Young Dreams

Kathie Blackwood FitzPatrick

The kiss of a stranger looms high
In the imagination of a girl.
Thoughts of warm softness
Glitter and whirl
Through her sensitive mind,
Until
She would rather sit and dream
Than meet the stranger once again
Lest her thoughts may prove to be
Only an unreal dream.

My Eyes

By Kathie Blackwood

My eyes can say so much
That our tongues cannot
Be moved to say.
How memories linger on
Of friends
I've made for a time or more
Through the silent language
Of my eyes.

Oh, Christmas Tree

By Kathie Blackwood

Oh, Christmas tree
If only we could be more
Like thee,
A symbol of God's love;
Evergreen and vibrant.
Cut down from the mountain
Heights to be with us,
And in our hearts
On this Christmas Day.
Thy branches, thy body,
Glorified and adorned,
Reach out to all the world

With peace
Beckoning them to see
And hear the message of our Lord.
Thy base but touches to
The Earth
With roots on mountains high,
Just as our roots are not on
Earth...
But up in heaven lie
Awaiting our return.
Thy branches twist not
Nor do they gnarl,
But stand out straight and right
With purpose and direction,
Bathed in glorious light
For all to look upon and see,
Just as our own selves should be.
The center of thy body points
Straight to heaven's door,
Wearing a star-like crown like
No other tree before
For truly thou art honored
Above all trees
To be adorned, used of God,
And of such an example be
To us here below,
Helping our Lord bring to us
One day of heaven on Earth.

Oh, Christmas tree,
If only we could be more
Like thee, A symbol of God's love.

THE HUMBLE SPIDER

By Kathie Blackwood

On a stormy afternoon long ago
In a land torn with hate
When there should have been love
In the hearts from the Christ
They claimed to know,
A man of God hid out.
He hid out from the Church who
Hated the truth about him.
From place to place he ran and hid,
For he feared for his life and chance,
To speak the truth and save those souls
Deep in darkness still.
One day on a chase for his life,
He lost the men
Long enough to hide.
Deep down inside
An old wine barrel in a cellar
Where he prayed and asked
The Lord
To help in his time of need.

Just as he asked, he saw
That a spider had dropped in heed,
And spun his fragile web
From side to side over that open end
Of his hiding place.
Up and down, and around and around;
He watched his curious friend,
And almost forgot why he was
There...
Because of the hate waiting outside,
Reaching and spreading through the
Countryside.
Voices entered in, and he froze
In fear.
The men had found his place.
They searched every cellar, and
Every closet
And of him found no trace.
"The wine barrel, there...
Take a look,"
Shouted the Captain of the men.
"No use, sir," another replied,
"He could not be within.
A gentle web of a spider is spun
O'er the end,
Unless you find a ghost inside...
'Tis no use, he must have gotten
Away from us again."

Soon they were gone, and away
From the inn,
Bringing peace and thanks to
The heart of a man,
Spared from a martyr's death.
He watched the spider in awe and
Prayer,
And coming forth he was aware,
This humble creature of God
Had spared his very life,
That he may go and do the same
As he,
The humble spider.

Help Him Across

By Kathie Blackwood FitzPatrick

In putting over a fact one
Should never have to look down to see.
If you want someone to believe what you say,
You must show him in every way
That you are the same as he,
Or have some common ground,
So you help him across.
Then if you strive to exceed yourself
In some pleasing way,
Soon he will not be able to help

Looking up, though he may not say,
"Please give me your hand,
So you may stand
Side by side on higher ground,"
But that is what he will feel,
And the truth is bound to happen
In his heart,
And bear forth life,
If you can do this one thing first.

THE SAGA OF VIRGIL AND NATHAN

Kathie Blackwood

In the mountains there lived two men
In a feud.
They worked the good land, and grew
Their own food,
But hated each other fiercely.
Long ago they started a row,
When Nathan shot Virgil's prize-winning cow,
Trying to hunt down a deer.
Neither remember that day long ago,
But trouble they pass back to and fro,
In the form of dirty tricks.
If there's salt in Virgil's water,
There's sand in Nathan's honey.
Or Nathan will sneak over, and pour

Out feathers plenty,
Over Virgil's hay, and much to his dismay,
If the chimney smoked black with a huff,
And a puff,
And blew back the other way,
It was certainly arranged by Nathan.
A hole in the fence the size of a cow is
Hardly a likely thing,
Or geese from the pen loose on the wing,
All in the same afternoon.
So that's how it went year after year,
Each one living in constant fear,
And hate of the other man.
One day thought Nathan, "This evil must
End,"
So he went back to his cabin far beyond
The bend,
Of the river that wound through the woods,
Vowing to stay there until he thought
Of a way to bring back peace.
The shack far away was a quiet release,
And he thought on many things.
He thought of the cows, and he
Thought of the geese,
And all the other bad turns.
It made Nathan wish he could take
His gun
And give Virgil what he earned,

In Nathan's own narrow mind.
How he wished he could rid himself
Of Virgil forever more.
His brand new axe that hung so nicely
On his hay room door
Might help him with his trouble…
Or Virgil could be run away,
And off his only wealth.
Then Nathan could be all alone,
With the mountains to himself.
"What a blessing that would be.
That evil neighbor must be destroyed,"
Was his final thought.
Then Nathan went to thinking,
And dreaming up a plot,
To bring back peace once more.
The place where he was,
Was quiet and still,
A place where a man can open and fill
His mind full of many thoughts.
Nathan thought hard of what he must do,
Choosing one way, then another way,
And thinking the whole thing through,
For a solid three days and nights,
He knew there was only one way to
Blot out his evil neighbor.
Nathan returned to his humble home,
And fetched the axe from the door,

His brand new axe that Virgil had
Swiped at least seven times or more,
Then went to pay him a visit.
The freedom of the mountains reveals
Many wonderful things,
In the creatures that sing,
And those on the wing,
Bursting forth with life;
And now through the beauty of the trees
Are seen two men who used to be
In hatred of one another,
With each an arm around his brother
Because one man saw fit,
That the candle of friendship again be lit
By a gift, and an honest word;
For evil cannot overcome more evil
By itself,
But must be overcome only
By more good.

Walls of Silence...

By Kathie Blackwood FitzPatrick

Fierce violence is like a roaring lion
That frightens away
The opportunity for understanding.
A child may cry out through the silence

Of the night.
I'll never hear that cry.
A mother's tears may comfort her fears
In a lonely room,
Lonely as a tomb,
Where no one can see into the heart.
Oh, if the walls of silence were lifted
That protect our happy dreams
We would have to feel others'
Most urgent needs
As if they were our own.

Trust

By Kathie Blackwood FitzPatrick

The forests and the woods live
A life of peace,
Tall and serene, beautiful
And quiet
If only man could learn to
Live by it,
And learn its wonderful
Balance of peace,
The world could be the same.
Man, the only rebel,
His nature may never be tamed.
His nature may never be the learned

In the ways that are really true.
Take the lilies of the field,
As we have been shown.
They toil not,
Neither do they spin,
And not one alone,
Has gone uncared for.
How much more important are we
Than one tiny flower of the field.
The world could be like the forest,
Serene and lush,
If every man knew where to put
His trust,
And brushed his worries away like
Dust
On top of the old family Bible.

Home Fire

By Kathie Blackwood FitzPatrick

I've traveled the countryside,
Met a lot of people,
Tasted their wine
Seen their smiles,
Heard their songs…
But when I come home,
That's where love is.

The glow of the home fire
Is always the best.
The embers die down low.
The fiery glow
Is gone,
As I think of days gone by:
Cold memories,
Cold lonely nights;
Remembering the home fire
Has kept my days alive.
Real love is here,
Never to die,
Like so many ashes to be
Swept away
Forgotten in the next tomorrow.

Old House

By Kathie Blackwood FitzPatrick

Old house, why are you so
Strong?
Your old oak timbers, and
Foundations have so long
Withstood these many years,
Protecting and loving through
Trials and fears
Of those who abode within.

Oh, old house, how rare you are.
Our new are built with timber far
From strong and hard like thee.
So many of those who live in the new
Are weak in mind and soul…
As if their walls cannot
Protect the fold

From the stench of an evil world;
And in a few short years their
Protective walls
Will crumble and fall,
While you still stand so straight
And tall,
And vacant.
As if your noble kind no longer
Inhabit the earth.

LOVE IS…

By Kathie Blackwood FitzPatrick

Love is not the roses that come,
And love is not the moon that shines
Over the head of two.
Love is not a lock of hair
That curls on a brow so young and fair
With "eye like limpid pool."

Love is not selfishness over a face
So vain,
Or scheming ways to find romance
Under a window pane
Deep in the midnight hour.
Love is not the words that promise
That precious "I love you,"
For how many are left by those untrue,
And by those who vow these words?
One who loves gives himself away,
Never wanting reward or pay in
Return for his own delight.
Love is quiet in a time of pain.
Love knows when he must refrain,
No matter who is right or wrong.
Love being simple is hard to understand,
If a heart is selfish,
Or must be grand,
For love is a humble thing.
How many tears must one people shed,
And how many hearts must they break
And Shred
Into pieces so small they contaminate us
All,
Before we see the plan that God
Will help us understand
What love really is?

Even a Rose

By Kathie Blackwood FitzPatrick

Beautiful is a silent glance,
And a mystery what he will say.
A scarf she wears;
A scent she bears,
That lingers in every place
Enchanting past memories
Until dawn,
After dawn
Of many nights to come.
We only love that which we don't
Completely understand.
For if we did we would reprimand,
And find fault with the very thing
We loved.
Hopefully, the one we love we will
Never understand
For even a beautiful rose must have
A flaw somewhere…

Only Love Can

By Kathie Blackwood FitzPatrick

Only love can make a rose grow tall
And wind above the garden wall
To bask in the gentle sun.
With no love the ground
Grows dry,
And the leaves must wither.
By and by,
Soon the beauty of the wall
Will quickly die, and slowly
Fall,
Piece and petal at a time.
Only the wind will some day find
Her remains.

Dreams...

By Kathie Blackwood FitzPatrick

Memories can seem to fade away
Like the leaves that drift
From the trees by day,
Forever to be lost
Beyond the next tomorrow.

Oh, for an everlasting Summer
Where everything
Is now,
Never again to fade
Or tarnish those most wanted
Dreams
So richly endowed us
Deep in the shadows of our minds,
Never to last beyond day break
For their reality can
Never be ours.

It's Christmas...

By Kathie Blackwood FitzPatrick

Snowflakes dance down from the heavens.
It's Christmas.
Untouched snow is marked by
Darting sleighs that brush
Over its magic surface on a snowy holiday.
The air is fresh, and smells so clean
And gay,
Of pine and maple candy from ovens
Near the way,
Where all the children gather
To sled and sing and play.
The land seems so silent,

Like a holy prayer,
As the sun sets slowly,
The snow has lost its glare.
The moon in its bright splendor could
Remind one of long ago,
And the star that led three wise men
To a manger low.
Snow dances down from the heavens
Like silver dust. It's Christmas.
The night is as peaceful as an Angel's dream…
It's Christmas.

Interpretation Of Colors:

By Kathie Blackwood

This verse should be read by one
Sitting in the country
Looking up at the sky on a
Beautiful day
So that everything may be illustrated
Before him:

Blue is the color of man,
And his highest aspirations:
What a fitting color for the sky!
Green is the color of the Earth,
All that is within,

And all that is warm and friendly.
Yellow is the color meaning life,
And sunlight, and every living thing.
Red can be the color of love,
Death,
Or worldly passion;
Measuring the color of yellow or blue
It holds within,
Is the secret of this hue.
Black is the color of sin and
Darkness
Where all men can stumble and fall.
White is the hue of heaven worn
Smudge free by no man.
The color of blue and green together
Can only mean
The ideal understanding sought
By all men on Earth,
Just as gentle white and red display
A woman's love,
Colors unlock deep secrets
That live
In the heart of every man.

To Be Cherished

By Kathie Blackwood FitzPatrick

A purple velvet pillow is a very
Beautiful thing,
To be proud of while it is cherished.
The attention of a man makes
A thing be cherished,
And any cherished thing will soon
Become beautiful,
As an uncut diamond,
A pearl down in the deep,
Or a dying ember hidden beneath
The cold, cold sleep of loneliness

On Happiness

By Kathie Blackwood FitzPatrick

For wealth makes not one
Happy,
But only understanding
And Love,
As wide as the sky,
And as small as one grain
Of sand
That lies on the shell-lined shore.

Even the sun in all his glory
Takes time to shine on
Her small face.

FREEDOM

By Kathie Blackwood FitzPatrick

Round and tender, bright and
Cheerful,
A cool sweet orange tastes exactly
Like
A fall breeze feels when the earth
Is warm,
And the sun shines on my face.
Oh, how I long to be free one day,
For life is much too short to be
Any other way.
Misused freedom is only wasted
Time,
And time is precious, and too hard
To find.
Almost anything on Earth can be
Regained,
But time and love,
Can easily be lost
Forever.

SOLITUDE

By Kathie Blackwood FitzPatrick

When a man is truly alone with himself
The eyes of his mind see much.
For what we see, and hear,
Then think
Can sometimes be a crutch
For the truth
Which lies within us all.
Oh fortunate is that one
Who can hear
The voice that speaks
From the soul.

TRUTH

By Kathie Blackwood FitzPatrick

Truth is something a man
Feels inside,
That strikes a distant bell,
Heard through the fog,
And stormy tide
And forever to endure
Deep in the heart of a man.

WEALTH

By Kathie Blackwood FitzPatrick

Money is the root of all evil,
Only when you have it,
And only when you don't.

THE BUTTERFLY

By Kathie Blackwood FitzPatrick

In the garden there grew a flower so fair,
With petals of gold and red
That flared,
And waved in the gentle breeze,
For she was a sheltered flower.
Under the petals, and close
To the stem,
A bundle of life was soon to
Begin,
And appear up over the rim
Of the skirt of petals.
Soon a butterfly did emerge,
And pulled himself out in the sun,
To show his tiny face,
And onto the petals he clung,
To bring himself up in place.

The petals gently caressed him
As he sucked his food deep from the
The pollen dens.
His wings were crumpled,
he appeared a bit crude,
And his legs were unsure of himself.
There he stayed, and until he grew,
Never leaving that place.
The threatening winds would blow,
But he would hang on tight,
Never showing a trace of loneliness.
One morning he awoke to see butterflies
In many great quantities,
And numbers, flitting from flower to
Flower.
They visited roses, and clovers,
And one by one said "hello" to the daisies.
This greatly troubled him,
But he clung on tight,
Never once loosing sight
That he loved this flower of his.
The others asked him why he did not
Choose to leave.
"Because I have all I want,
And everything I need."

They told him that he must go out,
And learn their ways,
To gather food, and spend his days
With other butterflies;
And to know the ways of the daisies,
And the sweetness of a rose,
The darkness of the forest, and
Where all the water holes,
And streams run free, and wild.
They told him he would never be wise,
Unless he learned from the other
Butterflies
About the ways of life.
He clung on tight to his flower, as the
Petals rose to caress him.
The others flew off, and away, as his
Eyes grew dim with tears.
I think it not impossible that he must
Have cried
To be the only butterfly who loved…
Who loved a flower that was soon to die,
Never to return to life the same,
Even though thousands of flowers
In the field
Would still wear her familiar name.

Flower Story

By Kathie Blackwood FitzPatrick

Once in the meadow on the field
There grew
A wild little daisy who was very blue
Because she couldn't be among
The tall, tall roses
Who abode in the garden yonder.
The place where she grew was
Friendly enough
With loveliness all around,
But she was just on an ordinary
Hill,
On such ordinary ground,
Which hardly was profound enough
For a daisy who longs to
Linger with the roses.
One day as she thought,
And dreamt
On the roses,
A young girl strolled through her field,
Softly singing, and dreaming, when
Suddenly she plucked
The daisy right out of the field,
And placed it behind her ear.

She wandered down low,
And across the hill coming very
Close and near
To the garden of lovely roses.
On a girlish whim that struck her mind,
Reaching through her hair to find,
She pulled the daisy and cast her
High over the garden fence.
The girl went back across the hill,
The place that was her home;
Fields and lands where new seeds
Were sown
And others have flourished before them.
As for the daisy that lay like a rose,
She was delighted and glad that
Luck chose
To bless one flower as she.
But her roots were back in the field,
Roots that were common grown.
As the little wild flower began to
Wilt away alone,
She wished that she was home,
Back on common ground,
Where she had her roots,
And where she could be found
With others from her field.
Looking up at a rose that stood so
So tall,

From lying on the ground,
She saw that there was nothing at all,
Nothing but petals soon to die.
Oh for the place that was her home,
Fields and lands where new seeds were sown,
And where others have flourished before them.
They, and a little wild daisy
That longed to climb like a rose.

THE GREEN, GREEN SEA

By Kathie Blackwood FitzPatrick

In a blue glass bottle on a
Table top
Lived a very unhappy fish.
He brooded all day and brooded all night;
To be anywhere else was his wish.
He swam up and down,
And from side to side,
Looking at a world that was not
What a certain wee fish really
Saw,
And thought
Things he should not have thought.
Being so unhappy in his blue
Glass house,
He didn't even see

All the nice things he had inside,
He just wanted to be
A fish that lived in the green,
Green sea,
Somewhere.
He swam in circles, and around
And around,
Waiting for that day of hope.
From dawn 'til dusk he swam,
And waited.
All he could do was mope.
One day as he slept in the bottom
Of the jar,
His Mistress brought in a dainty
Glass cup
Of hot chicken broth, and placed
It not far
From the little wee fish, to cool.
Not long from then he awoke,
And looked,
And thought, "Well, I'm no fool.
There's the green, green sea
I've been waiting to go back to."
With one mighty leap he sailed
Out the top
Into the green, green sea
Which he found out too late,

In a very sad way
Was not what he thought it to be.
So I'd say, my friend,
If you see the world
Through the blinding of the glare
Of a blue glass bottle on a table
Top,
You'd better be happy to stay there.

Attitude

By Kathie Blackwood FitzPatrick

Lemon, unlike lime.
Cannot be tamed by sugar.
Her disagreeable nip
Will always hence remain.

Rocking Chair

By Kathie Blackwood FitzPatrick

Rocking chair, back and forth,
If you have a thought to share,
Think it over, then rhythm again,
And soon you will believe it.

Innocence

By Kathie Blackwood FitzPatrick

A little girl sat on a wide
City bench
Watching the world go by her
In steady streams of life,
Unceasing and never ending,
Observing the ways of men.
Her wide, shadowed eyes invite
A meaningful glance
From someone, somewhere out there
In a land trodden by many who
Pass her by
Without a look of concern for one
So young as she.
On her feet and on her way into
The crowd she falls.
Somehow, her way, wise as a serpent
Yet gentle as a dove,
Into a world or ravening wolves,
…She may conquer them all.

Men Who Love

By Kathie Blackwood FitzPatrick

A man who loves his roses
Will stay in the meadow fair
For the beauty of a rose lives
Not in the desert glare
And sand.
The man who will choose the
Desert must live with the
Cactus instead,
The flowers and thorns,
But not like his rose
Back in the meadow
Bed,
So soft and pure and sweet.
How men do love the desert,
But want their roses, too.

I think the young men from
The desert will never learn
To be true…
If you ask a rose.

MATERIAL GAIN

By Kathie Blackwood FitzPatrick

He that has much had nothing
Left over, and less…
Than he that had little who
Had more, and enough.
—KEF

LIFE

By Kathie Blackwood FitzPatrick

We must not let life
Swallow us up like
A hungry beast of the field,
But in turn overcome,
And devour it, not to yield
To the dark Prince who rules
This world.
The size of the Beast who
Chases all,
Whether to win or break, and fall
Is only determined individually
By our own weakness,
Whatever it may be.

NAP IN THE PARK

By Kathie Blackwood FitzPatrick

Lazy afternoon…
Butterflies wing,
Birds sing
And flit from branch to branch.
This is the first chance
In a long time
We've had to be together.
Busy world…
Boys and girls
Running to and fro,
Playing on swings.
Buying ice creams…

But I just want to rest
In your arms,
Free from all fear and alarm.
And whatever tomorrow
And the maddening swarm
Of life may bring
Nuns sing…
Frisbees fling…
Warm breeze…
Children in glee…
Tell me
What's on your mind?
Grandpas hum,
Just for fun,
On a day away from the farm.
A little dog barks
At a sassy meadow lark,
But what's the harm?
Let me melt in your arms.
'Til the sun fades to dark.
I want to nap in the park
With you.

Nelly the Bell

By Katherin Blackwood

On a farm down the road at the countryside
In the back of the field there did reside
A cow named Nelly the Bell.
Nelly the Bell was a good cow, she was,
And loved to lay where the bees did buzz,
In the flowers near the fence by the field.
As she lay in the flowers, one day
Did appear
A graceful and dainty one bit of a deer
Grazing the grass by the hill.
Nelly the Bell stopped chewing her cud.
She blinked her big eyes, and stood up
In the mud
To get a better view
Of this creature so rare
That flit up in the air,
And pranced with great delight.
She took a bite of her cud, and a look at the deer,
And a look at her side and back.
With a look at her tail, and a look at her toes,
Thought, "What kind of cow is that…
Out there in the field near the fence
On the hill?"
Then with a darting of horns he
Fast disappeared.

Nelly sat down for her head to be cleared,
And thought, "Then what kind of cow
Am I?"
"I'm fat and round with stubs on my head,
Not graceful and grand with horns instead,
That climb and reach to the sky.
I am what I am, but I'm sure if I tried
I could be graceful and pretty, and prance
And glide
Just like that other cow.
So around the pasture she flit like a bird,
Prancing and dancing, and though a bit absurd,
Nosed up a branch on her head.
She raced and leaped, and though she tried,
Nelly sat down in her flowers and cried.
She just couldn't be like
That other cow.
She was so upset she couldn't chew her cud,
And her bees buzzed around her as she sat in
The mud
Seeming to try and cheer her.
"I wish I was that other cow.
She had everything."
And just at that thought, above the hill
A rifle shot did ring,
And a buck sailed down the mount.
Old Nelly the Bell raised up her head,
And saw the deer had fallen down dead

By her flowers near the fence by the field,
As two big hunters came and drug him away.
She saw what seemed to be one day
Was only a giddy dream.
Though sad for a while, she came to realize
That she was glad she was Nelly the Bell.
She nestled down deep in her flowers and mud,
And went back to merrily chewing her cud,
Soon asleep with a smile, and well,
Now there's just no happier than
Nelly the Bell.

The Blind Duck

By Kathie Blackwood

I took a walk by the lake one day
With a bag of bread.
In hopes to feed a crowd of ducks,
But I found instead,
That they fled, and flew away as
I approached the shore,
Skimming, leaping, flying off across
To the other side,
Causing a current and a tide
To lap up on the shore,
Bathing the large webbed feet of one
Who had been before,
But somehow chose to stay.

I bended my knee, and gave him some crusts.
He swallowed, and ate, moving closer
With a trust
I ceased to understand.
I pet his thick grey down that felt
Warm against my knee,
And cold where the water spots be
Like jewels in the sun.
He ate from my hand being not afraid
Or shy.
It was then that I noticed sores that lay
Under his body, and feathers plucked loose.
I wondered why he suffered this abuse,
When I saw his eyes were not afraid
Of my moving hands,
Even be them kind,
I knew at once, this poor old duck
Had somehow come to be blind.
How sad it is what it sometimes takes…
To make one be so wise.

UNITY...ONE HEART

By Kathie Blackwood FitzPatrick

All of us are really as one,
One inside the other,
Like a line a million miles long,
One showing through the other.
Everyone has the same kind
Of heart,
A heart that sheds the same
Kind of tear,
In a soul that lives in many
Lands,
From the city lights and
Desolate sands,
Baked by the cruel desert
Sun—
All of us are really one,
And the Lord only knows,
But may be that's how
God keeps track of His own,
And why He says to all the world,
To love thy neighbor
Even thine enemies,
As you love yourself.

A Wise Proverb

Hate only kills the one
Who hates...
What a fate for a friend.
—KBF

One Tiny Raindrop

By Kathie Blackwood FitzPatrick

We are each like one tiny raindrop fallen
From the sky
Born below to the earth.
In lush green meadows or through concrete
We try
To each one find our own worth.
Some of us fall on streets and walks
Where we die
Or struggle to live.
Other raindrops fall where life they can give
To a land so dry and lonely.
And some still fall on those lands rich
And green,
Those places so fair where it does not
Even seem they are needed.
Every one raindrop would like to fall,
And grow to the top of the mightiest tree,
Or live in the petals of the rose who is

All the very most lovely to see,
But some have to be that blade of grass,
A tiny plant, but together make
The mass
Of beautiful green that covers the Earth.
When the rain comes down, and brings
Its life,
Many kinds and ways there will be,
One of love or maybe of strife;
For a single soul to live and grow,
And learn to look up and see.
But there is no place more noble
For a raindrop to be,
Than growing next to the tendermost heart,
Of one precious daisy
He loves.

The Little Grey Mouse

By Kathie Blackwood FitzPatrick

Once there was a piano in a house
Where a little girl lived,
And so did a little grey mouse.
It was a big white house with
A flower bed and apples
Growing on the big front tree,
But no music was ever heard
To charm the flowers and the birds

Because the little girl never learned
To play.
Susan Hugh spent her days
Having fun instead of learning,
Never once wanting or yearning
To make the keyboard sing.
The big dark piano stood alone
At night
Covered by a shadowed veil,
And out of sight
Was the small grey mouse
Searching for a bite
Of cheese or bread to eat.
Now, over the edge a small thin tail is seen,
When suddenly he fell down upon the keys…
…Klink…Klink…Klink…
He stopped to listen.
What a charming sound.
Up the keyboard he went, carefully
Stepping around
All those big black keys…Klink…
Playing each note with his tiny foot,
…I think…
He began to like it.
Each night as the darkness fell
In the shadows over the house,
Soft music could be heard
Played by the tiny mouse…

Klink…Klink…Klink…
How hard it was to hit the notes
With his tiny foot
Deep in the darkness of the night.
No one ever came to give him
Any light.
The little grey mouse was glad,
For he learned to play best in the dark
With no one around to see.
Each night the mouse played his little part.
And the music became beautiful eventually.
The music enchanted the night like tiny
Little bells,
And no one would ever tell,
Even if they knew,
That a little grey mouse learned to play
Better than Susan Hugh.

Wisdom

The man who will believe
Everything he is told
Is wiser by a hundredfold
Than the man, the poor,
Poor soul…
Who won't believe in anything
—KBF

Four Clay Jugs

By Kathie Blackwood FitzPatrick

Four clay jugs lay in a line,
Smooth in the warmth of the sun;
All the same size and hue,
This group of only a few,
Looked the same they every one.
Inside, unseen by the eye,
The first had a morsel of grain,
Fed by the thin gray earth,
And nursed by the loving rain,
That seeped through the hole above,

Soon to climb to the top,
And to be free in the warmth
Of the day.

The second clay jug in the sun
That lay,
Let him drink up her rain,
Only an empty vessel under the
Eye of the sun.
She enjoyed her fruitless way,
Giving her life to no one.
The third clay vessel was filled
With sand,
And only a heavy weight

That held the water like a sponge,
Where even with lucky fate,
Nothing could hope to grow.
The last clay jug was filled with jewels
Encrusted deep below,
Hid hastily by a thief in a chase
A very long time ago,
And there they'll stay for who
Would ever know
The unseen truth that lies within
A plain clay jug that always has been
Like any other plain brown jug
Around her.
So, I think this proverb true:
That two and two…
Are not always four,
But an infinite number
Of totals galore,
Just like four clay jugs
That lie in the sun.
Though who shall know
Their secret?

Leadership...

From the ones who are loved
Does the silence come.
Ones who are not are the people
We hear from the loudest…
Whose effect on this world
May be the strongest.
Where are the people who love?
—KBF

Outward Appearance

Masks, masks…
But it's a good thing
We never see
What's really behind some
Identity
That's better left unseen,
Like a monster in a cave.
—KBF

Strength

Within ourselves we cannot
Find true strength.
Some may go to far greater lengths
This simple truth to learn.
In weakness of the flesh alone
Does the secret lie.
We, ourselves, first must die
Before this honor is earned.
For strength lies low, deep in
The heart of the weakness of men…
For only then
Do we learn to seek God.
—KBF

Weakness

A man's weakness is always in what
He hasn't,
But usually starts with what
He has.
—KBF

QUESTIONS

By Kathie Blackwood FitzPatrick

If a waterfall rages,
And plunges high from a
Mountain top;
Deep into a valley,
The water is bound,
But not a single soul is around
To hear it echo like thunder,
It has caused me sometime to
Wonder,
Wound there be any sound?

CHILDREN

Pure evil is not clearly seen
Than in children who have
Never been
Chastened, or whipped with a
Willow stick.
Children will not understand
Your reason,
Only a firm hand during
The season

When they are ripe for learning.
If they grow unguided
They will be sure
To endlessly rest on the brim
Of forever being a rebel;
Unhappy and striking out
At his own unknown enemy.
—KBF

CHILDREN

A man who is too wise
To understand a child
Must really be a fool
Caught up in his own
Veil of righteousness.
There is hardly an exception
To the rule…
Truth is sensed first of all
In the mind of a child.
—KBF

EVERY CHILD

Every child finds someone,
Even ceasing friendships soundly,
Ending contact for some,
Elevating certainty,
Far reaching,
Eternally calling
For someone.
—KBF

A FRIEND

By Katherin Blackwood FitzPatrick
I was sitting on the grass near a street one day,
Thinking of nothing in a peculiar way
When I sort of wished, and I kind of hoped
I had someone to talk to.
People passed me one by one,
But gee it wasn't any fun.
No one even saw me.
It was sad in a way. Just one of those days
A person isn't friendly.
I looked around me, and stretched my eyes
To see what I could see.
And lo and behold I saw a speck

Coming toward me.
It was far away down an empty city block,
Bouncing on down closer on the old gray walk,
A bundle of fur and two glowing little eyes,
I could plainly see,
As he stopped before me;
A pup—a mongrel at that.
With a wag of his tail and a wink of his eye,
I looked at his face, and he at I,
Wondering back at him.
Coming to me and my outstretched arm,
He seemed to know I wouldn't harm
A friend.
His nose was so cold as he touched my chin,
And his tongue was warm as he licked my skin
On my face, and arm and hands.
Fur so soft, and body so warm,
Eyes so big, and brown and almost forlorn,
And filled with love,
And I'll ever forget
How he slipped from me and on he went
Leaving me a little more content
In a world that sometimes can forget
About you and me.
The street was crowded, as I watched
Him trot
Through the crowds of people
Until he was a spot,

Ever so small,
With my eyes I peered,
Watching him as he disappeared,
Leaving a trace of happiness behind,
Kind of like…
A friend.

Future

The world is fading away,
The old and the young
All say.
This is the realness of
The moment.
Look up with happiness,
And look up with joy,
The soft wind whispers
The secret…
The tall grass whispers
The answer,
Like the gentle sweet voice
Of Jesus.
—KBF

Prayer of Life

By Kathie Blackwood FitzPatrick

Dear Lord I pray
The things I've done
Be help to some,
And harm to none.
The things of which
I'm not too sure,
Please guide me through;
An pray the things I
Try to do
Will always be conceived in You.
And if I waver along the way,
Just lift me up, Oh Lord
I pray.
For worthy though I can
Not be,
Your promise still abides
That this day I will have
My rest
Because dear Lord
You've done my best.

Touch

By Kathie Blackwood

What is a kiss without the tenderness,
Warm and caressed?
Touch adds warmth and confidence
To every thought you express.
What is praise without a friendly clasp,
Or a friendly pat on the head
To a child so young and wanting?
Touch adds warmth and confidence
To every thought you express
Making everything you say be real
Like a blind man who reaches out
Wanting to know
That the world is really there.

Friendship

By Kathie Blackwood FitzPatrick

I'm glad I'm not a four leaf clover
Lying in the sun,
With my tiny leaves perched
Up high
Waiting for someone to find me.
I could be most anywhere
Waiting in the sun or shade,
But the heart who seeks me out
May search until sunlight fades,
And never find me still.
But a heart with a will may search
The fields so green,
Even in the places it does not even
Seem I would be.
I'm glad that clovers cannot cry,
As her four leaves crumble
And die,
Within the gates of one poor soul
Who needed her most of all.

The Mind

By Kathie Blackwood FitzPatrick

All people live behind
The door of their own mind.
Wise is the man with a solid door
Who opens wide for truth.
Foolish is the man who shuts out
Truth,
Soon he will be destroyed,
For the mind is a powerful thing,
Only controlled by the truth of
Real love,
The mind's only protector.

Peace

Sweet Holy Spirit dove
Of peace
Can cling to nothing unclean,
Easily frightened away to flight,
And tenderly grieved by sin.
It's no wonder you are doomed
To flight,
Far above in God's heaven,
Never to rest yourself again
Upon Earth's troubled shore
Until the new day dawns
When the Lord's new Jerusalem
Rules upon the Earth
—KBF

Spirituality

Just as we tame the beasts
Of the field
God must tame His children
To Love
In a hating world.
Oh, how my own heart grieves
For the little sparrow
who will never come to me
Even though I love him.
—KBF

Eternity

We all seem to walk through
A forest deep,
And dark from the things of life
That shadow overhead
Never knowing what lies before us,
For we tread the path but once.
We can ask the way, but who can say,
There are so many ways to go,
And each of us plods our path
Toward some hidden goal,
That lies beyond all paths
That journey through the way.

Coming Out

There has been a painting that has hung on the wall of our home for many years, and since about 1993 it has hung on the wall of "Karen Street," right next to the large picture of Jesus and the wall writing, "Jesus, help me to love you with my life!"

The painting was done by me, (Kathie), when I was 18 years old. It was done with acrylic paint on a piece of cardboard cut from a Stetson hat box for lack of a canvas. It was done around the early summer of that year. I did a very basic pencil sketch at first. The painting was "born" after about three afternoons of work at home in my small apartment. After all the symbolism I've discovered in the painting since its creation, I wouldn't be surprised, if I took the commercial frame apart, to find it dated "July 10, 1966." I know it was painted in the year 1966, but I can't remember the exact date. It's on the painting, but it's hidden by the bottom frame and is not easily removable.

Both Jaina and Karen really liked this painting because it symbolized to them a young girl transcending from one plane to the next, rising into an abstract clearing of some kind. After the Thirtymile Fire, as I spent time in Karen's room writing about her on the same computer she used when she did her homework and composed her poems and essays, I looked up at the painting one day on the wall in front of me, and I had a huge symbolic revelation within the images of this early work I had created when I was Karen's same age. Here it is:

The figure of the young adult woman is exactly the same size and frame as Karen. The young woman has the same long, reddish-brown, dark hair worn in the hairstyle Karen loved most. The attire is a white blouse, symbolizing both her purity and the heavenly, angelic side of the Thirtymile fire day. The black skirt symbolizes the dark, demonic spirits that showed up to war for the possession of souls hanging in the balance of time between a thin edge of life and death. Those of us who know God and understand the principles of spiritual warfare in the unseen realm understand the forces at work that must have been warring against each other for the souls and lives of human beings, each with a unique future and destiny. In a tense and eventually fatal situation such as Thirtymile, angels loom unseen, like a host of heavenly military, waiting for orders. Will the humans be rescued and delivered, or is it their appointed time? When it's someone's appointed time, that overrules all, and redeemed souls are delivered into the presence of God by these heavenly hosts. It's a different kind of deliverance—an eternal one. Such was the case that day, precluded by intercessory prayer, heard by all nearby, the four of them, led by Karen, then Jessica.

Around the waist of the central female figure in the painting is the yellow ribbon—or waistband—symbolizing the classic color of the Wildland Firefighter uniform. And, of course, in the left hand, the single solitary red rose, Karen's signature symbol of her teen life. From a forest, the figure is walking into the light of a clearing of a new plane of consciousness and existence. In Karen's case, it was heaven.

Never Again So Close

This poem was written in 1969 while I was pregnant with my oldest daughter Yvonne. It turned out to be prophetic of her life, as she left home to live with grandparents at the age of 11 years due to stepfather issues. Although she continued to live with family in my same area, there was always somewhat of a distance between us compared to the daughters who were raised directly in my home. As a young adult, she did not follow us in our move from California to Washington but continued to flourish as an independent thinker and a big city girl who lived in both San Francisco and the East Bay. She worked as a personal trainer in athletic clubs and in recent years has developed her own business. Yvonne is married, and she and her husband, Jeff Heffel, are homeowners who reside in Alamo, California.

This very special poem has sometimes been read in mother-daughter events and Mother's Day programs over the years.

"Never Again So Close"

By Katherin Blackwood FitzPatrick
Written about my daughter
Yvonne Blackwood Heffel, while
I was still pregnant with her, at age 22.

Waiting to be a mother
Is a time of joy and pain,
Living through each coming day
Fighting back the strain
Of human love and anticipation
To see your image recreated
In a brand new soul.
Each anxious day slips by
With such gradual grace,
With the setting sun again
Showing his old familiar face
Reluctantly each morning.
"But never again will I be so close,
Myself and this child of mine."
In a few short years
They venture away,
Differences arise
And they choose to stay
Learning many things,
And all the world's ways,
Of evil and good and that understood
By all the wisest of men.
And when they've grown

They'll be far from you then.
In a lonely time of sadness
You may remember when
In those slow dawning days
You were together unending
During their creating.
"But never again will I be so close,
Myself and this child of mine."

I Caught a Glimpse of Karen One Day

It was in the spring of 2000, I think. She was in her room sitting at her tall art table where she often did her homework or read her Bible. She had her long, auburn hair neatly pinned into a tight knot behind her head. Suddenly she turned around, dressed in a cotton shirt and summer shorts, and stretched her tanned legs and bare feet straight out in front of her, bracing them on the computer chair next to her. She examined her toes, her feet, and her legs as if looking for flaws. I was carrying laundry into her sister's room, and stood silently near the doorway watching her, as if to evaluate her characteristics along with her.

"So, is this the short term, short life-to-live-version of a young girl you've given me, Lord?" I found myself thinking. How long will we really have her? Was her premonition of a premature death real or fantasy? How many times she had been spared from unusual accidents already! Surely angels had been working in her behalf on many occasions in the past.

In a matter of seconds, a quick flash of mini-memories of her growing up flashed through my mind. She was the brave, strong, and willful toddler, yet she was the quiet, shy, blond child who barely spoke a word. We even wondered if she was going to be speech impaired. Would she ever speak more than a few words? She was so jolted by the move from California to Washington at the age of 8 that some days she just put her head down on her desk at school and cried. "I think you'd better just come and pick her up," the teacher would tell me when she called. Who would ever have known that at about the same age, when she walked out on the soccer field for the first time for the Yakima Youth Soccer Association, what a champion player she was to one day become? All who knew her as she was growing up marveled at the huge transformation of Karen in her teen years to the beautiful, elegant, and dramatic swan-like young woman. Not only that, but Karen became an eloquent public speaker, gifted singer, and talented writer, artist, and poet.

I slipped quietly away from the door of "Karen Street" with my thoughts. Karen went back to studying her well-worn Bible, slipping into the deep and private world she loved most, coming away into that special place of communication with the God of heaven and earth who made her. To Karen, there was nothing like talking with and being with God. Only He really knew the answer to my question. Maybe that's all that really mattered.

In the early 1970s, while walking all alone on the ocean shoreline in northern California, the Lord seemed to speak to me about His endless, boundless love in a rare and beautiful way, using nature as example. During that meditation time, a song came to me with a rare and beautiful melody. Here are the lyrics:

Message of the Sea

Song Lyrics by Kathie Blackwood Fitzpatrick

I love the sea.
God's personality
Can be seen on every wave.
My Jesus, He walked there.
He prayed and He taught there
In days long ago.
As I walked by the sea.
God's Spirit showed to me.
A message left there since the first of time:
"Though your sins be like the sands
Of a thousand seas,
I will always be there to wash over thee.
Don't dwell in life's desert,
Come to the sea.
My love is unending to rush over thee."
When you walk by the sea
Let God's personality
Be seen on every wave.
Let each wave be a prayer
As you wash away each care…
As you hear the message
That God wrote on the sea:
That He'll never stop loving, you and me.

"Ye are the salt of the earth…"
"Build not your house on the sand…"
His words still ring out loud and clear.
He says, "Peace be still," when storms of life
Overcome us.
Jesus still abides so near.
As I walked by the sea, God's Spirit
Showed to me,
A message left there since the first of time:
Though your sins be like the sands
Of a thousand seas.
I will always be there to rush over thee.
Don't dwell in life's desert…
Come to the sea.
My love is unending…
To rush over thee.

Sisters: A Photo Album

Karen and Jaina: The "Mutt and Jeff" years.

Two sisters, three years apart: Jaina Christine FitzPatrick, born February 12, 1979, and Karen Lee FitzPatrick, born December 27, 1982. From around 1990 through around 1995, I doubt you would ever have seen such contrast in appearance and style between two sisters. As different as they were, they loved each other deeply. Jaina, the older sister, invested and infused love into her younger sister in rare and wonderful ways. But they were so extremely different, it was comical at times. We affectionately called those years, "The Mutt and Jeff years."

The tall, slender Jaina, already looking quite teenage by age 12 and often referred to as the "Living Barbie,"—especially in the very long, blond ponytail years—was a huge contrast to the young Karen, who was athletic and tan and often mistaken for Jaina's little brother. As a child, Karen was shocked and insulted to learn that her cousins had nicknamed her Ziggy after a popular but homely cartoon character who had a large round nose with spotted freckles.

As the years progressed past 1996, suddenly the young, blond, boyish-looking Karen began to slowly unfold as the classic, sleek, elegant swan! People who knew Karen as a child could scarcely comprehend the contrast between Karen, the tomboy-like young girl, and Karen, the tall, athletic, shapely young woman who was a dark-haired beauty who looked like Miss Cinderella in her homecoming and prom gowns! Jaina's emotions ranged from mild jealousy that Karen succeeded on so many levels with what appeared to be near effortless output to sisterly pride and happiness for Karen that she excelled so highly in academics, music, photography, and sports and had become so unexpectedly beautiful.

By 1998 to 2001, the two girls began to sense more common ground as peers and friends. Once their rooms were side-by-side, they often shared girl talk about life, dreams of the future, and boys late into the night.

If anyone could talk about loving her younger sister, it was Jaina FitzPatrick. She had a lot to do with who Karen became, a very great and amazing young woman who inspired many in her world.

Big sister Jaina with arm around little Karen while visiting Mt. Rainier Park in 1993. Watching them together was a delight. Jaina invested heaps of love and protection into Karen as a young child.

SISTERS: A PHOTO ALBUM

Reflected in a glass ball is big sister Jaina with her arm around Karen at Buchardt Gardens, in 1997 while on vacation. Though a dim reflection, the love still shows through.

Karen and Jaina riding bumper cars at the county fair in Vallejo, CA. in 1983.

Karen is on the picnic table; Jaina is in big sunglasses.

You have never seen sisters like this: Karen and big sister Jaina, "Queen Barbie," in 1984.

Above: Jaina already knew the inevitable snowball fight was only moments away.

Right: After pelting each other with snowballs, the girls call time out.

ANGEL PROMISES

Jaina and Karen with Grandma Ruby who was visiting from their native northern California: 1993.

The classic "Mutt and Jeff" picture, a studio photo of Jaina and Karen, 1991.

Karen and Jaina with me (Kathie) sitting by beautiful Rimrock Lake on Highway 12, in Naches, WA. about 20 minutes from home in Yakima. 1994.

Karen and Jaina at Naches River on Highway 410 near Whislin' Jack's Lodge in Naches, Washington, enjoying a little time together, summer 1993.

Karen and Jaina enjoying a shish-ka-bob while camping on the San Juan Islands in 1997. Karen is wearing a favorite Mighty Mouse T-shirt: "Here I come to save the day."

SISTERS: A PHOTO ALBUM

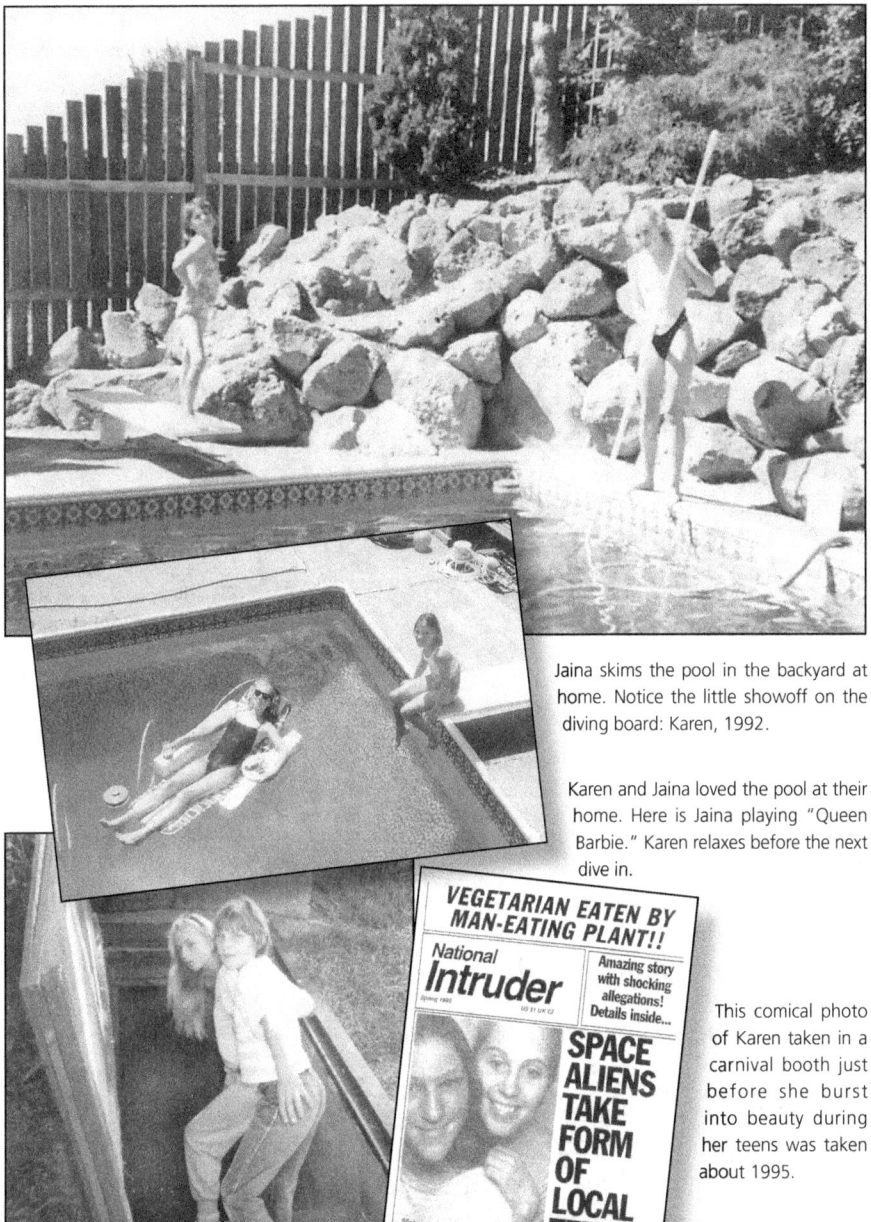

Jaina skims the pool in the backyard at home. Notice the little showoff on the diving board: Karen, 1992.

Karen and Jaina loved the pool at their home. Here is Jaina playing "Queen Barbie." Karen relaxes before the next dive in.

This comical photo of Karen taken in a carnival booth just before she burst into beauty during her teens was taken about 1995.

Jaina and Karen look like images on the front of a youth mystery novel checking out an old cellar while visiting family in upstate New York in 1994.

Jaina and Karen dive into a lake somewhere near Winthrop, Washington, as we stopped for a break on a family trip in 1997.

Jaina and Karen take a quick dip in the lake on a family vacation in 1997. After returning from the San Juan Islands, the girls slipped from the van into a lake near Winthrop for a refreshing swim.

Jaina and Karen at Washington Pass near Winthrop in 1997.

CHRISTMAS TIME, 1999

Although their relationship was almost perfect—

This was the closest I'd seen to sibling rivalry between the two. The "Perfect Barbie," Jaina, was beginning to encounter unwanted weight gain, acne problems, and occasional depression. Now, the little sister, Karen, often mistaken for "the little" brother in the past, was beginning to rise and shine, and find her "place in the sun." The two began to grow closer in a new way, as peers.

Of all the Christmas tree themes over the years, the Angel Tree theme was the favorite with the two girls. It consisted of angel ornaments both bought and collected, and ornaments the girls had made over the years dating back to second grade for Karen. One year, Karen decided the angel ornament with the white frilly netting for a dress needed to come down off the tree and hang on the chandelier in the White Room where she could look at it all the time, year around. It's still there. It needs dusting from time to time, but it's still there.

You could count the number of quarrels between Jaina and Karen on one hand. In this picture, one can sense rare sibling rivalry. The little tomboy Karen was all grown up and glamorous. It's Christmas time, and the tree was decorated in the girls' favorite theme. You guessed it, the Angel Tree.

THERE IS ANOTHER SISTER

Just for the record, Karen has two sisters! When we moved to Yakima in 1990, older sister Yvonne did not choose to move with us as she liked her job in San Francisco at a fitness center, had a serious boyfriend, and loved the beaches of California! She visits us occasionally, then returns to the land where she makes good money as a personal trainer! Yvonne and her husband, Jeff Heffel, are proud homeowners of a property they personally renovated. They reside in Alamo, California.

SISTERS FOREVER

"The thing I remember most about Karen is that we used to have so much fun laughing about absolutely nothing!"
—Yvonne

Karen's two older sisters, Jaina Christine FitzPatrick and Yvonne Blackwood Heffel, enjoying ice cream at Sherry's in Winthrop after a memorial visit to the Thirtymile Fire site in 2003.

Jaina and Karen as young ladies, sisters, and peers, now walking in a world of similar interests. Their rooms were next to each other, and they shared laughter, Bible verses, boy stories, tears, life disappointments, and joys. This photo was taken before Karen met her prom date in the White Room in 1999.

Jaina with Karen on February 12, 2001. It was to be her last birthday with her little sister Karen.

Karen, The Bear Chaser

Karen, packin' popsicles! Age, about 14 months.

So where does all this bravery begin? Where does that indefinable stuff that firefighters are made out of all start to formulate? Does it start in the womb? With Karen, it may have.

She was due on Christmas Day, like her older sister Yvonne, who actually did make it at exactly 3:59 P.M. on December 25, 1970. There must be something about April 4. But like so many babies are, she was just a little late in arriving. I managed to get through Christmas dinner and all the family festivities that Christmas. However, at about 1:30 A.M. the next morning, Karen got very active. She seemed to squirm around, kick around, and let me know in no uncertain terms she had had quite enough of the confinement and was coming out now! You would have thought she was kickboxing or breaking down heavy firewall barricades with strong shoulders, like a battering ram. But she seemed determined to exit from the womb immediately.

I remember thinking, It'll be interesting to meet this amazing little personality! Well, with all that stubborn kicking and flailing around with the strength of Sampson, she broke my water. "What a mess!" I wailed. I was rushed to the hospital. Karen was over nine pounds, closer to ten, and breach—feet first. The doctors tried, but could not seem to turn her around.

"No alternative birth center for you, honey!" the doctor announced. So those plans were put aside. It had worked well for her older sister, Jaina, who, three years earlier, had been born in the very same room we were scheduled to use again.

The determined infant Karen did not make it into the world until 5:40 P.M. on December 27, 1982. After her arrival, her father held her in a blanket and told her, "You will be my hiking companion, camper, and mountain climber, my sports champion!" That she was, indeed.

At times, Karen seemed like a quiet child but with smoldering determination and a "no fear" attitude that surfaced every now and then. One of those times was when we took her along on a family camping trip to Blue Lakes Campground behind Yosemite National Park in California. She was about three and a half years old.

When we drove up to the office to register, I already sensed we might be due for an unusual adventure with the bears. As I waited in the camping van with the kids for their dad to register inside, I noticed a humorous cartoon strip running along the outside of the building. A bear was sitting with a camper carrying wood to the campfire, then next frame, roasting a hot dog at a campfire with the camper, sleeping in the camper's sleeping bag, then carrying the camper off into the woods in the last frame of the cartoon. I wasn't too sure I appreciated this type of humor.

"Do you think this is a good place to be camping with our kids?" I asked in all seriousness when their dad returned to the van.

"Oh, it will be all right. You always worry too much!" was his answer.

We found an excellent shady campsite near the creek, not far from the road and other amenities, and got all set up with two tents. The first night we heard them all around the area. I woke up. Jaina was already peeking outside through a little opening in the netted window.

"Bears," she said quietly.
"Kathie, is all the food locked up in the van?"
"Yup."
"Just stay still and be very quiet."

It was near dawn, and the nocturnal bears were very active. They had it figured out that it was smart to raid all the garbage cans at every campsite before the campsite garbage trucks arrived. Once they had their feast, they were gone.

The next morning while going to the van for breakfast food, I could see the muddy bear paw swipe over the crack of the door opening. They could smell the food, but couldn't get to it. "Do you see that, girls? No hiding cookies under your pillow in this place! The bears will come right into the tent and get them!" They looked up at me with wide eyes and shuddered at the thought. The fear of obedience was upon them.

I told their dad that I was beginning to be worried about camping at that site with small children. He was not worried. "They are hitting the garbage cans every night. They're happy with that," he argued. "Don't worry."

Every night we heard the bears in the campsite and every morning we saw the new muddy paw swipe across the crack of the closed van door. Swimming and hiking was fun, our camp meals were great, but after five days, it was time to pack up and go back home to Benicia, California, the next day. I considered us lucky that we had no serious encounters with the bears.

The next morning about 10:30 A.M., showers were done and the kids were fed. It was time to pack up the van to leave for home. I noticed the muddy paw print on the crack of the closed van door at about 7 A.M. again that morning. "Persistent bear!" I concluded. Jaina and Karen played nearby as I laid all the coolers and food out on the picnic table to pack it up for our trip home. No one was watching high above in the tree that hung over our large wooden picnic table. Then suddenly a large, brown bear, maybe about 150 lbs, dropped down from the tree onto the table right in front of me!

Apparently the bear, who had been trying for the food in the locked van all week, saw his big chance! At first I froze in fear. Their dad was at the front of the van about 50 feet away. "Girls, come with me. Let's run to the van," I instructed them breathlessly. Other campers nearby began to holler when they saw the bear. Jaina ran to the van, but Karen ran for the bear! "Karen! Come here now!" I shouted frantically. Karen squealed in delight at the sight of the big brown bear and ran straight for him. The bear became terrified and broke into a gallop, then broke into a full run down the dirt road with Karen in hot pursuit behind him, squealing happily in her high pitched voice. The terrified bear finally ran up the nearest tree trunk, crawling and scratching up as high as he could go, staring down at Karen below, shaking in fear. Karen just stood at the base of the tree laughing and squealing in delight at the sight of the bear, arms out, looking up, full of wonder. What a sight she was with her bare tummy, baggy jeans, and wearing kid tennis shoes with loose laces. The campers from the other campsites just shook their heads. They couldn't believe it. Jaina peered safely from the van window. I soon scooped her up and carried her back to the campsite.

"Karen, when are you gonna learn to listen to Mom?" I said, up in her face, a little angry. Little did I sense at the time that, for Karen, this was the beginning of bravery. The Lord was also trying to show me—through a series of close calls through the years—that He, and He alone would choose her appointed time.

Karen at about 2 years of age. Her bold spirit was slowly emerging.

"Gelf-ling" Karen at about two-and-a-half-years at our home in Benicia.

"SHERMIE"

Gospel singer Sherman Andrus with Kathie, Jaina, and Karen at their home in 1991.

"Shermie" is a nickname for a favorite childhood buddy of Karen's, Sherman Andrus, legendary gospel singer.

We all have eras in our lives. Karen and Jaina remember 1990 to about 1995 as a time we often had some very interesting company in our home. I was the manager of Christian Artist's Associates, an offshoot of my Christian TV work in California in the 1980s, and often booked well-known Christian talent around the Northwest, around the USA, sometimes overseas, sometimes even in the White House.

Occasionally, the music artists that I often spoke with on the phone came to stay in our big lodge-like home in Yakima between concerts or TV dates. One such Christian artist was legendary gospel singer, Sherman Andrus.

Like the other guests who sometimes frequented our guest area, Sherman learned to make himself at home, practice music in the White Room, and enjoy our cooking for at least a week or so at a time. From the beginning, Sherman and Karen both seemed to have that crazy energy that drew them together like a cosmic magnet. Their first encounter must have been when Karen was about nine years old. Sherman's constant teasing sometimes wore me and Jaina out a bit, but never Karen. She would feed off it, and the two of them would absolutely go into orbit with laughter. Sherman and Karen would hit the mall and the movies, and it was "watch out world" when they were out on the town in Yakima.

One morning Sherman had the idea that he and Karen and I should go out for breakfast. I agreed, but I kept getting interrupted by calls. Karen and Sherman, the impatient and hungry ones, were getting antsy. While taking one last call, I heard the keys slip off the key rack in the kitchen. Within moments I heard the sound of my car starting, and Karen and Sherman roared out the long gravel driveway without me. Those rascals!

"I hope you had a very nice breakfast," I said when they returned about four hours later, looking very impish.

"We couldn't wait; you were taking too long," Karen answered with a wink.

"Yep!" Sherman agreed.

Sherman's wife, Winnie, kept hearing about this "amazing" kid as reports of Karen drifted back to Bethany, Oklahoma where Sherman and Winnie lived at the time. "Maybe you can come and visit with Winnie and me some summer. You'd like the pool," Sherman remarked. Although Karen was excited at the prospect, it never quite happened. Because Sherman and Winnie had a grown son, Sherman Jr. who was married and lived in Portland, Oregon, there were reasons to come out west every now and then.

Sherman sometimes called to check out booking prospects with me here in the Northwest when he knew he was coming this way. Karen would get on the phone and update him on the latest victories of her

Bobcat soccer team and whatever else was new. How Sherman loved that tomboy side of Karen! But then Karen started growing up.

"Hey, Shermie. You should have seen me when I went to prom and wore the most fabulous gown and black high heels!"

"You mean high heels and nylons and stuff like that?" Sherman asked during one phone call.

"Yeah, of course, you know?" Karen replied in melodic tones that only she could speak.

"I hate that!" Sherman said. I could hear him all the way across the room. "You're growing up. Why can't you just stay like that little girl I know? We have so much fun."

"Cause I can't!" Karen laughed.

"And boys! Are you interested in boys?"

"Of course, Shermie."

"I hate that!" Karen laughed some more at his silly comments.

Then, a few years later, Sherman called because he was coming to Tri-Cities. After talking business with me, Karen swooped in and took the phone from my hand.

"Shermie, how are ya?"

"Fine, Karen. How are you?"

"Shermie, this week I got saved, I mean really, really saved. I'm different."

Sherman was silent at first. He wasn't sure how to take it.

"Really? You're scarin' me now," he kidded at first. Sherman began to get an early glimpse of the new, emerging Karen—the real butterfly.

"Karen, I want to come to your high school graduation. Can you find out when it is?"

"OK, Shermie. That would be fun!"

Well, the best made plans can be disrupted. Sometimes we are just required to be too many places at once.

Year 2001.

"Shermie, graduation night is June 8, 2001."

"OK. What day does that fall on? Let me talk to Winnie."

Well, due to a family birthday party in Bethany, OK. Sherman was not able to attend Karen's high school graduation ceremonies and baccalaureate. I would have loved it if he had heard her sing in the trio with her classmates, Sarah and Kelly, "Circle of Friends." But some good things just never get to happen like you think they will. She walked across the stage at the Yakima Sundome on June 8, 2001, to accept her high school diploma from West Valley High School. On July 24, the community, the nation, and the world, honored and remembered Karen, Jessica, Tom and Devin, because they were no longer with us.

"Life can sometimes just throw you a curve ball!" as Karen would say.

Angel Stuff

A mighty angel towers over the city of Rome. According to the Bible, angels await orders from God. Their missions are many, but for the believers they either rescue or deliver into the presence of God at the appointed time. Photo by Kathie FitzPatrick, Rome, Italy, August 2006

One of Karen's firefighter comrades from the Thirtymile Fire, a young blond man named Scott, walked up to me at the reception of Karen's Celebration of Life service held at West Valley High School in Yakima.

"I want to see if Karen's mom has Karen's handshake," he said, taking my hand. I gave him the firm handshake the teenaged boys in Yakima County Youth Detention knew well. "Yeeee-ep!" He replied with a grin. Scott had escaped the catastrophic fire with only a few minor burns on his legs. He was one of the lucky ones. "I want to tell you something," he said, getting more serious. "Right before the fire blew up, Karen jumped up onto the rocks. I watched her. She turned around and smiled. Her face shone like an angel. Ten minutes later she was gone." I thanked Scott for telling me the story.

Now I have a few stories.

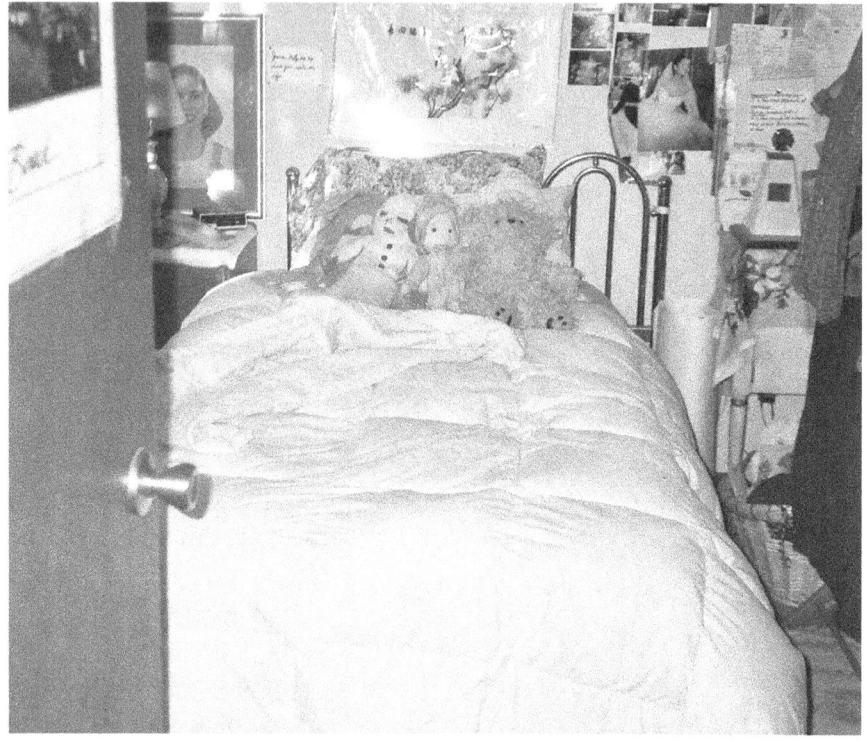

When I went downstairs to Karen's room the next morning, July 10, and saw she had only lain down for a brief time under her angel blanket, then threw it aside on her bed, I knew she had left quickly the night before to report to the fire.

Karen's Angel Blanket

Karen's angel blanket: It was a gift from the ladies at church who made crafts to sell for the foreign missions fund. But really, I think it must have been spun in heaven.

It was December 1981. I was in the last stages of pregnancy with Karen. I was huge, and she was very active and very large due to weighing well over nine pounds! Little did I know, some ladies in the church I attended, the First Assembly of God Church in Vallejo, California, were planning a very nice surprise for Karen and me.

After Karen Lee arrived into this world, my friend Barbie announced that she was planning a baby shower for me. When Karen was three weeks old, my friends and some of the church family assembled at

Barbie's home and gave me and baby Karen a grand time! They showered me with really wonderful presents. But the very grandest gift of all came last. Barbie handed me a mysterious, large box with a big, fluffy big pink bow on top. Breathlessly, I opened it. There it was—a pink quilt! I opened it and displayed it for all the guests to see. The ladies had skillfully embroidered the outline of beautiful angels on both sides. In the center was the well-known prayer: "Now I lay me down to sleep. I pray to the Lord my soul to keep. If I die before I wake, I pray the Lord my soul will take." I was stunned by the beauty of this gift of time and patience! This was not created by anyone I was especially close to, just some very nice ladies in the church who knew of me and that I had just had a baby girl.

When I got home, I placed it in Karen's baby crib as I tucked her in. There it stayed. It followed her to the bed when she was a little older. Later, when she was a toddler, Karen dragged it around over her shoulder with her thumb in her mouth. It followed her to the room where she lived until she was eight. Then, during our move from California in 1990, it comforted her as she wrapped herself in it for the car trip to Washington. There it went to her bedroom on the second floor of our very large home in Yakima. It was always on the foot of her bed or folded somewhere in her room. It moved downstairs to the room next to Jaina's because the girls wanted to room next to each other when Karen was about 13. There they proceeded to bond into best friends for life. In the years to follow, we often heard laughs, giggles, and even sobs from that downstairs realm of two girls who were truly very close sisters. Then came the high school years.

"Mom, tuck me in!" Karen would tease me, bounding into her bed with her pink angel blanket and her teddy bear "Pooky." Karen squealed with delight as I sat on her bed and wrapped her pink angel blanket around her over her white down comforter, giving her a peck on the cheek or her freckled nose. Even when she was 18, I was reminded daily that this beautiful young woman had a very delightful inner child!

On July 9th, 2001, I heard that she might be called out around midnight to join her crew in the North Cascades to fight fires up there. But I didn't hear the phone ring when she got the call. This time, they called her cell phone. When I walked into her room the next morning and saw the angel blanket on top of her bed, folded back, I could almost picture her rising up and heading for the door. I knew she had gone to the fire.

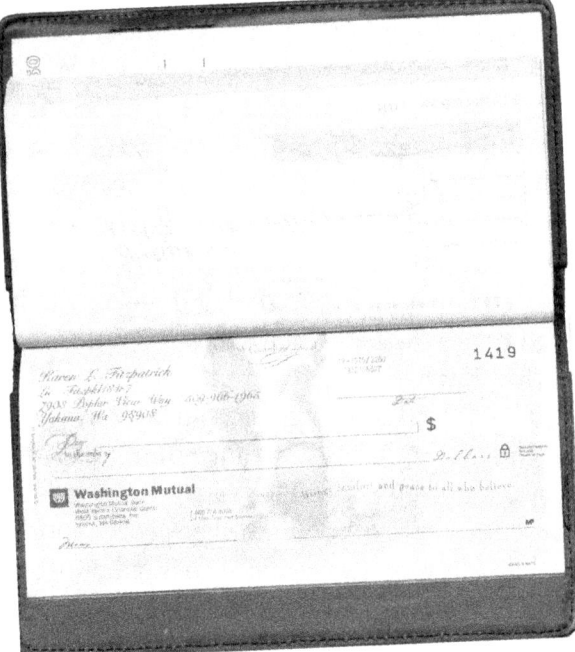

Karen's checkbook from her senior year in high school bought everything from prom dresses to school supplies, and she also used it to give generously to others. Karen was known as an extravagant gift giver. Her checkbook design bears the Guardian Angel and the Bible verse Hebrews 1:14 and the phrase, "brings comfort and peace to all who believe."

THE GUARDIAN ANGEL THING

"God speaks of his angels as messengers swift as the wind, and as servants of flaming fire" (Hebrews 1:7).

"Are they not all ministering spirits, sent forth to minister to them who shall be heirs of salvation?" (Hebrews 1:14).

Karen never said much about angels, but they seemed to surround her life—both seen and unseen. They were embroidered on her favorite childhood blanket and one even found its way to her personal checkbook. She seemed to walk in divine protection as she survived a number of life threatening, close calls in childhood. Then, only seven months before the Thirtymile Fire, Karen walked away from a car wreck on a

December evening. She was hit from behind by a teen driver who had only had his license for two days. Her car, the silver Acclaim she loved, was totaled. A little sore, but unscratched and virtually unscathed by the accident, the paramedics and emergency workers who arrived on the scene could not believe her near-perfect condition. She was trying to cheer everybody else up, especially the boy who hit her. "I'm really not mad at you," she said, peering through the windshield of the other car, trying to find him. "Are you all right?"

Everyone who knew Karen was quick to point out that her Guardian Angel was certainly watching over her that night, and working overtime for sure! So what happened on July 10, 2001, when she was "taken" in the swirling flames of the Thirtymile Fire? Was the lighting band from heaven sleeping? I think not. Angels dispatched by God himself were definitely present! In the Bible it is said that we all have an appointed time to die. Only God knows when it is. When that appointed time comes, if we have been living for God with our lives and are bound for heaven, our Guardian Angel—or band of angels—now has a new task. It is to deliver us up into the presence of God, to be with him forever.

This moment was the one Karen lived for, but we could not have guessed it would happen so soon, when she was only 18 years old. Isaiah 57:1 points out God's wisdom in sparing the righteous who die young—or too soon as we perceive it. Only the Lord who made heaven and earth and every cell in our bodies has the power to see ahead on a life pathway and make the decision to "spare them from future trials, persecutions and temptations."

So what did God see ahead for Karen that was so fearsome? The ones who knew her could only speculate what God saw ahead that caused Him to take her rather than rescue her on that hot July day. Or was the picture even much bigger than that? We can only guess. We can only speculate.

Window of Destiny

There are a few things that happen by chance, and then sometimes you get the distinct feeling other things happen that are connected to destiny.

"Hey, 'Mommy-O', I've got my own personal forest out here by my window!" Karen Lee commented to me one day as I dropped off some of her freshly laundered jeans to her room downstairs.

"Yeah, you do, don't you?" I looked out the large window in her room at the pine trees and a variety of forest foliage. The view of the valley was almost obstructed by the trees and bushes. That little corner of the world was the only spot on our half acre lot with trees and plants like that.

A few pictures were taken in the forest where she worked around the time of the Thirtymile Fire tragedy. As I put up in her room one of the photos sent to me by the Forest Service, it suddenly struck me. I looked out her big window. I could almost hear her voice, "I've got my own personal forest." Yes, she did. It was the same foliage as commonly seen in the Chewuch River Canyon in WA., and the area where she worked the previous week in Oregon. It was another amazing coincidence— or was it really destiny?

Karen spent the last part of June 2001 and the first part of July in the national forests of Oregon working for the USFS and then the Chewuch River Canyon, WA., July 10, her last assignment. Oddly, the foliage in the picture and in the Chewuch River Canyon itself resembles the same small patch of foliage that grew in her "own personal forest" just outside her bedroom window. See the comparison in the photos.

Angel Stuff

Thoughts from Paula Hagemeyer

Bruce and Paula Hagemeyer had been camping somewhere behind the Chewuch River Canyon area for a few days prior to the July 10, 2001, episode. On the day of July 10, they had driven their SUV into the area where the fire had been ablaze earlier in the day. Driving along the Chewuch River Road and then back out on to Highway 20 to make a grocery run to Gary's Red Apple in the small town of Winthrop, they had seen no indication of the fire or any signage to warn the public of the fire.

Later that afternoon, unknown to Bruce and Paula, as the fire in the Chewuch River Canyon was worsening and the fire management officers knew they were losing their battle with the small campfire that got away, this fire was now transitioning quickly into a soon-to-be huge and violent fire that would burn many thousands of acres. Meanwhile, from their campsite, the Hagemeyers noticed a rosy glow on the horizon in front of them. Out of curiosity, they got into their vehicle and drove toward it. Within minutes of crossing the bridge into the Chewuch River Canyon area, they found themselves suddenly entrapped by the fire that originated from the Thirtymile campsite. The scene had become frantic as the tall trees were ablaze all around them. Sideways tornadoes were about to formulate that would later rip out large trees and toss them around like small toothpicks in the hot whirl of the firestorm. In the midst of the formulating chaos, Karen came over to Bruce and Paula's vehicle and spoke briefly to them with friendliness and kindness. Soon after, she hopped up on the rocks with other crew members, and about 10 minutes later she was gone forever into eternity.

Meanwhile, Bruce and Paula struggled with the sudden and shocking emergency immediately before them. Within moments, they were sharing a one-man aluminum fire shelter with USFS firefighter Rebecca Welch, fighting for their lives in the 70 mile-per-hour firestorm winds that had so suddenly formed. They struggled and prayed with the rest of the crew who had deployed their fire shelters on the road. Rebecca Welch used every bit of the skill, training, and wisdom she could muster to keep all of them safe within the confines of the tiny foil shelter. It was the longest 15 minutes of their lives. When the fire finished the worst of the burn-over, they were still alive, suffering only a few minor burns. Remarkable. Never had three people survived such a fire emergency in a one-man fire shelter.

At the first anniversary commemoration of the Thirtymile Fire in Winthrop, Washington, Paula handed us a note with some of their thoughts about Karen. She said she had carried it around with her for a year.

> "Attached are some thoughts I had about your daughter and our brief encounter with her. I meant to read it at her memorial, but at the time it did not seem appropriate, after all. I have carried this with me in my backpack since that day. A year later, I still have these warm feelings for her in my heart. There were no heroes that day, but your daughter was the only one who tried to comfort us, and I thank you, your husband, and Karen for that.
>
> Sincerely,
> Paula Hagemeyer"

Our Brief Love Relationship with Karen FitzPatrick:

When we were driving down the canyon road in what Bruce and I hoped would be an uneventful exit, we came upon several firefighters blocking the road. They waved their arms for us to stop. I believe one of those who waved us down was Karen FitzPatrick.

Two young people came up to our truck that day and spoke with us one at a time. A young man, and a young woman I now know was Karen. She stood outside the driver's side of our vehicle, close to Bruce who was the driver that day, and spoke with both of us. I felt an instant parental connection with this young lady. I remember thinking later that we were probably close to her parents' age, and she could be our daughter. During our short conversation, Karen treated us with utmost respect, kindness and, I feel, love. She shared a little of herself with us, speaking of where she was from and her recent training and her total excitement about being a firefighter. In expressing her feelings about the current fire, Karen said, "Oh, this is so beautiful. Look at the sun!" It was the most incredible red I'd ever seen

ANGEL STUFF

in my life. She said, "You'll never see anything like it again in your life!" She said some were taking pictures and that if we had a camera we should take one too. Our verbal conversation ended there.

In ending, I would like to say, I felt your daughter was an angel. And I felt honored to have known her those last few minutes before she went to heaven!

Love, Paula Hagemeyer

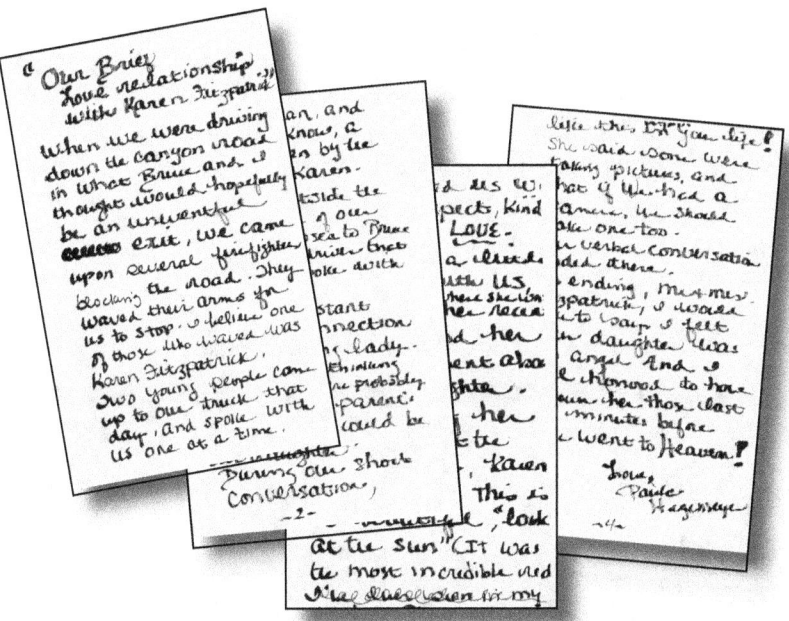

Angel Promises

"It was Winter of 2007, and I found myself suddenly really missing Karen," Jaina FitzPatrick, now 28, recalls. "I had gone to Seattle with a bunch of students and friends for some training. Once over there, I discovered a very pretty and friendly girl named Karen. I was just thinking to myself how much she reminded me of my sister, Karen. It made me miss her all the more. After some small conversation, I discovered that she knew my sister Karen Lee from some church group activities. We had a nice talk about it. Then she said, "You know your sister Karen is watching over you and protecting you—she is helping and supporting you now." I wondered about that as it did not seem biblical, but was a nice idea. As far as I had been taught once in heaven, they are not aware of our activities down here.

I found myself pondering over this for quite sometime. A few days later, after coming home, I was thinking about this some more. I asked God to give me a sign if it was true. I was in my room and reached for a little golden book about friendships. It immediately fell open to a passage that read, 'If you wish for perfect friends, best look for them among angels.'

Hmmmm. Now that really made me wonder! I guess I will have to think about that some more!"

—Jaina FitzPatrick, sister of Karen Lee.

The prophetic cloud which formed over the four firefighters, bearing 4 white galloping horses aligned one behind each other.

The Sign in the Cloud

The Thirtymile Fire Cloud

Then it happened...the unthinkable. A small abandoned campfire smoldered and rekindled into a much larger fire that began to spread across the area next to the Chewuch River not 30 feet from a paved road. Spotted high above by a Canadian smokejumper plane by 9:30 P.M. on the eve of July 9, the FMOs and other management of the U.S. Forest Service began to make decisions about what to do about this "small fire" near the Thirtymile Campground in the Chewuch River Canyon.

At the time, most of the resources, water, and equipment were going to a larger fire about 30 miles away called the South Libby Fire. At midnight, the Okanogan Sheriff's Department sent a big fire suppression rig out to the site. Unfortunately, the hot shots who were on the fire at the time, turned the water source away and began to light "control line" fires, hoping to create a barrier the fire would not cross. This did not work and made the fire worse.

At about 9 A.M. the next morning, when Karen FitzPatrick, Tom Craven, Devin Weaver, and Jessica Johnson arrived on the scene with their firefighting crews, the small fire had become a much larger "initial attack" fire. The unfortunate details that followed are now history, and for other researchers to tell. The sad conclusive facts are that this small fire that began from an abandoned, runaway campfire ultimately burned in excess of 9,300 acres and took the lives of four young firefighters, Karen FitzPatrick, 18; Tom Craven, 30; Devin Weaver, 21; and Jessica Johnson, 19.

During their dramatic and tragic entrapment that occurred late that afternoon, Karen and her three ill-fated firefighter colleagues deployed their aluminum fire shelters on the rocky slopes above the Chewuch River near the site of a dead-end canyon road their more experienced supervisors thought was an escape route. Unfortunately, their supervisors in charge did not bother to check a map, one of a myriad of deadly mistakes made by the fire management that day. Karen died on her knees in her aluminum fire shelter, praying as an intercessor with the other three trapped firefighters who were about to enter the point of eternity, and for the safety of the remainder of the crew trapped down below on the road, and the in creek who ultimately did live. Karen, a strong young woman of faith, was ready to meet with eternity, and interceded loudly for the others with her. They died at 5:30 P.M. from smoke inhalation and from breathing products of hot combustion. At 6 P.M., a huge cloud formed above them in the sky, bearing four linear steps at the top. We call this the "Stairway to Heaven Picture." This very special moment was captured on film by local photographer, Sandor Feher of Santila Studios, Winthrop, WA.

More than the four steps, now the four white galloping horses.

It was Karen's grandmother, Ruby Lee Horace, of Walnut Creek, California, who first noticed the outline of a galloping white horse in this rare and beautiful cloud formation. She sees the back legs and tail of the horse on the left of the cloud with the front legs folded under, and the head of the horse on the right following the top of the cloud line. Can you see the galloping horse as if he is leaping up over the mountain? The steps seem to mount to the back of the horse. Shortly after this, a friend of the family called, and said, "I see multiple horses."

This is also very interesting in view of the Scripture found in the Revelation 19:11-14, as Jesus returns to earth in the clouds on a white horse with his people behind him on white horses. Also seen on www.youtube.com. Enter ANGEL PROMISES, then click on the frame to view.

Ruby Lee Garrison—age 22. She was later known as Ruby Horace, originally Ruby Horacek. She is Karen's grandmother.

The Sign in the Cloud... Karen's Legacy

By John FitzPatrick

Her valiant smile; a "no fear" display.
"Wholly bright," with joy and peace...
Like a beacon's shining ray.
Do you know the mystery...
Why Karen trod "this Way?"

She knew it was her time,
...some heard this girl say.
Ready was she; but then who else,
For their sins would not pay?

Three stayed close to Karen,
Then midst Providential fire and fray.
Drew strange comfort from this lass;
As "bearing cross," she knelt to pray.

With gospel truth and earnest plea,
Echoed her words in souls that day.
In those hearts prepared came grace;
Then "the few," burst from their clay.

Those pitched upon that rocky mount;
Only earthly shells there lay.

Neath those thin and silvery shrouds,
Spirits with God; no more to stray.
"New born" souls for Heavenly glory!
Behold, "The Cloud"…now no dismay.

Karen, having a reputation in the community and on her high school campus for being a dynamic young woman of God for only 18 years old, recognized the last few minutes between 5:15 P.M. and 5:30 P.M. as their last moments before facing eternity. She died on her knees on the rocky ground, inside her aluminum fire shelter, praying with the other three firefighters, Jessica, Tom, and Devin, and also for the safety of those deployed on the road who did live. She did not pray for her own safety, nor did she expect to be rescued. These facts were established through eyewitnesses at the site at the time and also how she was found after her death. It is also interesting that her friend Don, who saw Karen on her knees crying out for the salvation of others in a vision only one month before, saw her surrounded by swirling flames! He was very puzzled by what this could possibly mean.

The Sign in the Cloud

Approximately thirty minutes after their passing, at 6 P.M., a huge, white billowy cloud formulated high above them in the bright blue summer sky, bearing four linear steps at the top. This famous photo of the Thirtymile Mile Fire Cloud was named "The Stairway to Heaven Picture" by Karen's mom, Kathie FitzPatrick.

"I was preparing my message for the one year anniversary commemoration, when I looked at the picture of the cloud on the U.S. Forest Service brochure, and suddenly there it was, as plain as day—what looked like a stairway to heaven! For the first time, I saw it! I believe it was a sign from God for something we already knew in our hearts."

Photo courtesy of the US. Forest Service Visitor Center, Winthrop, Washington, Thirtymile Fire Memorial Site. The photo is on the front of the brochure about the Thirtymile fire, available to the public before going in to view the site, now a national monument.

Karen Lee, cousin Cherlin Johnson, Aunt Suzanne, friend Pat, and pet parrot, "Cherub"—June 13, 2001, in Laguna Beach, California. During Karen's after graduation vacation.

THE FIREFIGHTER BOOTS

We had just come home with them that afternoon. The price tag was a real heart-stopper—around $350.

Earlier, as we were leaving the store where the boots were purchased, we ran into Karen's friend and the Fire Chief from our local city, Yakima. Karen enjoyed her time job-shadowing there at the city fire department very much.

"Tom! I just got my boots!" she beamed, carrying the big box in an even larger big bag. "I just got hired on by the U.S. Forest Service!"

"Oh, hi, Karen. Hey, so did my sons! Be sure to break them in before you wear them to work, even if you just wear them around the house or yard. Your feet will be sore if you don't! My sons have been practicing for the Pack Test this week, each carrying a backpack of 40 lbs of rocks around the track at West Valley High School!"

"Really?" Karen laughed. "I'll be in Laguna Beach, next week at my Aunt's house near the beach. It's my graduation gift from my family."

"Well, you'd better at least make it twice that week to the gym to work out with your Aunt Suzanne or you'll be sorry." I warned her, "You may not be ready."

"OK, Mom. But I want to get nice and tan. The beach is calling!" She laughed. "Aunt Suzanne says I'll like playing volleyball on the beach. There's a tournament too!"

"Well, you will get off the plane on Saturday night about 8:30 and the Pack Test is the following day, Sunday afternoon," I reminded her. We had a nice time visiting with Karen's fire chief friend for about 10 minutes, then left for home.

It was early evening now. We had both had a few errands, and I even made a stop by my real estate office. Dinner was on slow cook in the oven, and I slipped down the stairs to the laundry room to do a few things. The lower level of our home is like its own world, separate drive up entrance, family room, bath, two bedrooms, and storage areas. I could hear Karen rustling around in her room; "Karen Street," we called it. Suddenly her door opened, and she appeared. "Mom, can you come in here for a few minutes?

"OK, Hon. Let me put this detergent in and get the laundry started. Dinner is almost ready." I walked over to her open door. I could see she had the box with the new boots open, and apparently she had been looking them over. They were the brown leather wonders that were supposed to take anything this earth's disaster zone could dish out.

"Mom, look! There's a date stamped inside each one of these boots—the date they were made. Can you see it?" She held the open shoe up to the light.

"It reads, June 20, 2000. I wonder what that means."

"Wonder what what means?" I asked, clueless, at first.

"It was the date I was 'born again.'" Karen replied. Oh yes. This was a date I had heard about. It was hard for me to grasp because I had seen evidence of it much earlier, at least a few years prior. Her dad and a friend from Bible study, Tom H., had keyed in on this date.

"So why is it you think it was that date?" I asked. She got really quiet on me. "Is it because that's the date you gave up the bad boy, Mark?"

"Yes. I put Jesus first and put the bad relationship behind me," Karen replied.

I remembered the night. I could hear her sobs emanating up from her room below, way up on the second floor as I worked in the living room. I knew she was on her knees by her bed on what came to be known as her little prayer rug. I had slipped quietly downstairs and looked silently through the slightly open door from her sister's room. She was deep into the presence of God, on her knees with a tear stained face. I shut the door and went back upstairs. These were deep moments between her and Jesus. Back to the present tense.

"Soooooo, the date June 20, 2000," I stated. Do you have any clues on what that means?"

"I think it means that it was written in destiny that I would be a firefighter," Karen replied, matter-of-factly, tucking the mysterious boot back into the box.

"Well, Miss Firefighter, dinner's almost ready if you are."

"OK, Mom!"

Looking back, I suppose it was written in destiny that she would be a firefighter.

Firefighter boots atop Karen's bed. Note the white tag at the top of the boot marks the date the boots were made. Karen thought it was an unusual coincidence that her boots were made on the same date she was "born again." Some of us thought it was unusual she claimed this late date, but to her it signified when she became totally focused on God and no longer distracted by lesser things or bad relationships.

The Sign in the Cloud

She Knew

For quite some time I had come to grips with the reality that in Karen's world she had come to believe—or walk in a premonition—that she would not live to be an adult who would enjoy a long career or get to raise a family. But it was her desire, and it was her dream. The picture of the fantasy wedding dress is still on her wall today. But she had a knowing that something would interfere with her dreams and cut her life short.

It started when she was about 15, I think. I still remember Karen coming home from school one snowy day. She looked kind of sad and dark, very rare for her.

"Mom, I don't know what to do. At school, all these counselors want to talk to me about college and what I want to be when I get out of high school."

"Yes, Hon?" I said, putting another log on the fireplace in the kitchen.

"I won't ever live long enough to have to really worry about it," she said, dropping the bomb squarely.

"Really?" She looked serious, and I perceived it was a spiritual issue. "Well, the best thing to do is plan anyway and let God decide the matter," I nodded with a smile. "Don't you think?"

She cracked a little smile. "It's kind of hard to plan at all. I can't take career planning seriously, feeling as I do."

"I'll tell you what. Let's keep this secret between you and me. The teachers and counselors at school will never understand this kind of thinking. I'm sure you'll get into something you're interested in. Dr. Buehler would just love to see you train for dental hygiene," I said, referring to our neighbor and family dentist. "Weren't you just talking about it on your last visit?"

"Yeah, I kind of like that choice," she smiled.

"See there. It's all settled."

But then there was that fire on the fourth of July. It changed her life forever. We called it the "Shorty Pajama Fire." A late-night fire that started in a dry field next to our home by careless teen neighbor boys, became a much larger fire that almost took our house and another house. The firemen from the local fire department seemed helpless. The high tech, new, yellow fire truck was parked on the road above our house. However, it was obviously at the wrong angle to effectively fight the fire.

"What good does it do to have a quarter million dollar fire truck if you don't know how to use it?" I wailed impatiently to the fire department operator on the phone, as the fire crept closer to our house. In all the commotion, Karen woke out of a sound sleep, came upstairs, and quickly sized up the situation. She rushed outside in her flannel shorty pajamas and met with some guys hauling hoses. As I backed my car out to move it out of range, I caught a glimpse of Karen sailing over the fence, hoses blazing, wetting down the side of our house and meeting the flames head on. The fire was soon quelled. The rest is history.

Midnight, July 4, 1997. "Thank you young lady for helping us put out the fire," said a very tired West Valley Fire Chief. Yes. Thank you. But life would never again be the same for a tall, blossoming beauty. The path was set. Little did she know that she had a date with another fire on July 10, 2001, in the North Cascades. That one would not be so kind.

Coping with Grief

The unusual thing about this piece of work is that I wrote it around the latter part of June 2001. It was a new entry for my "Extreme Teen Rescue," the Young Lion's Youth Ministry Program manual (See: www.younglions.org)

I had run across numerous young people in our youth detention ministry who had lost a family member—sometimes tragically—and I decided to add this to my list of topics. At the time I wrote on this topic, I had a strange feeling overcome me, like something unexplainable was looming. I ran off copies from my computer, put one on Karen's desk in her room, one on Jaina's desk, and one on their dad's desk. About three weeks later, I had to take my own advice. I realized God had already begun to prepare me for the terrible tragedy. It's still good advice for anyone:

God provides His strength at the point of tragedy and at the time of our human weakness and grief.

"I have strength for all things in Christ who empowers me—I am ready for anything and equal to anything through Him who 'infuses inner strength' into me. (That is, I am self sufficient in Christ's Sufficiency)" (Philippians 4:13, Amplified Bible).

"Bless the Lord, my immovable Rock. He gives me strength and skill in battle. He is always kind and loving to me; he is my fortress, my tower of strength and safety, my deliverer. He stands before me like a shield. He subdues my people under me" (Psalms 144:1, Living Bible Translation).

Humanly speaking, we hit the wall and shatter at tragic news and circumstances. But then our frail human side collapses on the Immovable Rock and quietly rests there, experiencing God's strength, not our own.

When we have been completely and emotionally drained and saddened, when we have been deflated by life, that's when we feel His infilling, like the filling of a balloon, channeling to us His strength, not our own. It's no wonder God likes to show His strength in weakness. It becomes a shining beacon of light, a testimony of the reality of God's promises, that they are truly real and are available to all who will live for Him!

We are praying too, that you will be filled with His mighty, glorious strength, no matter what happens—always full of the joy of the Lord (Colossians 1:11, Living Bible Translation).

THE MYSTERIOUS ANGEL

In April 2006, while standing in line at the checkout of a local grocery store, a woman I did not know at the time turned around and said to me, " Kathie FitzPatrick, I have something I've been waiting to give to you. It's been about three years now. It's an angel."

I thought this was very kind. I was often still recognized by people in the community as one of the Thirtymile Fire parents. Many people gave me various things after the tragic fire, poetry, inspirational messages, artwork, quilts, and crafts of all kinds.

"I can't even describe it," she said. "I just need to give it to you." We exchanged phone numbers. Her name was Carol.

It should have been simple, but we had a hard time getting hold of each other on the phone. Then I had a hard time finding time to meet her. Weeks went by. One day she said in a phone call, "You know, I don't live too far from Aspen Real Estate. Call me when you are there, and I'll come over with it." With the busy season in real estate coming, I continued to be sidetracked and distracted even further. In the meantime, I got the open door, bright-light-shining-down-from-heaven call to do the book, *Angel Promises*. I wondered how I would ever find the time. I was already overwhelmed. I started accumulating the poems, photos, and artwork, and started on faith. A professional photo shop I used downtown began scanning photos and artwork for me.

On the way to the photo shop one day, I got call from a secretary of another real estate company. "Carol Lane left an angel here for you to pick up. Can you come and get it?" I was coming down Yakima Avenue, practically driving right by the very establishment at the time.

"I'll be right there!" At the same time I was wondering, Now why did she leave it there? May be God knew exactly how busy I was. Within moments, I was walking into the entryway of that office.

The secretary pulled it out. I gasped in amazement. It was the most beautiful and perfect art piece of an angel I think I have ever seen. It was very large. It was framed in a wide silver frame. The angel was reaching toward Karen's extended hand, and they were going up. The young girl figure in the white robe had the long reddish brown hair that Karen loved. Tears came to my eyes. This wonderful and kind woman had never even known Karen. I looked closer. The work was lovingly made in tiny, intricate cross-stitch. On the back it read, "Presented to Kathie FitzPatrick in memory of her daughter Karen, whom I did not have the honor of knowing, but somehow she touched my heart." Later, I measured it. It was 20" by 27." This work is thousands upon thousands of intricate, tiny stitches

I called her, but had trouble reaching her. I left her a thank you message. "Thank you for the angel! I'm sure you thought I was rather late in picking it up, but I was actually was right on time." I went to the photo imaging studio and took it upstairs to be photographed for Angel Promises. It was then that some very interesting circumstances began to take place.

Delays in my busy work schedule caused me be a couple of weeks late in getting back to pick up the disc with what I hoped would be an image of the angel to place in the "memories and stories" section of the book. Geri gave me the disc, and I went downstairs to the "box" to print out a few for my files. I loaded the disc. The reader showed zero pictures on this disc. That was strange. I had used this photo service for years for everything from real estate to vacation pictures to business cards, and everything was always perfect. I went back upstairs.

"Geri, the angel is not on the disc," I announced.

"It has to be; I put it on there myself," she replied. Into the box it went. It was the same thing again—zero pictures. Geri, who had done much work for me over the years, went back to her main computer to look for the angel.

"It has disappeared," she said, her eyes bugging out. "But I saw it myself. It was on there, then I put it on your disc."

Little did I realize at the time that if I was going to use this angel creation in Angel Promises, this was definitely going to take some standing firm and fighting a little battle with a few feisty demons from hell.

"Okaaaaay, Geri! There are a few things I'm going to have to explain to you." I was about to ask her what church she went to, but decided to skip it. "Getting this angel on this disc is going to take a little more effort than we bargained for, but if we stand firm and don't give up, it'll happen. I need your help to understand that." She looked back at me with wide eyes, but agreed. I was there for hours. It should have been an easy pick up—in the store and out of the store. Hours went by. I needed to get back to work! Finally, since the angel mysteriously reappeared in her computer upstairs, I asked her to run a few 4 x 6 copies for me in case that's all I was going to have to work with. Finally, she was able to do that. But what I needed was the high quality photograph taken of the angel piece on a disc so I could save it to Word documents. Weeks of trying went by.

Finally, Geri called. "I have it ready!" The effort to get the angel on the disc succeeded in part, but the mechanism needed to save it was not on the disc as usual, so it was no good to me. Finally, I went back again, after countless tries. The angel was finally on the disc and the "save as" mechanism was also there, so I could use it in my book. Phew! "Thanks Geri. You are a trooper," I smiled. I had guessed right. The image of Karen with the angel would have important spiritual impact, and I was feeling the dark resistance. In Ephesians 6:10 we are reminded to "Stand firm." We did.

Now, you have to see how beautiful this angel is. Ooops! She has disappeared again! Well, I'm sure she will reappear somewhere in this book. If you watch carefully, you will see her, I'm sure!

Thinking About Psalms 91

> "We live within the shadow of the Almighty, sheltered by the God who is above all gods. This I declare, that he alone is my refuge, my place of safety; he is my God, and I am trusting in Him" (See Psalms 91:1-16, Living Bible).

After Karen's death, this was the really big question in my mind. It was the closest I ever came to being mad at God. "So why didn't you protect her?" I asked Him in those early dawning hours of July 11.

I thought of my own life as it flashed before my eyes in a few winks of time. There certainly had been times of danger for me in my youth and other times. I remembered back to angry satanists who came storming through our outdoor park Crusades for Christ in San Francisco, tipping over tables and ripping up tracts with their teeth. It was a miracle they didn't do more. I remembered almost being blown up four times in the span of about two weeks over in Israel during a tense political time. We just happened to barely miss those incidents. When I was about Karen's age, I remember being chased down in my car at 11 P.M. on a Saturday night in California by Hell's Angels who tried to force me to pull over. I almost wrecked my mom's car, but I would not pull over. They finally left me alone and rode their bikes away into the darkness that night long ago. Then there was the high speed chase with the infamous Zodiac Killer in San Francisco back in 1978. No one ever got that close to him and lived to tell about it. My list was pretty long. So why was Karen's list so short? God knew I needed some answers.

The afternoon of July 11, 2001, the day after Karen died, there was a knock on the door and a couple, good friends of ours, appeared to spend time with us and comfort us. "Let's take a look at Isaiah 57:1," Jere said, opening his Bible. Then he read the passage: "The good men perish; the godly die before their time, and no one seems to care or wonder why. No one seems to realize that God is taking them away from evil days ahead. For the godly who die shall rest in peace." (Living Bible Translation)

Jaina and I knew there were choppy waters ahead in Karen's future, and we wondered how she would handle navigating them. This was mainly centering around making the right choices regarding relationships. I wondered at times if I would have the "same Karen" in five years. Maybe God indeed knew that the pressures would be too great. Perhaps He wanted to flash-freeze-frame Karen in time, as the delightful and inspirational young woman she was on July 10, 2001, somebody who was close to Him, first and foremost.

"Surrounded By Swirling Flames"

Karen had a favorite restaurant. It was a Chinese restaurant in Yakima, and the owner's name was Don. She and her friends often met there for lunch on Sundays. Don was a bright, shining Asian gentleman with a deep relationship with Jesus.

When Don learned Karen wanted to work as a firefighter for the U.S. Forest Service, he asked Karen, "Karen, so why do you want to work on the mountain?" his eyes were wide and bright.

"Because it's closer to God!" Karen replied playfully, with a little wink. Karen and her friends and family were regulars at the favorite restaurant on one of the main thoroughfares in Yakima. Don and his wife, Cheryl, and their family had often seemed like family to Karen over the past seven years or so. Don also sometimes attended the Bible study Karen attended.

After her death, we learned of an amazing phenomenon that Don had experienced. Fast forward in time to July 17, 2001. It was the outdoor graveside service for Karen Lee at the beautiful West Hills Memorial Park in West Valley. Her sister Jaina leaned over and whispered to me,

"What's the matter with Don C.? He's pacing around nervously like a cat on a hot tin roof."

"I don't know—who knows? Maybe he just misses Karen," I replied. I glanced back over my shoulder at Don and his wife, and he looked very nervous and upset as he walked around and around the grass area near us.

Fast forward to September 2001. "Don, why were you so upset and nervous at the funeral, pacing around and around out there?" John Fitz-Patrick asked him after finishing lunch at the restaurant. Don became very quiet at first, but then spoke.

"About four weeks before Karen went to the fire, I had a dream—like a vision of Karen. She was on her knees crying out for the salvation of others, but as she was on her knees, she was surrounded by swirling flames!" Don's face was full of pain. Suddenly, Karen's dad knew what the mysterious emotion was behind Don's behavior that day. "I didn't understand it, so I never said anything," Don admitted.

"Don, I don't think anything would have changed what happened that day. If you had talked to Karen about it, she wouldn't have read it that way at the time." Some of us remember how she used to talk about "snatching them from the flames" those last few weeks. Well, it looks like that's what she she did!"

"Ye are the light of the world..."

> *"Ye are the light of the world. A city that is set on a hill, cannot be hid. Neither do men light a candle, and put it under a bushel, but on a candlestick; and it giveth light unto all who are in the house. Let your light shine before men, that they may see your good works, and glorify your Father which is in heaven."* (Matt. 5:14-16)

Karen, along with her father and her sister Jaina had been part of a small group Bible study since 1996. I called them, "the church with no name." Their leader, Tom H., was a pretty radical guy even for conservative Christians. You might call him a purist or an isolationist. After observing the group and the leader's theology off an on for about two years, I had to pull away and not be a part of it. Formerly, Karen and I had also been going to Stone Church Assemblies of God in Yakima where she enjoyed participating in the youth group and in music. But by 1998, she had decided to just attend "the group."

If there was one good thing about her participation there, it was the encouragement by the leadership to spend long, large blocks time reading the Word of God, the Bible. This she did, and out of it she grew a deep walk with God. By the age of 18, she was a talented, very intelligent, caring, and amazing human being who had many friends, not just her own age, but adults who were close friends that drew inspiration from her. Karen Lee was definitely not a product of our decadent modern society, but reflected the character of a wholesome young woman much like that of our American culture of past eras when the Bible was the cornerstone of our society. But one thing continued to haunt me. Karen felt as if she could not attend church anywhere else—not even to visit or for something special such as a Christmas program or a youth conference. During June 2001, the month before her death, she made an unusual decision to attend a five day regional youth conference held at Stone Church Assemblies of God in Yakima, and enjoyed it immensely. Karen met, studied, and worshipped the Lord with many other teens her own age and was greatly lifted and encouraged. That week, as she left the house each morning, she would say, "Don't tell Dad, don't tell Tom!" and winked. Of course I wouldn't tell them. It was a healthy and balanced spiritual environment she was going into there. I knew it well.

I had hoped it would break the pattern, but it didn't. My heart ached. Karen needed to share her Bible knowledge, her leadership, her musical talents, terrific singing voice, and spiritual brilliance with the world at large. But the leader, who was not a pastor but an irrigation district employee, was going to be sure the lid was kept on Karen, and only for "The Group." He had a strong influence and an ironclad grip on everyone in that small group. It both scared and concerned me. I prayed about it all the time—constantly, in fact. I also got quite verbal about it from time to time to others in the household.

"I can't just go to that little group. I have certain things that the Lord has asked me to do that only I can do," I said, referring primarily to the Young Lion's Youth Ministry Program that I had helped form for youth detention ministry and that now has groups active around America and Canada and overseas. "And Karen—same thing. She is 'hiding her light under a bushel' being over there!"

I guess I sounded like a broken record on this principle for about three years prior to her death in July 2001. As a result, there was no video, no audio recordings of her playing the piano or of her great singing voice passionately delivering her favorite songs. Only the memories of those who were honored enough to hear her when she was alive. A friend of the family who read Isaiah 57:1 reflecting on why the righteous sometimes die young and we wonder why, caused a chill up my spine. Maybe I did know why.

In June of 2001, as Karen was preparing for her high school graduation from West Valley High School in Yakima, I walked into her room about the time she was hanging up her blue cap and gown. She had just pressed it. I took a deep breath. I had to try again.

"Karen," I began, with all the motherly influence I could muster. "On June 8, you will graduate high school."

"Yeah, Mom?" she said, standing by her dresser, putting away a pair of jeans.

"Listen to me now." She turned around and looked at me full force, with those huge blue eyes like none other.

"So this fall are you going to go back to your high school campus and sit in your old classrooms?"

She looked back at me, puzzled.

"No, you aren't, are you? So when are you going to 'graduate' from 'the group?' Isn't it time to branch out? Isn't it time to be out there spreading your light—your talents—with the whole world, the mainstream of life? They need to hear from you, Karen."

She was quiet for a moment. "I'll think about it, Mom." We both stood there silent for a few more moments. Somehow, even then, I knew I had lost the battle.

Fast forward in time. In 2004, I was listening to the televised memory services for the former president, Ronald Reagan. I had been listening downstairs, then went upstairs to work for a while, and flipped on the TV up there on the top floor. A man who knew Reagan personally was speaking about some of his memories of the former president.

"I remember his favorite writer was the American statesman, John Winthrop, who did not believe in 'isolationism.' Winthrop used to always say something Ronnie believed in very strongly: 'When you have something really great, don't hide your light under a bushel, but spread it around for the whole world to see!'" This comment stopped me in my tracks breathless. Had I not said it myself time and time again?

Karen died July 10, 2001, in the small mountain town of Winthrop, Washington. Another signpost, another stroke of destiny, it would seem.

THE ROSE, THE ROSE, THE ROSE

Somewhere around the age of 15, Karen developed a favorite symbol that came to be on so many things that represented her—the single, tall, long-stemmed red rose. It was on a poster in her room; dried red roses lay on her window sill, the first tall, long-stemmed red rose given to her by her first date, Dan, upon arriving to go a Valentine banquet at age 15, still hung upside down in its plastic wrapper from her ceiling by a poster that read, "Overboard!" Her address labels had a single red rose on them, lying across black and white piano keys. (Oh, how she loved to play the piano!) The single red rose became her signature and a way by which she was still identified, even after her death.

THE ROSES ON THE WALK

Our house in Benicia, California, had an amazing rose garden growing on either side of the front entry to the house. The roses were many various colors—red, pink, white, yellow, multicolor with pink, yellow, and red in one bloom, and the favorite of Karen, the lavender rose. The name of this rose was—you guessed it, "Angel Face."

Every January, the roses were carefully pruned back to only about 10 inches tall. By April, the new green growth was full and bushy and around 4 feet tall. The girls watched for those rosebuds. They knew their favorite roses would soon appear, and they knew them all by name. Oh, the fragrant bouquets that filled our home back then!

When they were small, I used to talk to Karen and her sisters about the roses, using them for examples. "What if all these roses were all the same color?" I asked. "Wouldn't that be a little boring?"

"Roses for My Love," a pastel drawing by Kathie FitzPatrick, 1979. One of the art pieces Karen and her sisters grew up with.

They looked back at me and nodded their little blond heads. "It's kind of how God created all the various peoples, nations, and races. They are all beautiful to Him, just like our rose garden is beautiful to you. It's the variety and makes it so pretty, don't you think?"

Our family grew up in the multicultural society of the San Francisco Bay Area, so it was natural for our neighborhood to be filled with many races, but our girls often thought of the illustration of the rose garden, especially when we moved away. The first time we attended an all-white church in Washington State, my girls looked at me very puzzled afterwards and wanted to know where "everyone else" was.

"They have different rose gardens up here!" I winked.

THE ROSE BEYOND THE WALL...

Near shady wall a rose once grew,
Budded and blossomed
In God's free light,
Watered and fed by morning dew,
Shedding its sweetness day and night.
As it grew and blossomed fair and tall,
Slowly rising to loftier height,
It came to a crevice in the wall
Through which there shone a beam of light.
Onward it crept with added strength
With never a thought of fear of pride,
It followed the light
Through the crevice's length
And unfolded itself on the other side.
The light, the dew, the broadening view,

Coping with Grief

Were found the same
As they were before,
And it lost itself in the beauties new,
Breathing its fragrance more and more.
Small claim of death cause us to grieve
And make our courage faint and fall?
Nay! Let us faith and hope receive—
The rose still grows beyond the wall.
Scattering fragrance far and wide
Just as it did in days of yore,
Just as it did on the other side,
Just as it will forevermore.

—from the writings of A.L. Frink

*With Sympathy from the West Valley
Firefighter's Association*

The White Padded Mailer with the Single Red Rose on It

Even the mailer the anonymous letter came in bore the single red rose running up the side. How could they have known? They didn't, but God did.

After the tragedy of losing Karen, four spectacular funeral/memory services individually commemorating all of the young firefighters unfolded that week following the fatal fire. Karen's was the last service, and was held on July 17, 2001, at Stone Church Assemblies of God, in Yakima. Then one very large service to remember all four jointly was held at the Sundome at the fairgrounds in Yakima on July 24, 2001. Thousands from the community attended, dignitaries from the White House were present, and the current governor of the State of Washington at that time, Gary Locke, spoke in the service. Fire trucks from all across America hit the road toward Yakima to be there on July 24. The procession to the services at the Sundome included many fire vehicles from around the nation and was more than seven miles long. News agencies from around America carried the story and showed the overhead helicopter view of the procession.

Around that time, we received baskets full of mail from everywhere around the nation. It was mostly from people who knew Karen or from firefighters and firefighter families, some who had lost young adult firefighter children as well. I was determined to find time to read it all. Each one had its own unique heartache and heartthrob. I sifted through the mail and pulled out a medium-size, white, padded mailer with a single red rose imprinted on it that ran upward along the left side.

"This must be someone who knew Karen," I concluded logically. Only personal friends and family knew about the single red rose.

I opened the mailer, and inside was a letter printed on a computer, an audio tape, and song lyrics printed on the back of the letter with musical chords along with the lyrics. It was from an anonymous woman who had never met us or Karen. But she wrote a letter that turned out to bear a very important message for us to hear with our hearts.

IT WAS HER APPOINTED TIME.
SHE KNEW IT, BUT IT WAS OK.

July 15, 2001

Dear John & Kathie FitzPatrick:

My husband and I are Christian ministers and would like to share this story with you.

Two weeks ago we began planning a short vacation in Canada when the Lord began to impress on us to head east of the mountains to Yakima, about a three-hour drive. I have relatives in Yakima and was feeling that the Lord was directing us there instead. I began to have visions of the highway and the scenery alongside of the road. The impressions began to get stronger and stronger and we prayed and cancelled our reservations. We both felt God was guiding us here for some reason, not just family

We arrived on the 12th and saw the newspaper about the fire. I saw their faces and my heart broke. I was tired from the long drive and went to the pool. On my way back, I began singing an unusual song. I felt God's peace all over me and heard myself singing about going home to be with God. I wondered if it was about me or someone else. I get a lot of songs for others from the Lord. The voice I sang with was quiet and young like a young girl's voice. I was confused and fell asleep. I woke around 2 o'clock in the morning and felt God was telling me it was not about me but one of the young girls who died was a Christian, and that God had been speaking to her heart that she would die and go home to be with Him, that she had known about this before she died as God had told her and given her His peace about it. I told my sister here in Yakima about these things. She got me your names and address.

When I was young, I had a death experience. I was absent from my body and present with the Lord. There was no talking with the mouth, only with the heart. Total love. All I needed to know or understand, every question in my heart, was answered instantly in my heart. Jesus said it was not my time, and that He was sending me back. It was painful coming back.

I wrote this letter up to this point on Saturday the 14th. Early in the morning on the 15th, my sister called. She had been up since 5:00 A.M. Not sure why. She had made a pot of coffee and read the morning newspaper confirming that she had known ahead of time, and God had prepared her heart.

I am enclosing a copy of the words I felt God was sharing with me. There are some areas that you can fill in much better than I. I hope this brings comfort to you during this difficult time. I am not the greatest singer and musician in the world, but this is what I got.

As my husband and I are headed back home, the landscape took me with such beauty and God showed me she had such a love for nature!

Sincerely,
Ministers in Jesus Christ

Following are the lyrics of the song that was on the audio tape sent by the anonymous woman. She played the piano and sang the song on the tape.

GOING HOME

Maybe it's my time, and I'm going home
To My Father in Heaven
Who will take me in his arms
And hold me closely to His heart
And wipe every tear from my eyes
Maybe that's why I saw old friends last night
And_____ at the grocery store, and Mary at the mall
So many faces and memories to hold
Should I tell them God has told me, I'm going Home?
And why, oh why, do I hear my heart cry
"You know it's time. You know it's time"
I feel His heart of peace in mine
And I'm ready as I'll ever be
I only want His perfect will for me
Do my mother and father know…why I do the things I do?
Does my family know the reason why
I'm acting so strangely? It's my time to go
And I know, I know because my heart tells me so
It's His heart inside calling to me
And I know. It's my time to go
To my heavenly Father's home.

The Thirtymile Firestorm

Twenty minutes before the fire blew up, the firefighters watch as if to sense keenly something in the air—something on the wind was coming. Karen holds her camera above her head, taking a picture of herself. Photo by Matt Rutman.

Conversation with Matt Rutman

There were many. But I'll never forget this brief little story from the U.S. Forest Service firefighter who took amazing photos of the blazing red sky, the raining embers, and scribbled the diary in the last moments before going under his fire shelter for his dramatic dance with life and death. Seventy mile per hour winds threatened to rip the shelter from his body in those last, very critical, and dramatic fifteen minutes or so of the killer Thirtymile Fire. However, he was not destined to die that day. He seemed to know it clearly, to the depths of his very soul. Matt yelled out to the dark forces that howled, whirled, and whipped through the canyon, hovering ominously above him. "It's not my time to die!" It wasn't. He had many an important story to tell, and facts to reveal about the fire and what went wrong that day that resulted in the deaths of four firefighters and certainly the near death of all who were trapped at the fiery scene.

"I didn't know your daughter, but she worked alongside me that day, digging line," Matt began in a telephone conversation to me only days after the fatal fire. "In certain areas, the little trees were only about ten inches apart. It was hard to even walk through the thickest part of it. Karen and I were digging line, and the branches of the little trees ripped the fire shelter from the Velcro holder on my belt. It fell to the ground. I kept going; didn't pay much attention. You always hope you're never really going to need it. Karen stopped and ran all the way back to get it. She came running up to me, and with a little smile, pinned it back on me."

We talked further about the events of the afternoon and the escalation and transition of the small campfire that got away and became the huge, fatal firestorm that it became. "If she had not pinned the fire shelter back on my belt, later that day I would have died for sure! She will always be part of me. She saved my life. We're bonded forever."

Twenty minutes before the blow up and the burn-over that took the life of Karen, Tom, Jessica, and Devin, Matt Rutman took a very important photo. Karen is looking up, with a big smile. She lifted a camera above her head, and suddenly took a picture of herself. We know now, she had a premonition she would die. Knowing her, it seems as if she is looking up into the face of her Father in heaven, thinking to herself, "See you soon!" She did.

The Forces Gather

There was an alert in heaven, then a loud rumble in hell.

It was July 10, 2001—midnight. A 21-man fire crew had been dispatched from Naches and surrounding areas to fight a "small fire" near the small mountain towns of Twisp and Winthrop, Washington in the Northern Cascade Mountains near the Canadian border.

At 9:03 A.M. they arrive on the scene. The fire has now grown. It is now an "initial attack" fire. In the unseen realm, it was already known that in the human world inflated egos would fly, negligence and ignorance from fire superiors would reign supreme that day, and all reasonable safety would be overlooked, putting lives and eternal destiny on the line for the mortals involved. A young fire crew of varying backgrounds, spiritual strengths, and weaknesses would potentially face death before the day was over. It is exactly the sort of climate that attracts the demons from the far corners of hell like a magnet to see if they can succeed in claiming those lives not yet secured and reserved for heaven, and it causes the Creator of earth and their very human lives themselves to dispatch angels from the far corners of the universe to hover near, to watch and wait for orders from God himself over the lives present on the scene and caught up in this soon-to-be mighty whirlwind of explosive, fire, wind, and chaos that would settle in life for some and death for others. For even Satan had to ask God for permission to take the life of Job, which was denied, although Job was severely tested, and sometimes wished for death, which seemed kinder than the test from God.

Amidst these unseen forces, both light and dark—about to barter for the souls of men—walked a bright light named Karen Lee. Her peers kept noticing that she walked in such enthusiasm and light. It was rare, and very special. Most others in the crew had never given their eternal destiny much thought. It was more fun to think about at which bar they would meet their friends for a drink or two on a Saturday night. Death seemed far away. Distant.

As the darkness gathered, and the king of hell appeared, he raged angrily over this young woman of bright light. She knew his deep secrets. She had stolen many from his dark kingdom, "snatching them from the fire," as the Bible had put it. Karen had even written about it in her own personal journal. She considered it to be her most important mission in this life. The Great Dark One began to delight in the prospect. She was in the midst of impending disaster. A beautiful plan. The fire officers were blinded to the potential dangers. Soon he would stake his claim for souls. And could it be—would it just be possible that he could rid himself of this young warrior princess who had caused so much damage to the kingdom of hell? He erupted loudly with laughter in the dark wind of the skies. What a delightful idea, indeed! He roared and screamed out again toward heaven, begging for her. "I want her. Her voice against me must be silenced!" he screamed, within the thunder of the fire. "Give me this Princess of Truth! She must die!"

Great and mighty angels hovered near, waiting. The mortals had already given so much attention to the great idol, the god of the environment, and the "endangered species" fish, over protecting the lives of the humans, that the avenue and ovens of hell were opened doubly wide now, for the dark philosophy of pagans had prevailed. God, for a moment, seemed to turn aside. But not really. The Dark One sensed permission to proceed. Joyously he began to move in. The crown fire moving quickly over the tops of the trees of the forest worsened and gained speed. The crew heard the sound of the "locomotive" approaching. A great explosion suddenly occurred. Five fire fighters who were up on the rocks began to outrun flames—Jason, Devin, Jessica, Tom, and Karen.

Then they heard the command from their crew boss, "Deploy, deploy!"

Silver aluminum shelters flew out. Soon they were inside them. Down on the road below, the others were in their shelters. Some made it to the creek. Flames swirled; seventy mile-an-hour firestorm winds howled; two sideways tornadoes twisted; Matt Rutman cried out from his fire shelter on the road to the dark presence hovering above, "It's not my time to die!" In the midst of the dark storm, God listened. Meanwhile, the angry forces pulled giant trees out by the roots and tossed them around like flimsy toothpicks.

Jason Emhoff, soon sensing the rock scree was a dangerous place to be, ran for the road and his truck. But he forgot something very important. Jason forgot his fire gloves. In sheer shock, he sat in his truck, gripping the steering wheel, watching the flesh melt off his hands. He was badly burned, but lived. Thom Taylor, further up on the rock scree, could hear Karen praying loudly. She was interceding for the lives and the souls of herself and the three immediately with her. Then Jessica prayed. Karen prayed for salvation. She prayed for the safety of the ones on the road and down below, who later did live. Positioned on a rock scree, a firefighter cannot get as good a seal in the shelter as the ones who lay on a flat surface. Breathing the smoke from the fire and products of hot combustion soon took its toll, searing their lungs. Within only a few minutes, by 5:30 p.m., four silvery shelters became their shiny death shrouds. Thom Taylor, realizing he would be burned on the rock scree, put the fire shelter up over his head like a tent and skillfully made his way down over the large boulders, through the dark smoke, toward the sandbar and the creek.

"As I passed by the four, I could see they were still and silent, already succumbed to smoke inhalation," Thom later explained. He somehow miraculously made his way to the creek, and quickly plunged in, with his silver aluminum shelter over him like a protective tent, shielding him from falling fiery embers.

Meanwhile, The Great Dark One rejoiced in a great victory. A fireball of his presence rolled through the forest, taking one half of the trees as he went, singeing and burning them. Onward he raged, hitting the rocks where the four lay, like the blast of a mighty torpedo. Thom Taylor, from his safe haven in the creek, peeked up from under his fire shelter just in time to see the large fireball, estimated at about 1,600 degrees, roll over the top of the four of them, reaching and stretching over the spot where they lay, like a three-pronged claw out of hell. It was done. Soon it was silent.

About 15 minutes later, firefighters emerged from their deployment spots to take inventory of who was where, and who was still alive. Cries were heard, and the tears flowed hard, as it was realized that the four comrades on the hill did not survive. Eternal destiny was decided. It would appear that the forces of hell had won that day. But then, they have always been greatly shortsighted! Angels who hovered near did not get orders to rescue but to deliver into the presence of God, instead. It would appear that a wise and ultimately kind God, looking into both the near and far future, would decide for eternal destiny forever with Him instead of continued life on earth now. Later, fire behavior experts would puzzle and scratch their heads trying to logically explain what happened out there that day. "An act of God," they would ultimately call it. "The fire just didn't do what we thought it was going to do." Oh, the ego of mere man. The entire earth and universe suffers and groans under the dark weight of it.

But at 6 P.M., against the clear blue summer sky, a great and gigantic cumulous cloud formed over their site of departure from this earth. At the top of this magnificent cloud formation was clearly seen four linear steps, as if representing a stairway to heaven. I can picture Karen and her comrades meeting bright shining angels who announced, "You shall be ushered into the presence of God forever!"

Oh, now who was it really who had the won the victory? Four souls "snatched from the fire," as the Bible says, and Karen wrote in her personal journal. For, you see, eternity is for a very long time. And God has a way of leaving His fingerprints and signposts along the way for others to find, especially when you just can't "hide a bright light under a bushel basket!" And especially, you can't "hide a bright light under a bushel basket" in Winthrop, Washington.

Firetraining — June 2001

In June 2001, after the completion of their intensive weeklong fire training classes held by the U.S. Forest Service and other related fire agencies in the area, the 200 new Firefighter Rookies were required to now prove themselves. On a Friday morning they were transported up Hwy 410 to the Gold Creek area. Three fires were lit…and the Rookies had to put them out!

News Anchor, Jay Cowan of KAPP-ABC Television was on hand with a video camera. "Who's local?" he called out to the group. Many had come in from far distances for the fire training. In the quick interview process, he discovered Karen, a recent young grad from West Valley High School in Yakima, WA. He instructed her to walk through the story, and describe what was happening.

"We're going to dig line around the fire..." she explained. "It's our final test! I'm not sure what to expect..." It was a day for putting all skills to the test, including using chainsaws. These are a few still photos from the KAPP-TV news story televised only about 4 weeks before the Thirtymile Fire tragedy.

"For two years Karen FitzPatrick has been waiting to fight fires..."

Karen center, standing with her Rookie classmates

Photos courtesy KAPP-TV, Yakima, WA. Used by permission.

Images from the Fire

The narrow valley floor, between the mountainous, hilly area of the Chewuch River Canyon area. The spot within the circle indicates the location of the Thirtymile Fire. Courtesy of the US Forest Service.

The Thirtymile Firestorm

The fire had gotten away from them, but none of the supervisors wanted to admit it. For them, it was too soon to quit fighting the fire. This is another midday scene of the Thirtymile Fire. Photo courtesy of the U.S. Forest Service.

A firefighter stands on a log fallen across the Chewuch River. This was the state of the Thirtymile Fire about noon on July 10. Photo courtesy of the U.S. Forest Service.

Angel Promises

The Thirtymile Fire crew during lunch on July 10, 2001, watching the soon-to-be fatal fire from behind the trees in a meadow. This photo survived the firestorm and was later recovered from Devin Weaver's camera. Photo courtesy of the Devin Weaver family.

Photo courtesy of the U.S. Forest Service

View from inside the van: The other USFS van, driven by Pete Kampen, with some of the firefighting crew inside, burst through the flames as the fire moved quickly and aggressively across the road in front of them—the only escape route. This van in the photo saw the unfortunate view of the burning, fallen logs in front of them and could not follow. Here they are turning around. Karen was a passenger in this van. "We're going to die," said Karen.

Last moments, about 5:15 P.M., with the sound of an approaching locomotive, the crown fire became a firestorm that finally blew up. The falling, burning embers showered everywhere. Courtesy of the U.S. Forest Service. Some of these photos were taken by Matt Rutman before going under his fire shelter on the road by the creek.

The blowup from the air as seen by the pilot of the smoke-jumper plane above the fire. This was the beginning of the formulation of the huge cumulous-looking cloud above the site. By 6 P.M., the cloud resembled the four-tiered "Stairway to Heaven" and also the form of a white horse leaping over the mountain.

The Thirtymile Firestorm

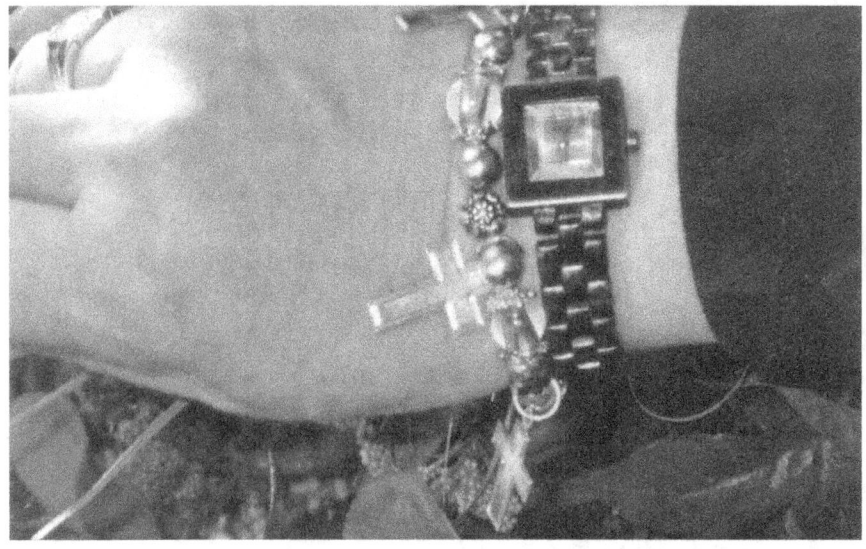

The burned, charred, silver watch taken from Karen's lifeless body, eternally frozen in time at 5:29 P.M. "The U.S. Forest Service waited two years to turn it over to me."

They say all four of them died at 5:30 P.M. on July 10, 2001, from smoke inhalation and breathing products of hot combustion. Their bodies were thought to have been burned post mortem. If the heat was strong enough to both stop and burn the watch, I guess we will always wonder.

I have worn the watch a few times when I met with the press or some other important occasion connected to the Thirtymile Fire. I wore it the first time up in Winthrop, Washington, at the third year anniversary and a visit to the monument site. Little did I know their newspaper write-up on the third anniversary would begin, "Kathie FitzPatrick sometimes wears on her wrist the burned silver watch of Karen's, eternally frozen at 5:29."

I have worn some of Karen's favorite shoes as well, as if she is in a sense coming and walking with me at times. At the time of the memorials, I told the press I was out of the black dress. I stepped into the memorial services wearing a white dress and Karen's favorite white high heel sandals. "I'm wearing white as a symbol of hope and resurrection," I explained at the time. In meetings with Senator Maria Cantwell and others to discuss the formation of possible new safety legislation to better protect all firefighters in the future, I wore Karen's favorite black high heel boots. To me, at the time, they seemed as if they were "battle zone" boots!

Karen, wearing the silver watch. It was one of her sweet-sixteen birthday presents from her mom, Kathie.

Obituary: Karen L. FitzPatrick

Yakima Herald Republic
—July 12, 2001

> Karen Lee FitzPatrick, 18, passed away on Tuesday, July 10, 2001. She was one of the four firefighters who lost their lives in the Twisp, Washington, forest fire.
>
> Karen was born on December 27, 1982, in Martinez, California, to John and Kathie (Horacek) FitzPatrick. Karen and her family moved to Yakima in August of 1990. She had just graduated from West Valley High School, June 8, 2001, where she was a member of the Honor Society, Key Club, and was a noteworthy weightlifter, photographer, musician, and volunteer. She was known for her smile, her laugh and her exuberant personality. She also was much appreciated for her artistic skills and her frequent gourmet cooking and baking. She was voted by her fellow students as "Most likely To Be The Next Martha Stewart." Karen loved anything that brought beauty and comfort to the lives of others. A teen with great life contrasts, she had a collection of numerous evening gowns, and hardly missed a prom or homecoming event. On the other hand, she was strong and fast, and had a history of excelling in athletics including 10 seasons of soccer during elementary and junior years. While playing for the Bobcats, her team succeeded in bringing home the American Cup, State Championship Award out of Seattle in 1994. She was also the drum major for the West Valley Junior High Panther's Band and participated in many parades statewide during that time.

But as much as anything, Karen was known for her vibrant religious faith. Spirituality and faith were a big part of who she was. Rediscovering a verse in the Bible, Romans 5:8, "But God shows and clearly proves His own love for us by the fact that while we were yet sinners, Christ the Messiah, the anointed One, died for us" (Amplified Bible). After years of "church going," Karen became truly a born again Christian and a light and an encouragement to all who knew her. This new spiritual revelation rolled into her and her father's lives, like its own kind of fireball, about one year ago. Karen thought it a strange coincidence that the manufacturer's date on her firefighting boots was the same date she was "born again," and had commented on that to her family.

"It's almost like God decided she was at a point where she was so close to Him, He decided to take her. Think about Isaiah 57:1," commented her sister Jaina, age 22. "She's in a better place. No more hassles!"

On Monday evening, July 9, she and her father John FitzPatrick practiced driving the Suzuki sidekick up to the mountains so she could get more used to driving the vehicle. While out for the evening they visited their pastor, Tom Hagerman, in Cowiche. They had a very rich time of just talking, praying, and reading the Bible for about two hours. It was a very special, close time. Karen and her Dad got home about 11 P.M. Monday evening. Karen got called to report to the fire at 12 midnight.

"You just never know what the next day will hold," commented Karen's mother, Kathie. "It was a preparation for her 'homegoing.' God knows the day we will be born and the day we will leave the planet. We're responsible for everything in between. Life is a test you don't want to fail!" she continued. "It's moments like these that you begin to understand verses like, 'I can do all things through Christ who strengthens me. (infuses me with inner strength—), and Psalms 144:1, 'The Lord is my immovable Rock, and my fortress' really truly mean, This where the rubber meets the road. If it wasn't for the reality of that, we would both be caving in. We feel it so strongly now. We cried buckets, but then you have to let go sometime," Kathie said.

"The natural flesh part of me grieves over the loss of my daughter," her father said. "But the soul part of me is leaping for joy for my daughter being in heaven."

"People have asked us so many questions over the last few days," said Karen's mother. "We're not blaming God, just trusting God. He loved her even more than we did!"

Karen is survived by her parents, John and Kathie FitzPatrick of Yakima, her sister Jaina, a student at YVCC, her sister, Yvonne Blackwood, 30, of San Francisco, her grandparents, Sophie FitzPatrick of Canajoharie, New York, and Henry and Ruby Horace of Walnut Creek, California.

Funeral services will be held Tuesday, July 17, 2001 at Stone Church, 3303 Englewood Avenue, Yakima, Washington. A committal service will follow at West Hills Memorial Park. Memorial contributions may be made to the Okanogan Wenatchee Firefighters' Memorial Fund at any branch of the Yakima Valley Credit Union. Keith and Keith Funeral Home is in charge of arrangements.

Heroes Remembered

Some of the Monuments

There are various monuments and memorials to the four firefighters who perished fighting the infamous Thirtymile Fire and wildland firefighting in general. To view additional information see: www.wildlandfire.com/docs/memorials.htm or www.wa.gov/wsp/fire/memorial.htm

Winthrop, Washington

In the small tourist town of Winthop, Washington, since July 10, 2001, there is now a new sight to see. At the actual location of the huge drama which was the last few minutes of the Thirtymile Fire, when life and death were on the line for a young 21-man fire crew, there is a national monument to remember the four young firefighters who died there, Tom Craven, 30; Jessica Johnson, 19; Karen FitzPatrick, 18; and Devin Weaver, 21.

Just above Leavenworth, Washington, the Swiss Bavarian village so often frequented by visitors, one can take Highway 20 to the small mountain town of Winthrop, named after the American Statesman. The town is full of old western flavor, great eating places, and cute, picturesque inns. As one is driving on Highway 20, look for the ball field on the right and the U.S. Forest Service Visitor Center on the left. Going inside, you can pick up a color brochure about the Thirtymile Fire that includes bios of the four young firefighters and a map to get to the site. It's easy. Just cross the street, that's West Chewuch Road. Drive all the way back, it's about 30 miles plus. I don't think I was ever counting. When I drove back with Forest Service personnel to see the death site for the first time, I remember saying to the fire behavior expert who was driving us, "The thought of a flame on the loose in this place is a horrifying thought!" He remained pretty quiet at that comment. It's all I ever think about when I drive back there ever since then.

We know the spot where the rocks made the fire ring where the campers left without putting it out. It's on the right. You probably won't find it. It's overgrown with new greenery now. A few more miles down the road you can see the fallen log where the young crew viewed the fire that had jumped to the other side of the creek. I'm sure they wondered where the helicopters were that were supposed to be bringing and dumping water on the fire around them. Sigh. No chance of that. Endangered species fish in the water. Cannot disturb them.

At the end of the canyon near the burned out bridge, you'll see the national monument to the Thirtymile Fire, named after the Thirtymile Campground nearby. A natural rock wall graces the rocky area, with pictures of each of the four digitized in marble. Impressive. The Chewuch River is there, the road and the sandbar, which was the illusive eye of safety in this horrific catastrophe.

The first year when it was dedicated, each of us from the four families were given a two hour block of time to hike the canyon and place a bronze plaque on the rock where our family member died. Karen's spot looked like a little Gethsemane, like a little kneeling stone. As she prayed with the other three at the end of their lives, I doubt that she was aware of it. One can still hike up and visit the spot where the four bronze plaques are and capture a small part of the catastrophic moment. Looking out over the sweeping vista, one can see the burned forest, the large trees pulled out by the forces and tossed around like small, light sticks. They say there were two sideways tornadoes here, and a fireball that came around like a mighty fury and hit the rocks where they were, flashing up and rolling over them with a flash of fire formation of an estimated 1,600 degree heat. But sweet, eternal victory was had. God in His mercy gave a sign in the cloud that formed over them at thirty minutes later that appeared to bear four clearly marked steps in the huge billowy cloud, pointed upward toward heaven. We love to affectionately call this photo, "The Stairway to Heaven Picture."

The first year after the fire, there was no way to adequately describe the heavy, profusely dense bloom of purple fireweed flowers that grew out of the ashes of the Thirtymile Fire. It must have been growing in a three mile circumference. It even showed the fire behavior experts the patterns of the fire itself as it swirled around the site. As I walked around the area, I picked some. It was the same color as the purple fallen firefighter ribbon. They say it's called "fireweed," but I'd like to rename it the fallen firefighter lily, if I could! In each tall plume are a series of flowers, each with four petals. At the time, it seemed like even nature itself had paid its own special tribute to the four bright shining stars who died an untimely death there. The purple blooms still appear each year at the anniversary time, the week of July 10. As the years pass by, the amount of flowers dissipate as the ashes slowly disappear and dissolve into the soil, just like the ashes of our loved ones. In a way, the deployment site high up on the rocks really is their true burial place. When you stand there, think about that. We do.

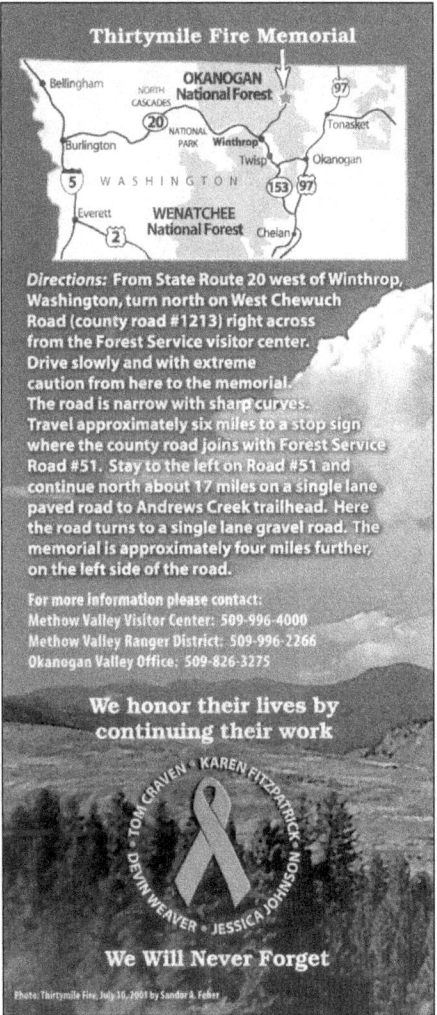

The U.S. Forest Service brochure maps the way for visitors to view the Thirtymile Fire site.

The National Memorial Site in Winthrop, WA.

Karen L. FitzPatrick, Devin Weaver, Jessica Johnson, and Tom L. Craven: The four young firefighters who perished in the Thirtymile Fire July 10, 2001.

Her "Gethsemane." The bronze monument with her name marks the spot where Karen Lee FitzPatrick knelt at this rock and prayed with her three trapped firefighter friends, Jessica Johnson, Tom Craven, and Devin Weaver. Karen also prayed for the safety of those firefighters who deployed their aluminum fire shelters on the road and elsewhere nearby, even in the creek. The other firefighters, mostly rookies who fought desperately for their lives amid firestorm winds of 70 miles per hour, two enormous sideways tornadoes nearly on top of them, and large trees being ripped out and thrown all about them in the midst of the fierce winds, did survive the horrific episode.

Heroes Remembered

Karen's image in marble at the Thirtymile site in Winthrop, Washington. One of four photos depicting each fallen firefighter at the national monument located at the end of West Chewuch River Road off Highway 20 in the small mountain town of Winthrop.

Karen, standing on the balcony of her home during the spring of 2001. Many feel this photo most resembles the bronze face monument.

Karen's face in bronze, as sculpted by Lyle Carter of Naches. This bronze bust is one of four; also memorialized are her fire fighting comrades, Tom Craven, Jessica Johnson, and Devin Weaver, all based out of the Naches Ranger District.

The Monument at the Naches Ranger Station

On Highway 12 in the country town of Naches, next to Yakima, Washington, stands a beautiful monument to remember the four young firefighters who perished battling the flames of the Thirtymile Fire of July 10, 2001.

Directly in front of the U.S. Forest Service Ranger Station where the four were based, stands the carefully crafted monument with a memory garden and stone bench for sitting and pondering and remembering those who lost their lives battling forest fires. Four natural basalt rock pillars stand tall, with bronze, life-size faces of the four Thirtymile youth, Tom Craven, age 30; Jessica Johnson, 19; Karen FitzPatrick, 18; and Devin Weaver, 21. A local Lion's Club and other nonprofit organizations and private citizens worked together along with the U.S. Forest Service to create this amazing and strikingly beautiful monument, which was dedicated in the Spring of 2003.

The bronze artist who created these faces, was talented local Naches artist and sculptor, Lyle Carter. It was quite a process that began with photographs—lots of them!

I had to bring Lyle a whole new set of photographs of Karen that I really had to dig out! The issue was that in most of photos of Karen, she had the very big smile. In bronze, it is rare that a bronze artist does a big smile on the face of his subject—only little smiles. Lyle explained that to me. So I drove out to Lyle's quaint studio in Naches, tucked away down winding country roads and a little stretch of woods. I thought I'd never find it. Finally, I drove up to a building that looked like a little red barn with abalone shells and deer horns nailed above the doors for decoration. Is this it? I wondered, after driving up and down the dirt road a few times. Then Lyle came enthusiastically bursting out the front door of the studio.

"This is the right place! Come on in!" he welcomed me, with a friendly grin.

We pinned up a variety of pictures of Karen by his work easel. Then he went to a box behind me and reverently removed the plastic from a red clay mold of a woman's face and lifted it out to show me. I froze over at first. It looked like a death mask, or the "Wicked Witch of the East," I wasn't sure which.

"No, no. The face is too long. She looks too sad!" was my first reaction. Lyle put it up on the easel and began to mist the clay mold with water. "Her face is not this long. She had a very angular jaw line here," I said, instructing him, as I stood over his shoulder speaking to him about Karen's face. His hands moved over the image as I spoke, working the clay carefully, artistically.

"I see a certain part of your face in hers, especially in through here," he motioned to my cheek line. "Stand right there for a minute," he said, as he continued to work the soft red clay. It took time and many visits to Lyle's studio, many talks, more photographs. I sympathized with the artist trying to capture an accurate look of Karen's face, as she was so animated and had many moods and looks and hairstyles! I mean, was it only I who knew how often she wore the ponytail?

Lyle put the figure of Karen's face away for a while to think it over. Back into the plastic wrap it went and back into the box. He was going to take a break from it as he was working on the faces of all four young firefighters during the same timeframe. It was October of 2002. The family went away to the huge, majestic ceremonies given in Washington D.C. by the Fallen Firefighter's of America Association to remember all the fallen firefighters of the previous year—2001. This included the more than 300 firefighters who were lost on 9/11. To meet their families and join with them in their loss was an amazing experience! The music and the honors paid to all were amazing and fabulous!

When we returned, we went to see Lyle. He had some time to think more about the sculpture of Karen and look more at photographs. He pulled the red clay mold out from the plastic wrap and the box and placed it on the easel. Was it Karen? I wasn't sure. "It is Karen—there is something about the expression," her father said tearfully. I rarely saw Karen without her big smile, but the expression on the sculpture Lyle Carter had created was one a mother would recognize. To me, it looked like the expression she gave to me when she was truly listening and connecting to what I was saying when the message was important. It was the expression of Karen taking in the truth. We decided we liked it. And the hair—well, what can I say—it was a neutral hairstyle, since she had so many revolving around the long reddish brown hair she loved.

From there, the faces went to a silicon mold process. Once dry, this is what the bronze would be formed with. It is an amazing and expensive process. A few months later, the faces were attached to the basalt rock pillars, and the beautiful monument was complete. Some people think the bronze face looks like her, and some don't. But the artist captured in the face an expression from Karen that I definitely recognize!

Angel Promises

Kathie FitzPatrick with Lyle Carter at his art studio in Naches with a clay mold of Karen's face.

Lyle Carter puts the finishing touches on Karen Lee's facial expression for the mold for the bronze of her face.

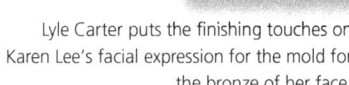

Bronze faces in process: The clay molds of Tom, Karen, and Devin have gone through the silicon mold stage. Jessica's mold is now in silicon, drying. Soon they will all be bronzed.

Part of the awesome Thirtymile Fire Monument and memory garden in Naches, Washington; also a tribute to remember the passing of all Wildland Firefighters.

Spring 2003: Kathie FitzPatrick speaks to the crowd gathered in front of the Naches Ranger Station in Naches, Washington, as part of the dedication ceremony of the Naches monument. The four bronze faces were unveiled that day.

Kathie FitzPatrick stands next to the bronze of her daughter Karen, sculpted by Lyle Carter.

Karen's Bronze Face at Night

One weekend evening, John had an idea that he would like to drive to the mountains and enjoy a picnic dinner. So Jaina and I got together some sandwiches, chips, fruit, and soft drinks, and off we drove in our little white Suzuki Jeep toward the peak of Mt. Clemans. We got a very late start, but the cool of the evening was pleasant and we caught the end of the lovely sunset before darkness fell.

After our sunset picnic, we bumped back down the gravel road, which was a little smoother going down than it had been going up, and headed for Yakima, some 32 miles away.

When we reached the small town of Naches on Highway 12, John pulled into the Naches Ranger Station. He wanted to spend a little time at the beautiful firefighter memorial there to remember Karen, Tom, Jessica, and Devin. I had not been there for a while, so I got out to join him. Jaina, who was a little carsick from the ride, rested in the back seat. John sat on the stone memory bench and gazed up at the bronze of Karen and her three friends. Their handsomely crafted, life-sized images were each mounted on individual five foot basalt pillars of stone. It was dark now, and the only spotlights shone to light the memorial.

Then I saw her in a whole new light. In the darkness, she shone brighter than ever! "John, do you see it?" I asked, studying her face a little more closely. The light caught her left eye, her cheekbone, and the subtle smile on her lips. Her illuminated eye seemed to twinkle with life! For a moment, I saw the "maverick" Karen, the bold witness for Christ. Her expression seemed to say, "I have a word from the Lord for you. Are you listening?"

Some think the bronze looks like Karen, and some don't think it looks like her. But the sculptor captured perfectly the spirit of her expression! I told the public at the dedication that Karen was rarely seen without a big smile, which is not normally done in bronze images. Usually, bronzes are done with subtle, little smiles. To me, the expression also represented the "Karen listening to wise advice" look. One hardly ever saw such a serious look on Karen's face. But I did; I'm her mother. And you know what? Karen did heed wise advice.

At night, under the lights, the bronze of Karen's face seems to come alive.

Is this the new Mona Lisa smile? Lyle Carter's rendition of Karen's face as it stands at the Naches Ranger Station Memorial next to her three comrades in death, Tom, Jessica, and Devin.

Virginia Craven, Tom Craven's mother, looks at the large Thirtymile Fire scrapbook on display at the Naches Firefighter Memorial Room. Kathie and daughter Jaina are to the right.

Kathie FitzPatrick stands next to Karen's picture on the dedication day in spring 2003. She is wearing the National Fallen Firefighter ribbon on her lapel.

Monument of remembrance, the Thirtymile Fire, in Boise, Idaho. National Interagency Fire Center

Bronze statues of Wildland firefighters seem to work silently in the fields. National Interagency Fire Center, Boise, Idaho.

The gravesite of Tommy Lee Craven in the quaint town of Roslyn, Washington, located in Mt. Olivet Cemetery, is more than just a remembrance of him; it was created by Will and Virginia Craven, Tom's parents, as a monument to all four firefighters. Tom Craven, at age 30, was the eldest of the young firefighters to perish fighting the Thirtymile Fire on 7/10/01.

July 17, 2001, late afternoon, the 21 white doves released into the sky circled above at the end of a very meaningful service. It was an unforgettable moment for all present. Karen is laid to rest at West Hills Memorial Park in Yakima in the Garden of Eternal Life in the shadow of a 25-foot cross that lights up at night. I think she would have approved. There is a very nice hillside view for visitors to enjoy. Jessica is in the nearby Garden of Inspiration.

The Four in the Okanogan

A Folksong,

Verse 1: *Well the skies were clear, the summer was here, way up in the Okanogan. The tourist crowd had all come out, and the campgrounds they were hoppin'. But in the air, there was something there that would soon drown out the singing, and four brave souls from a mountainside to heaven they'd be wingin'.*

Verse 2: *Well a call came in that a smoke was seen up near the Chewuch River. When the crews arrived the fire was high, and building ever stronger.*

From an acre or two in the pine and brush near the thirty mile campground, from a campfire spark came the birthing arc of a deadly monster wildfire.

(To Chorus)

When the Pine Tree forest glowed with fire, and the wind blew as hot as a branding iron. The sky grew gray that July day that will not be forgotten, when the forest burned and the families learned of the four in the Okanogan.

Verse 3: *There were twenty-one on the hill that day, making trail up the canyon, with McLeod, shovel, Pulaski axe they kept right on a-fighting. And then a shift in the valley wind sent a rain of ashes falling, as the fire crowned above their heads and the canyon turned to oven.*

Verse 4: *They could hear the rush of the burning brush and the pitch and pine explosions. There was no way out, when they heard the cries of two hikers up the hillside. With a wall of fire on either side, and a sky of flying embers. One shared a tent, and all but four would live to remember.*

Chorus: *When the Pine Tree forest glowed with fire, and the wind blew as hot as a branding iron. There were heroes born that July day that will not be forgotten when the forest burned and the people learned of the four in the Okanogan.*

Verse 5: *When the solitude and the silence of the forest flares to fury, and the scent of the heartache from the trees, for miles fill the valleys. When the sun turns brown and the stars dissolve in the smoke and heat you will find them, and all who fight the wildfires are the heroes in this poem. From Mann Gulch in Montana to the pinion pines of Tonto, from the chaparral of the Angeles, to the bison range of Yellowstone, Colorado, even Idaho, and the forest down in Oregon, well they all have known the pain they felt that day in the Okanogan.*

Chorus: *When the Pine Tree forest glowed with fire, and the wind blew as hot as a branding iron. Now the fireweed will blossom in those places not forgotten, where the forest burned and the people learned of the Four in the Okanogan.*

Words and music by Marian Mustoe, Ph.D.—Nighthawk Mountain Music, B.M.I—2001. Used by permission.

"The first time I saw Marian (Myles) Mustoe, he sang this song at the National Memorial Service for the four young fallen firefighters, held at the large Sundome complex arena in Yakima on July 24, 2001. I was so impressed! How could anyone write such a great a song like this so quickly after the tragedy?" Kathie remembers. "The song found its way to a few various radio stations, and I had a few copies on disc at the time. I had always hoped the song at some point in time in the future could be more widely appreciated," said Kathie, now in March 2007, and working on the book "Angel Promises." I called Myles, a professor at Eastern Oregon University, in La Grande, OR., and said, "Next time you are out in Wenatchee, come on out to Yakima. Let's talk over lunch."

Last month the invitation was accepted, and Kathie and Marian Mustoe sat down over Italian food at Russillo's in Yakima for a talk about the song. "It's such a great song, I commented, "Such detail. It needs to be more widely heard by more people. Better get those radio DJ's here in the Northwest going again...let's try to get that song back on the air. My book, and John Maclean's book about the Thirtymile Fire, are about to come out!" He talked to me about a few contacts he had in the music industry and in broadcasting, and promised me he would give it a go. But then he talked to me about the writing of the song.

"I was in Omak at the time of the fire," Mustoe recalls. "When I saw that big ominous cloud in the sky, I knew something very serious must have happened. Once I learned of the four deaths, I felt a song coming to me. It came so suddenly it was as if it was 'delivered,' if you know what I mean." Yes, I did. I had certainly happened to me before on different levels. And I was amazed at how many other people I was not even acquainted with at the time of the fire, had their own such experiences. Marian Mustoe is also an artist, and designed a very nice art piece to go with the song as well!

A Beautiful Expression

On the week of July 10, 2001, the Pacific Northwest was engulfed in a dark cloud of grief and sadness over the deaths of four young firefighters who perished while fighting the Thirtymile Fire.

No one had seen or experienced anything like it—sheer, raw emotion. Young people seemed to project and absorb the sadness as if they were their closest friends, family, brother, sister, son, or daughter. In the community of Yakima, Washington, everyone pulled together to celebrate their four lives. Each firefighter had an individual service. Tom Craven's service was held in his town of Roslyn, Washington, where he grew up. But Devin, Jessica, and Karen were celebrated and remembered where they had lived and grown up in Yakima.

As Karen's hearse, a U.S. Forest Service fire fighting vehicle, pulled up to the Stone Church on Englewood Avenue, city fire trucks lined the streets along the way with firefighters solemnly standing at the curb all up and down Englewood Avenue, each standing at a frozen salute as the vehicle carrying her drove by. The service, a Celebration of Life, was filled with music, photos projected on screens, and stories from her friends and music performed by her friends to remember her. To this day, people still pick up the phone to call Blue Ribbon video in Yakima to order the video remembrance of it.

On July 24, 2001, at the Yakima Sundome, the community, the nation, and the world remembered them. Many city fire trucks hit the road toward Yakima to join the service. The procession of vehicles, with the white limos carrying family, was seven miles long. Video of the procession taken from a helicopter was broadcast on national and world news.

One of the many wonderful expressions from the community was a beautiful sixteen page booklet that was quickly created, printed, and given out freely. I would like to share it with you. It was later learned that the work was compiled and created by Patricia Claire Renner, a school teacher from Escondido, CA., firefighter Matt Rutman's Mom. Thank you Patricia!

Heroes Remembered

The four firefighters who died July 10

Tom Craven, 30
Ellensburg, career firefighter
Married, with two small children. Once scouted by the Dallas Cowboys. Beat O.J. Simpson's junior-college yardage record.

Jessica Johnson, 19
Yakima, student at Central Washington University
Athlete and adventurer; wanted to be a dietitian. Worked as volunteer firefighter in West Valley.

Karen FitzPatrick, 18
Yakima, graduated a month earlier from West Valley High School
Loved academics, sports, home arts. Took it as a sign that her fire boots were made the same day she became a born-again Christian.

Devin Weaver, 21
Yakima, athlete and camper
Loved baseball; planned to study electrical engineering at the University of Washington this fall.

MILLE not NNIUM

Forever
Ebbs and flow

Forgotten

See the trees in sunlight?
Their strength lies deep inside.
They may bend, even break,
Yet their inner sap, though loosed,
Will also seal the wound.
The tree continues to grow as do we—
Pain for us may be growth too....

Who will answer for the fallen four,
Tom, Jessica, Karen, and Devin?
Who could know that the fires, twisting and joining,
Would cut them off from safety,
When the roar became too loud to hear
And a blood red sun seemed to sear
All that was alive?

I embrace a son and mourn the others-
I look for answers, for images, for words
That will give meaning to the lost-

I did not know then, yet, a mother knows
The anguish of another mother, of the other mothers-
And their grief is my grief.

This, then must and will give meaning to their being.
As I find a flower drawn by my own so long ago
On September 1, 1985,
I look for and must give meaning
So that all will not be lost...

Once the millenium called us, all of us,
To a new future (and the young are our future.)
Now, I hear the howling of wolf mothers,
Wondering what they should do,
After burning embers fell upon the fallen four.

No easy task, to begin to piece together,
To weave the sunlight,
Among the threads of the darkest days.

Beyond the streams and rivers,
The valley holds her own, close to her heart,
Embracing the ember blazoned four
Who are hers no more,
No more to run through the hills and curves
Of a thousand pine trees and smile their greetings
To the new day.

8,700 acres later....
What could any of this be for,
For Tom, Jessica, Karen and Devin?

When the nights come,
With wild wind and the memory of the terror
Of a vast and menacing fire,
When you, who are still here, feel death
Coming from behind, once again,
To overtake even the fleetest-
Remember, again, each time,
As have others who have gone before:

"What lasts is what you start with."

    We started with the hopes and dreams
    Of those who will always fight battles none of us
    aspire to fight.

    We started with their love and laughter
    And even now, on moon lit nights,
    We know that we will not leave them
    With empty words
    When their arms welcomed us
    And maybe even freed our own laughter...

    So, when sunsets drip nightfall
    In heated colors against the sky,
    When the scent of honeysuckle urges to linger
    By the soft breathing of a stream...
    Remember, that once, they filled our lives
    Even as the moon now fills the night.

Lanie Wolf Snavely

ANGEL PROMISES

Heroes Remembered

243

Happily may I walk.
May it be beautiful before me.
May it be beautiful behind me.
May it be beautiful below me.

a new day dawns
steps in the sand can leave a lingering impression

"My amulet is the wind of change blowing over the winds of creation/ I stand and allow all that is of nature and healing to pass through me. I am the instrument of the power of healing, a vessel without boundaries.

I seek the flow of existence, and in that search, I dispense love. The gifts you would know lie at your fingertips. Reach out to touch the wind and with the spirit of your power, change the direction as you so will it to be. With these words, I rest. See how you will direct the winds of change over the lifetime of all your endeavors.

THE BEGINNINGS OF THINGS

Karen with her dad, John FitzPatrick, standing at Washington Pass, near Winthrop, Washington, in 1997. Karen is wearing her favorite Mighty Mouse shirt.

August 1997: Winthrop, Washington... the Only Other Time Karen Had Been There.

I was planning a family vacation in the San Juan Islands for our family of four. The only missing piece was that I needed the Islander Motel—or somewhere in Friday Harbor—for a couple of nights. Everything seemed to be booked. I wondered if I would ever put this together. I was planning and booking this vacation only three weeks ahead. Unheard of, but not impossible.

The last of the Himalayan kittens were going out the door. We had raised them for years in California, and this new litter was finally close to six weeks old. This time, the mamma kitty had produced six "pet quality" kittens with very nice blue eyes and very nice markings. They were due to be sold for $100 each. This time it was going to be vacation money. I finally got a call from the Islander. "We have a cancellation for the days you need," the female voice on the other end of the line announced. I was ecstatic. It was done, and we were going!

I planned the route, the ferries, the Cherry Bank Hotel in Victoria, B.C., the whole trip was taking shape. We planned to take the gray van that had been transformed into the camping van with seats, sleeping area, a little refrigerator, and other amenities for traveling. We had used it in the move from California to Washington. It had been an invaluable vehicle in our crazy, mixed up, move northward that had seemed more like a funny Chevy Chase movie than a real life situation. Now it would go throughout the San Juan Islands and British Columbia on our new vacation adventure.

On August 20, the last of the kittens went out the door, as an Asian man handed me a one hundred dollar bill, carefully cradling the fluffy little kitten in his arms as he walked out toward his car in my driveway. The bill went into my purse. $600 vacation money! We were out the door and on our way that very afternoon.

We had never ridden on so many ferries, and thank goodness for all the "kitten money" to pay the way. Our family was beginning to think we were on a cruise. The waters on the way to British Columbia and the San Juan islands were blue and glorious, and if you watched carefully, you just might see the black and white "killer whales" jump out of the water a time or two The girls' eyes dazzled at the sights, the beaches, the birds, miniature monkeys, exotic butterflies, and other animals at the Crystal Gardens in Victoria, B.C., the sea walk, the intense colors and beauty and design of the Buchardt Gardens. It was a great experience. It was one of the few times in years we had all gotten away together for a trip. After six days, we headed back toward the mainland of Washington State, and Anacortes. We decided to take the winding mountain route through the Okanogan National Forest and Winthrop, Washington, toward our home in Yakima.

As we pulled into the quaint little western mountain town of Winthrop, I was amazed. It was obviously a tourist town set in the beautiful mountains on Highway 20. I had no idea it even existed. It was the first time visiting there for all of us. We parked the van and started walking. As we popped in and out of the picturesque shops and took in the sights, Karen suddenly said, "Mom! Look at these bees! They are living in the window! Beeeezzuzzit!" She laughed. "What is the deal?" Karen popped inside the shop for a closer look.

We followed. It was Doug and Sherry's wonderful shop with all kinds of homemade candies and homemade ice cream, huckleberry jams, chocolate huckleberry cordials, panda claws, and other unspeakable treats.

"These bees are living in the window," Karen remarked gleefully. "Kind of like a bee version of an ant farm!" She gave a hearty laugh as she peered closer at the active buzzing bee colony between two panes of glass. I'm sure Karen was not the first curious onlooker who had been drawn inside the store for a closer look. In the discovery, we went back outside where the tables were, and found that more food and fresh homemade ice cream flavors were available. All of us ordered ice cream cones. Karen ordered lemon custard and strawberry cheesecake in a waffle cone. Doug scooped it up and handed it to Karen. We all made decisions on flavors and soon went on our way, licking and slurping. As we finally meandered across the street to continue our exploration, we got a quick picture.

We spent a couple of hours exploring the cute shops, inns, and restaurants on the main street

Kathie, Jaina, and Karen move across the street after eating ice cream at Sherry's. Karen is still finishing her cone.

of Winthrop before moving on to the surrounding areas and finally heading home. It was a day filled with smiles and laughter and good memories.

Little did we know that in a few short years ahead in the future on a hot, dry, July day in 2001, a huge tragedy would occur there. As news media vans and satellite TV trucks from all over the Northwest jammed the entry from highway 20 to West Chewuch Road, they got the sudden news that they were not yet permitted to enter due to needed federal investigations which had to be conducted first. Emerging medical emergency vehicles would then turn off of West Chewuch Road onto Highway 20, driving slowly and silently through the town of Winthrop, as many individuals lined the streets and sidewalks with teary eyes. They already knew about the deaths of four young firefighters. Lights off, through silent streets, past those same shops and happily buzzing bees, but now with the lifeless bodies of Karen and her three firefighter friends as a grief-stricken world looked on.

The "Essence of Karen"

I sometimes used to wonder what it would be like if we could just bottle "the essence of Karen." I used to watch her just bubble and shine, as she seemed to bring warmth and happiness to anything and anyone anywhere, even a grouchy pot-bellied pig we met in the desert on a trip through Arizona. Did she ever soften up that grouchy creature! Perhaps her true calling would have been to be a politician, you say? No, I think not.

She had a smile and a laugh like no other. It seemed that her destiny was to bring warmth and love and caring to people of all ages, not just her peers. I was amazed at how many adults were affected by her young life. And it seemed one didn't usually just have a mere acquaintance with Karen, but a strong bond that was always fondly remembered. As a young woman, she was open and verbal with some of her questions and struggles about life, love, and the hereafter. But ultimately, in the end, at age 18, she achieved a deep and dynamic walk with God that left the people who knew her awestruck and gave them a small glimpse into the heaven to come.

I guess the Lord himself decided in His own unique way, that He would bottle the "essence of Karen" for everyone to learn and know of. It was in a way we didn't expect. It's happening right now.

Unforgettable and magical laughter. Karen Lee in Laguna Beach the week following graduation.

Just Heartwarming

Karen Loved a Dog Named Cici

Cici. A joy and a love to all: Cici, the Chow dog.

She came to us back in 1993 as a three-month-old puppy. Our friends, Doug and Donna Burrill, loved Chows, and owned two themselves. When we came over to their house on Wednesday nights for Bible study group, the first thing Jaina and Karen did was play with their two fabulous fluffy dogs.

"We work hard to 'people-ize' them," Donna explained with a cute laugh. Chinese Chows can be very much one-person-dogs, and can also be very territorial and not accepting of others. They are premium watchdogs and have powerful jaws, shoulders, and forearms. You don't want to be the subject of a Chow's anger, for sure. But at the same time they are capable of extreme love, affection, and humorous personalities if they are conditioned with much love and attention. It's a real commitment to raise them right. As it turned out, later that year, the same breeder was trying to place a female puppy. "I have to place her soon or she will not adapt well to the new owner," he explained. Surprisingly, we got a call from him not long after offering the female puppy to us. "I'm more concerned about her having a good home," he explained. Jaina and Karen were thrilled. Finally, their very own Chow!

She was an adorable, fluffy bunch of red fur—meek and lovable. It was hard to imagine that this puppy could either grow to be a loving pet or a mean, killer watchdog, but it was all in the upbringing and training. Regardless, Chows are known for killing any cats they can find. Their strength and speed mean almost instant death for any cat that unwittingly crosses their path. Since she was a puppy, I had high hopes she would adapt well. We already had three cats!

"Oh, brother!" Our friends just rolled their eyes. "Well, good luck with that!" Unknown to us, our housecats were ready and on the alert for the new intruder. We put the dog outside in our fenced yard with her food and water. A few hours later, when we went to check on her, she was no where to be found.

"She must have gotten out somehow!" Karen wailed. "Jaina, let's go try to find her!" The girls searched and searched and inquired of our neighbors. "She must have gotten out through the loose board on the fence," they guessed. All efforts turned up no puppy.

"Karen, someone must have stolen her," Jaina announced sadly to Karen at the end of the day. The girls went to bed with heavy hearts. They only had their puppy for one day, and she was already gone—probably forever.

The next afternoon the girls were out skimming the pool. They heard noises coming from the deck above them. Karen looked up, and there was Cici! She had been hiding under the deck! "There she is, Jaina! Look!" It took some coaxing and a little raw hamburger on the end of a stick, but she came out. The cats were waiting. Sugar, one of the female Himalayans, hissed and swatted at her immediately. Cici ran the other direction, but Jaina caught her.

"Awwww, poor baby. The cats have been scaring you!" she said holding her tenderly. "Come on, you are staying in my room, little puppy."

Well, I'm not sure how it all turned out, except over time the cats seemed to train the dog well, and they developed a very good understanding and respect for each other. Karen took Cici to dog obedience school, and the girls also invested a lot of love into her.

After Karen's death in July of 2001, Cici sensed keenly the absence of Karen. We gave her some attention as we had the time, but she knew the laugh, the energy, the melodic voice, the unique love of Karen, the doggy baths the grooming sessions, the petting by the magic massaging fingers, were somehow over and gone. She was now nine years old. One day she was fine, and the next day she just passed away. I looked out the window, and she appeared to be sleeping on the lawn by the fence. But when we checked on her more closely, we discovered she was dead. Not only did the dog pass away suddenly, but Karen's cat, Tigger, and her beta fish she talked to every day and called out musically by name—Sobe, or Sobe-meister,—also passed away shortly after Karen's death.

A few years ago there was a book titled, *On the Other Side,* by Marvin Ford. It was an interesting compilation of stories and accounts of individuals who had died and even had death certificates issued by the coroner, yet came back. This included Marvin Ford himself of Anaheim, California, who had died of a heart attack. Although he had no vital signs and had a death certificate issued by the hospital, around 35 minutes later, he was back.

Cici quietly studies Sugar, one of our housecats.

It was not the appointed time for these people apparently, and some had been told so by God or by an angel. Instantly they came back to earth, their spirits within their bodies alive once again as they woke up revived completely, much to the shock of those who were around them. The amazing thing about their stories is that they all had stories of heaven that were remarkably similar in great detail. A couple of individuals commented that during their brief glimpse of Paradise they saw pets who had endeared themselves to them and captured their hearts in life. Well, who knows? The story of Karen's pets suddenly passing on could certainly give rise to the curious prospect of such. We can only guess.

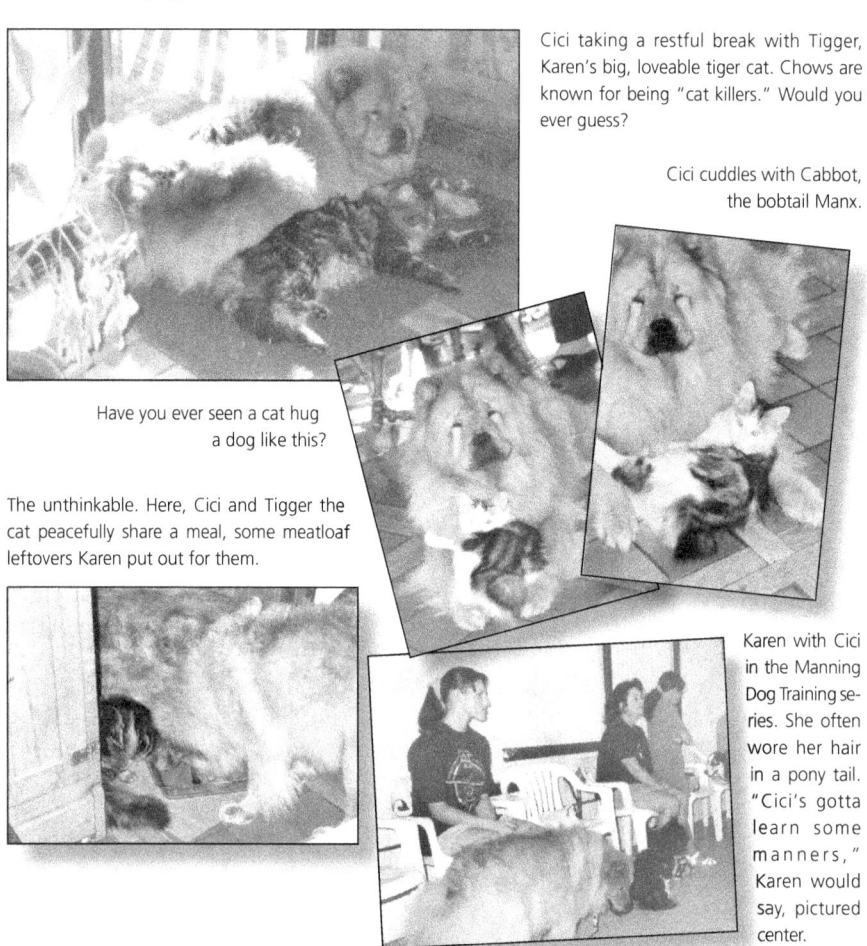

Cici taking a restful break with Tigger, Karen's big, loveable tiger cat. Chows are known for being "cat killers." Would you ever guess?

Cici cuddles with Cabbot, the bobtail Manx.

Have you ever seen a cat hug a dog like this?

The unthinkable. Here, Cici and Tigger the cat peacefully share a meal, some meatloaf leftovers Karen put out for them.

Karen with Cici in the Manning Dog Training series. She often wore her hair in a pony tail. "Cici's gotta learn some manners," Karen would say, pictured center.

Just Heartwarming

The Parades

I'll never forget them. I didn't see them all, but I saw enough. Karen participated in both junior high and high school marching bands in various parades in cities around the Northwest.

These events provided unforgettable experiences for Karen and her classmates—the prancing horses, the clowns, the floats, and classic cars carrying the beauty queens are what youthful dreams are made of. I never saw so many as when Karen was in the marching bands. I was so proud of her as she led her West Valley Panther Band, white gloves flying—under the direction of band teacher, Rich Reis, through the downtown avenues of many northwest cities, collecting top awards for their excellent artistic presentations. Her co-drum major partner was the pert and very cute, Cheryl Purcell, another close girlfriend. They would be positioned, one girl on one end and the other at the front or rear. At a certain point in the dance routine, they would stop the band, dance down the middle of the group to the drums and music, passing each other and changing ends. It was a sight to behold. I sure would love to find one of those parents somewhere out there who was doing home video!

In high school, the soccer coach wanted two hours after school every day. Karen was a soccer champ, but didn't see how she could do that much and keep her grades up. For the time being, the soccer ball went on the shelf, and high school band became her new love. During this time, Karen became first chair in flute. Her new band teacher was our next door neighbor, Dave Walter. Once again, being the high school drum major was such a huge time commitment, she was relieved to see another best friend, Jessica Dean, get the post for the next stretch of time. Karen dropped back to march and play flute in the sharp looking red, white, and blue West Valley band uniforms. Karen also learned to play keyboards, trumpet, and saxophone. She loved playing in the pep band for basketball and other high school sporting events. It was during these years it was also discovered she had a wonderful, amazing, and expressive singing voice. Karen began to sing at various events. One of her favorites was the song "Hero." After she passed away, her close friend, Cheryl Purcell, who was about to become a voice major at the college she was to attend that fall in Redding, California, sang "Hero" for her at two different memorial services while Jessica Dean accompanied her on the piano.

Fortunately, some of these photos were captured by me because, since I did not have real estate appointments that Saturday, I made a last minute decision to board a West Valley High School bus at 6 A.M. to join Karen, her teacher, and her friends for an unforgettable day!

Karen as drum major. "Fall in line now!"

Karen leads and marches with the West Valley Panther Band just before they break into a musical routine. Spring 1998, Wenatchee, Washington.

Karen looks over her shoulder at the banner wavers, checking their form.

Karen blows the whistle, bringing the band to attention.

Angel Promises

Marching, marching. "Has it been miles yet?" Being a drum major takes great strength and endurance. Often it was miles.

Karen getting ready to lead the next song.

Getting ready! Selah Days Parade, 1997

"Attention! Get ready. Time to move out!"

Karen Lee and close friend Cheryl Purcell: The two drum majors.

Karen: The Hairstyles

Karen was a girl who loved variety, creativity, and trendy fashion. She loved her long, auburn brunette hair. Occasionally, she had it cut a little shorter, but not so short it could not be done up in curls or swept up into a French roll, pony tail, or fashion clip!

Late in the spring of 2000, Karen had the sudden compulsion to try a very short haircut—hadn't done that one yet! But afterward, she became unusually depressed that she cut off her hair and could no longer enjoy variety in her hairstyles.

"Mom, I didn't know I would be this depressed over cutting my hair!" she wailed unhappily. Well, Karen had some of her own money from working as a Barista at Valerie's Espresso after school and also from doing three housecleaning accounts. It's where all the beautiful clothes, shoes, make up, and first class prom and homecoming gowns came from. Soon, I started to hear something like this—quick comments as Karen passed through the kitchen on the way to her room or dashed from the bathroom in her white satin dressing gown on the way to her room.

"Mom, I understand I can get a very realistic hairpiece. Jaina, what do you think? They can weave it into my existing hair. I just hate this 'boy' haircut!"

Well, I didn't know the half of it until I got a call at work from a hair salon owner. "Are you Kathie FitzPatrick, Karen's mom?"

"Yes."

"I just wanted to let you know that she is considering the purchase of a very expensive hairpiece that will weave into her existing hair. It will make her look like she is wearing long hair. But I don't think she will be happy with it."

"I see. I'm not surprised. I heard her talking about it," I replied.

"I just don't like to see a high school girl spend that kind of money, about $500, on something I don't think she will ultimately be happy with," the female salon owner explained.

"Thank you for calling me. I did have some idea about it, but I will talk to her more this evening when she comes home from work."

About 7 p.m., Karen returned home from working at the espresso coffee bar.

"Karen, honey, I got a call from a hair salon manager about the hairpiece."

"Oh, you mean Sharon?"

"Yes," I replied. "Why spend that kind of money on a hairpiece you probably won't like? Your hair will grow out soon enough. Everybody thinks it's very cute. It makes you look very chic and European."

"They do? It does?" She replied, wide-eyed.

"Yes. It's a just a new experiment for you—something different, but your hair will grow out soon. Just enjoy it for now. Soon, you'll be able to do big curls or sweep your hair up on top of your head or pigtails or whatever. Just have fun with it. Soon it will be over and your hair will be a little longer and you can do something new," I reasoned.

"OK, Mom. I guess you're right. It'll grow out soon enough," she sighed. "Not fast enough, but it'll grow out. Jessica and Lacy say the same thing!"

So Karen waited. By early summer 2001, her hair had grown out enough for a little variety in style, but not back to the long hair she loved. I think it was truly part of her very psyche—an unmet longing.

After receiving the news of the tragic fire the morning of July 11, 2001, I sadly slipped on my little black cotton dress and went in early, about 8 a.m. to my real estate office located in the Chinook Tower in downtown Yakima to drop off files to my broker to deal with my on-going transactions, as I was not going to deal with people that day or for a while. I went to my desk and retrieved the one last graduation picture of Karen in the black and silver cardboard holder and the one taken at the high school wearing the blue top. I certainly thought that her big, bright, shiny smile made up for the short haircut. It had been taken that last fall as her senior picture. That one senior picture of her in the blue top and the short haircut was the one I handed over to the media, and I sent copies to the Forest Service. It was duplicated and seen on TV and in print news around the world.

"Sorry, honey," I winced. She would have been very upset for the world to see her in her short haircut. But it was the most recent school picture of her at the time the tragic event happened, and the easiest for the press to use. I think I'm making up for that now, Karen! Forgive me?

Striking a Pose for the Camera

When Karen expressed an interest in modeling at about the age of 10, big sister Jaina just rolled her eyes.

It just didn't seem to be in the cards. Karen excelled in athletics, gymnastics, and sports, but the beauty thing—well, it just didn't seem to be happening.

However, as the teenage years progressed, Karen did an amazing and magical transformation. In 1998, while visiting San Francisco with Jaina and spending time with her older sister, Yvonne, a career girl who lived there, all three girls went shopping in the city for a day of sister fun and madness. In their journeys, they wound up at the San Francisco branch of the DNKY store. Apparently, from the looks of it, all the big management was present, in from New York. The runway was out, and a fashion show was soon to commence. It was around 1 P.M.

Oblivious to the event and the presence of the big-wigs in the store, Karen immediately started shopping for her size 6 on the designer jean round. Balancing shopping bags and looking at the styles and sizes intently, she was not aware of the presence of bodies gathering around her. Finally, she pulled out a few selections to try on. When she looked up, she was surrounded by a group of important-looking management.

"Would you consider being a model for our store?" one of the women asked, wide-eyed. Karen was breathless. Then she laughed at the comical sight. Jaina looked on with pride as older sister, Yvonne, came up on the rear of the scene.

"I used to live here, but I moved to Washington," she explained. I heard the conversation second hand from giggling girls on the phone later that evening. Knowing the boldness Karen was developing, I kind of wondered why she didn't jump on the stage on short notice. Oh, yes, I guess she did find her perfect pair of jeans too.

Modeling poses, Karen Lee FitzPatrick, January 1999.

Karen, changing the look a little in these poses with her long hair swept up.

Just Heartwarming

Karen by the "sparkle bush." January 1999.

Karen poses briskly on the railroad tie steps, January 1999.

Posing for the camera on a sunny day in January 1999.

Karen's time-out from modeling poses, January 1999.

Kathie's birthday with Karen and Jaina, November 1999.

MOTHER'S DAYS AND BIRTHDAYS; NEVER AGAIN QUITE THE SAME

I awoke one Mother's Day morning to brightly colored balloons being thrown and lightly bounced all over me along with giggles. It was Karen's idea, and her Jaina went along with the delightful prank.

"Happy Mother's Day!" Karen and Jaina squealed merrily. "Your special breakfast is almost ready. Get up now!" The girls did amazingly well with breakfast: scrambled eggs, Danish, fruit, toast, coffee, and orange juice. We always had a nice time on Mother's Day. In her teen years, Karen came to be known for a new tradition on Mother's Day: her four layer lemon-pansy cake with live flowers on it. Did you know pansies are edible? She learned it on her favorite TV program, "Martha Stewart."

Birthdays were always celebrated in grand style with dinner and presents at home or in favorite restaurants. After Karen's passing, it was a real adjustment to get through these special occasions without her. I had to try to not be overwhelmed by the lack of her presence, but enjoy the family that was present and the two lovely daughters I still had with me.

Just Heartwarming

At our kitchen table at home the girls put out the flowers and card before the Mother's Day breakfast was about to be served.

Yvonne, Karen and Jaina, celebrating Mom's birthday in California, in earlier youth days.

The Red Dresses

    I'm not sure when it started—those red dresses. Maybe it was in high school. Karen was definitely one of those "winter" colorized people who looked good in the dark reds and burgundy shades. It seemed that her favorite party dresses and prom dresses were red. Not every time—but often. It fit her romantic, dreamy attitude about the events she was going to, and with her long, back velvet dress coat—well, she was quite smashing. As she wrote about her experiences, the mention of the "red dress" made its appearance in poems such as "Crimson Lips."

    In a favorite art piece Karen created, it seems to be she in the center of a white pavilion, wearing a red gown. After her passing, I looked at it one day as it hung on the wall of her room, and it seemed to represent Karen in Paradise. I wonder if she gets to wear the red dress over there. Do you suppose?

Just Heartwarming

Karen: "The Athletic One"

Karen at Eagle Beach in the San Juan Islands, doing a handstand. Also pictured with her older sister Jaina in swimsuits in 1998.

Karen in weightlifting class her senior year at West Valley High School. She won first place in the women's bench press in the spring Lift-a-Thon, 2001.

It seemed like from the very beginning, Karen was destined to become some kind of athlete. She was strongest of all my babies in the womb. When Karen kicked with those strong little heels, I gasped, eyes bulging! Unhappy with her dark little space there, late on the eve of December 25, 1982, she decided she was busting out, ready or not.

The strong-willed baby Karen broke my water in the process and off to the hospital we rushed. Once there, the doctors determined she was breach—feet first. They tried to turn her around but were unsuccessful. Karen was a large baby, 9 lbs 8 ounces. Well, she finally made it into the world at 5:40 P.M. on December 27, 1982. The rest is history.

As a young child, Karen was often mistaken for a very active, tan, blond, little boy. She got to wear pink lace dresses, but in her play clothes, people often could not tell the difference. We noticed early on that Karen was strong and fast, especially if I was chasing her when she was chasing after a kitten or a ball headed for the middle of a busy street. When she was in the first grade, Karen came home one day with a ten foot banner the kids and her teacher made for her. It read: "Olympics 2010—Karen L. FitzPatrick—Fastest Woman in the World!" It had a drawing of an Olympic gold medal on it. By the time she was nine, she was running and bringing home awards, placing first or second in Junior Olympic track events in Cheney, Washington.

Karen and Jaina were members of children's gymnastics teams when they were very young. After enrolling them in a local gymnastics program shortly after moving here from California, I went back to pick up eight-year-old Karen after her evaluation session with her new coach. As I entered the gym, he looked at me wide-eyed.

"So what planet did you say this kid came from?" he joked as he talked to me in detail about Karen's abilities. "The sky is the limit for her!" he explained. "She is naturally gifted in athletics and probably could train for the Olympics."

Well, this came up often over the years. It would appear that Karen could have chosen her field: track, women's weightlifting, swimming, or diving. And if soccer was ever a division, certainly that. As she and her Yakima Youth Soccer Association team, The Bobcats, developed over the six years they were together, it was a joy to watch them become

Just Heartwarming

Karen in California, doing a high dive.

Karen, with her soccer team, the Bobcats, Washington State Champions, 1994. Karen is on the far right, age 12.

skilled players. Their coach, Chuck Maissen had endless patience. In 1994, they won top honors in Seattle—the State Championship. It was a great honor.

As a busy Realtor, I sometimes had trouble driving Karen every weekend to the far distances where these tournaments took place. The parents willingly chipped in to take Karen along, as they could not imagine competing without her. One time it was my turn, and I transported Karen about 200 hundred miles to Gig Harbor for a tournament there. I'll never forget her getting into the game and then aggressively running toward the swiftly flying ball, taking body shots on her back, shoulders and upper chest while the amazed and cheering crowd looked on. I wasn't particularly a sports fan, but I was pretty "wowed" at the sight of this technique, just like the other spectators. "Wow, Karen…I'm gonna have to get you a t-shirt that says, 'body shots!'" I said to her after the game was over. Soon she was back in her mean-looking, black leather coat and ready for lunch with her teammates.

The Coat

It started as kind of a joke, really. "The joke coat" we sometimes called it, that very mean-looking black leather jacket. About a year prior she had been shopping with her teammates after a tournament near Seattle, when the group decided to stop off in North Bend and shop a little at the outlet mall there. Karen was looking through a clearance round in one of the stores, and spotted a black leather jacket marked down from $350. to only $50. She pulled the jacket off the hanger and quickly tried it on. The reflection in the mirror and the cheers from her gal pal teammates at that moment was just the beginning. It was a match. It looked like a motorcycle gang jacket. It was so out of character for Karen, it was comical. However, it was due to serve a new purpose. When Karen donned the jacket over her orange and black Bobcat's uniform, and strutted out like a warrior princess to the next tournament, she was a stunning and serious looking rival. The other team was beginning to feel fear before they even got started with the game. It served a purpose, and served it well.

In junior high and high school, Karen gravitated more toward music and marching band. Karen was often approached about training and traveling more seriously with sports and for the Olympics. Karen and her father and I decided not to take that on as a lifestyle or primary focus. In the latter part of high school, Karen made the decision to use her strength and speed to go to work as a firefighter. She envisioned being able to help others and possibly even being able to rescue children from emergencies. From there, Karen planned to train to become an Emergency Medical Technician with the Fire Department.

In her senior year of high school, she was involved in weightlifting training. In May of 2001, Karen won a first place medal in the spring Lift-a-Thon, breaking a women's record in the bench press event. She went to work for the U.S. Forest Service in June 2001.

Karen was strong, swift, and intelligent, and could think and evaluate situations quickly. If you were ever trapped somewhere and it was up to Karen and her team to rescue you, by golly, you would be rescued! No doubt about that!

Watch Out World! It's Photography Class

Karen had another favorite class in high school—photography.

Along with music, band, and English, Karen also had a blast in photography class. She made a whole new circle of friends—her dark room buddies who learned to make magic with photographs. Karen never thought of taking black and white pictures until it was one of the requirements of the class. She tried reverse negative pictures and various types of subjects and buildings indoors and outdoors out on location.

She liked to use my camera and often had it loaded with black and white film for her class work. I was always changing to color later when I had to take pictures for my real estate work. The worst goof up I made was not changing the film back to color at graduation time.

"Oh, Mom! You mean those pictures are all in black and white?" Karen wailed unhappily.

Oops! Fortunately, I was able to get color photos from her friends and the professionals who were on duty that night. But in a few cases, the black and white ones have served well, such as the nice one of Karen and her friend Matt on graduation night.

I really don't know where all of the pictures from photography class are—only what turned up under her bed in her high school binder after her death. Here they are.

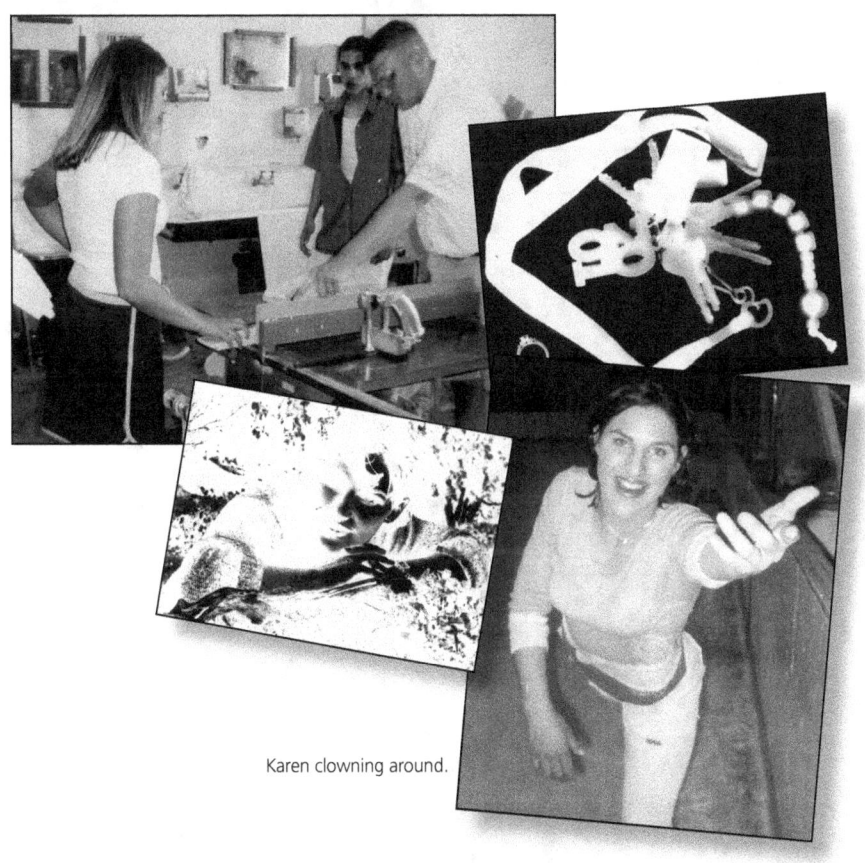

Karen clowning around.

Karen Lee FitzPatrick, 18. This black and white portrait was a favorite graduation photo, a product of her senior photography class.

Karen FitzPatrick
5 - 23 - 01
Photography per. 1
Picture Story

Most everyone who has cats in their family can remember witnessing interesting times in their history. Every cat is different; some active and playful and others lazy and sleepy. In my family, we have three cats; Tiger, Azmon and Mufferrd. Once, my mother was given a box of chocolates by my dad and soon after, the box was empty. My mom tried to find out who had eaten them all. My sister, who had probably eaten most of them, blamed the sinful deed on my two lazy cats, Tiger and Azmon. She also claimed that Mufferrd had told her on them. Sure enough we found the two cats slumped in their chair with tummy aches from eating too many sweets. If you made them get out of the chair, you could probably find the wrappers there as well.

Just Heartwarming

The pasture by the blue barn and the pony Karen grew up with. He actually belonged to a neighbor friend. His name was Charley Brown.

Left. St. Joseph's Church in Yakima, late winter 1999.

Below. St. Joseph's Church is a landmark in the Yakima Valley Region. This photo was taken by Karen in late winter 1999, probably January or February, and was before the arson fire. In July 1999, an intentional flame destroyed this beautiful building. It took several years and millions of dollars to rebuild.

Angel Promises

Another senior portrait in the woods in the fall of 2000. A gift from her mom, Karen is wearing the watch she wore the day of the Thirtymile Fire.

Another senior photo from the "Fall Woods Series," taken by classmate Aleishia, at the Cascade Gardens in Yakima, October 2000.

Assorted Poems, Letters, and Memories

Karen's fire pack from the Thirtymile Fire episode, and her fire boots. These are some of the quotes taken from the USFS brochure about her life.

Karen Lee FitzPatrick

Karen Lee FitzPatrick, born December 27, 1982, died July 10, 2001, battling the blaze at the Thirtymile Fire, near Winthrop, Washington.

She was the youngest of the four firefighters who perished, only about four weeks out of high school. Karen was often the youngest in her class, earning the nickname, "baby Karen" or "BK." Although she was often the youngest among her peers, she often excelled in the areas of music, art, academics, and sports. Since 1990, Karen had been a member of the girl's soccer team, The Bobcats who grew to excel greatly and take top state honors only four years later. She was the drum major for the West Valley Panther Band. Karen was also a member of the National Honor Society at West Valley High School, where she graduated June 8, 2001. Karen had plans to enroll at Yakima Valley Community College in the Fall of 2001 to study Fire Science, and eventually hoped to become an EMT with the fire department.

At the senior breakfast, Karen was honored to receive the Spirit award, and she was also voted by her peers the "Most Likely To Be The Next Martha Stewart." Karen was known for her gourmet cooking and baking, much enjoyed by all! A notable weightlifter, she also received an impressive medal at the Spring Lift-a-thon, May 2001. Karen was the music director of the small church where she attended, and was known for her beautiful and expressive singing voice.

Amidst all these talents, the thing she was most known for was her vibrant and alive faith in God, which shown like a lighthouse from her life. Karen had written on the wall of her room these words, "Jesus, help me to love you with my life." This she did, every day of her life, and even now, in death, her memory and her spirit go on!

Assorted Poems, Letters, and Memories

July 17, 2001: the "Celebration of Life" service for Karen L. FitzPatrick, held at Stone Church Assemblies of God Church, Yakima, Washington. Pictured above, U.S. Forest Service men in uniform pray. A close-up photo of this scene was published in the September 2001 issue of *Newsweek*. As additional guests and firefighters filed into the service, the attendance was estimated to be about 1,000.

THE DAY THE ANGELS CRIED

(Thirtymile's Fallen Firefighters)

For all of us in Washington's Yakima Valley
The month of July will never be the same.
We will remember it as a time of loss and tragedy,
Families changed forever by Thirtymile's flames.

A campfire that was carelessly forgotten
Was the bell tolling Death's grim call
On a beautiful summer's day, who could have imagined
How our forest's guardians would fall?

Angel Promises

The fire was small enough at the start
And that was thought to be quickly and easily contained
When the "hand crew" went in to do their part
Mopping up and making sure no hot spots remained.

Into the Okanogan's Chewuch River Canyon they went
A place of wild beauty and steep terrain
A team full of adventure, and youthful spirit
Hearts full of future dreams that Fate would never ordain.

Confident and strong, they went about their chore
Cutting fire lines and putting out small flames
Happy to be working in the majestic outdoors
Keeping the capricious hunger of wildland fire in rein.

The danger of their career they learned from day one
Survival and protective training was constantly taught
But when a rapid chain of events has begun
Even the most veteran and elite can be caught.

On that day in July when the angels cried
Circumstances came together too fast to understand
Timber exploded in an instant wave of fire
And for some in the "hand crew it was their final stand.

Assorted Poems, Letters, and Memories

Tom, Karen, Jessica, and Devin
Four people doing a job they loved
They're still watching over our forests from heaven
Helping to protect their fellow firefighters from above.
Though they're gone they'll not be forgotten
We'll always keep their memories alive
Every time we're in the mountains
The strength and love of their spirits will be by our side.

As we gaze upon the evening sky
And perhaps watch an eagle's last flight
As the tears slip from our eyes
We'll see their faces, hear their laughter
In the golden light.

—*Tami R. Miller, 8-10-01*

Kathie FitzPatrick holds a quilt sent to her with a card and a note inside that read, "These squares were hand ripped, because that's how our hearts felt when we received the news." The note pinned inside the quilt reads, "Made in memory of the fallen firefighters—gone, but not forgotten," Liz Miller, Pine Springs, Culbertson County, Texas.

To the Parents of Fallen Firefighters

You did the right thing, you know;
You gave your children wings and let them grow.

Although you may have thought the job was too tough
You taught them the courage to be brave enough

To look fire in the eye and dare it to spread;
If it got out of hand they could keep their head.

They were strong, brave, and courageous too.
You know, I bet they were a lot like you.

Assorted Poems, Letters, and Memories

> I know these words will not take away your pain
> As you will never get to see your child again
>
> But know that in this time of woe
> You gave the country a great hero.
>
> Thank You.
>
> *Teresa Martin and Family*

To the Parents of fallen firefighters:

You did the right thing, you know
You gave your children wings and let them grow

Although you may have thought the job was too tough
You taught them the courage to be brave enough

To look fire in the eye and dare it to spread
If it got out of hand they could keep their head

They were strong, brave and courageous too
You know, I bet they were a lot like you

I know these words will not take away your pain
As you will never get to see your child again

But know that in this time of woe
You gave our country a great hero.

Thank You.

Teresa Martin & Family

Goodbye to My Childhood Friend and Cousin, 7/11/01

By Danielle Ware

Such good times we had,
And so much to remember.
Times of children's play,
Many times of running around
Grandma and Grandpa's house;
Times of make believe and potions
In the backyard;
Many games of house, doctor, school,
In the old blue Ford truck,
To the numerous adventures within
Heather Farms Park.
The times where you dared me and
Challenged me…where most times
I was too "chicken" or "baby" to do.
The times where Grandpa would go
Behind Grandma's back to get us ice cream.
Your flavor was "orange sherbet,"
Mine, "chocolate."
To the memories and occasions at
Your old house,
Where we would bounce up high
On the trampoline;
The countless times we'd try to hangout
With the big kids and be "mature."

Assorted Poems, Letters, and Memories

Never will forget Cherlin doing our hair,
And pictures,
And tagging along with Jaina and Irene.
So many memories to remember!
I will always remember our fun times
And adventure.
Until we meet again,

Danielle Ware, childhood partner in crime

In the month of May 2002, I went to Karen's grave to put flowers in the vase and found this note from one of her best friends. It was on a card, curled up and inserted inside the flower holder. It was a little water stained, but still readable:

You've been on my mind now for nearly ten months, and although you're not "here," it would do my mind some good to write you a note. I just finished my freshman year at Wheaton (College). How weird it is that you're not here for me to tell you about it. I have a lot of new friends now, Karen, all of them Christians. I almost left Wheaton this year. It wasn't everything I had expected, so I tried to escape. But God knew better. He has some great things in store, I know. Today, I remember your "Crimson Lips." How do you spell that? Anyway, I brought you a rose like the one from Dan hanging in your room, and it's like the color of the poem you wrote.

You grow dimmer in my mind's eye as the time progresses, but I still remember your smile and your laugh. One day I, too, will die, but you've given me the assurance that it will be okay.

Love, Jessie.

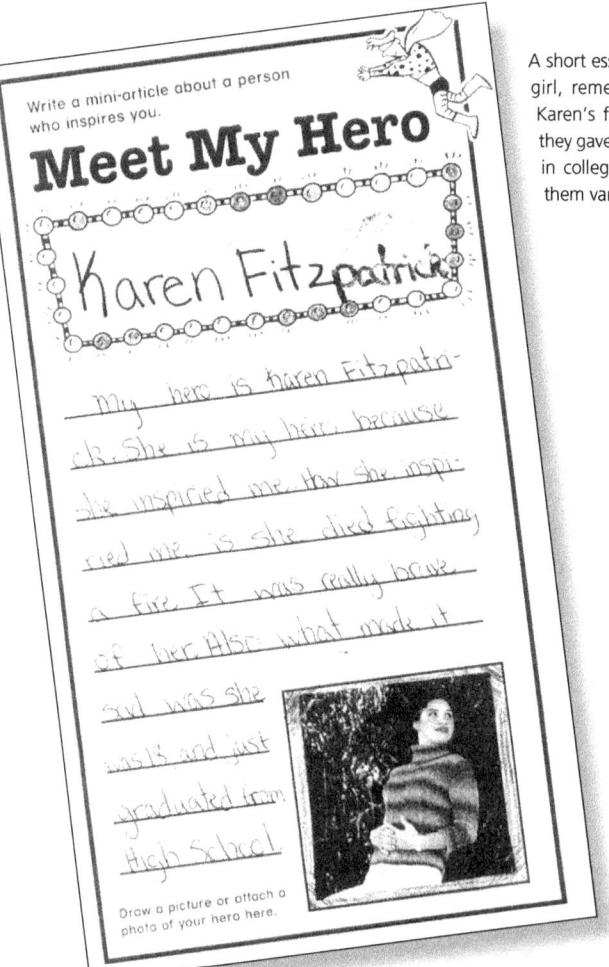

A short essay written by an 11-year-old girl, remembering Karen. Several of Karen's friends have mentioned that they gave oral reports and wrote essays in college about how Karen inspired them various ways.

Assorted Poems, Letters, and Memories

A Letter from the Gottlieb's,

a family Karen was close to: July 6, 2002

Dear Kathie, John, and Jaina:

Our hearts and prayers are with you as we approach the one year anniversary of Karen's ascension to light. Her radiant spirit continues to exercise its positive influence in this realm of dust.

The purpose of this note is to let you know that our family is leaving shortly for a three week teaching and service trip to Panama. We will be leading a group of 20 teens and will work under the direction of the Bahai's of Panama, teaching children's classes, painting buildings, visiting Indian villages high in the mountains, providing medical services at a small clinic, planting gardens and hopefully love and joy, and sharing the Word of God.

With your permission, we would like to dedicate this trip in Karen's name.

With Love, The Gottlieb's —Steve, Randie, Jordan, and Jonathan

---

O Son of Spirit!

Noble have I Created Thee,
yet thou hast abased thyself.
Rise then unto that
for which thou wast created.

Bahá'u'lláh

Children of the Universe ©1994 Harlan Scheffler
Quotation from *The Hidden Words of Bahá'u'lláh* A#22
Published by Special Ideas 1-800-326-1197

Cheryl Purcell, a close friend of Karen's, wrote this wonderful note to us! How amazing it was to see Cheryl blossom over the years. She, Jessica Dean, and Lacy Chambers had all been very close to Karen growing up. Cheryl was about to leave for Bible college in the fall, and would attend there as a voice and music major. She also sang the song, "Hero" in both the local service for Karen and national memorial services for all four firefighters held at the Yakima Sundome on 7/24/01. Later, while attending Bible college in Redding, California, Cheryl daily carried a view binder with Karen's photo in the front, along with her other books. Her friends often asked, "Doesn't that make you sad to look at Karen all the time?"

"Oh, no. It makes me very happy to look at Karen all the time!" Cheryl replied wisely. This is the answer Karen would have loved to hear.

Aug. 21, 2001

Dear John & Kathie,

I want you both to know what a blessing Karen was to me. She inspired me since I met her in band in 8th grade. And now, more than ever, she has given me a precious gift- a hunger to draw closer to my Savior.

Philippians 3:10-11
"I want to know Christ and the power of his resurrection and the fellowship of sharing in his sufferings, becoming like him in his death, and so, somehow, to attain to the resurrection from the dead."

That verse is truer than ever now. I also have a newfound love for hymns. It's exciting to find one that says it so perfectly and expresses your heart just right. In speech class, Karen was always willing (& eager) to share the gospel. I admire her zeal to win souls for the Lord. She will always be with me in heart & spirit. And I will never forget what I learned from her shining example. Thank you for allowing me to share in song at her Memorial & the Sundome Memorial. It meant so much that I could offer you comfort. May God's spirit continue to comfort you and bring peace. All my love & sympathy, Cheryl Purcell

Assorted Poems, Letters, and Memories

July 17, 2001

Dear Mr. and Mrs. FitzPatrick,

I don't know you, and I did not know your daughter, Karen, but I felt compelled to write to you. I heard about the fire that took Karen's life last week, and have been following the press coverage on "firehouse.com", on the internet.

I can not say that I know exactly how you feel, but I did want to let you know that we are sharing in your sorrow, and we are keeping you in our prayers.

We are also rejoicing in the fact that Karen was a Christian, and that we know for certain where she will be spending eternity. The press has touched on her Christian beliefs in great detail, and that alone has been a wonderful testimony. Perhaps, by someone hearing or reading about her faith, they too, may come to know the Lord. Even in death, Karen continues to be a shining light for Jesus.

There are several firefighters in our family, including my 19 year old daughter, Nicole. She has been firefighting for over 3 years now. She worked for C.D.F.- California Department of Forestry and Fire Protection, this summer and last.

During the off season, she has been actively involved in the Fresno City Fire Department Explorer Program, where she is the Assistant Fire Chief, and is currently finishing classes for her Associate Degree in Fire Science. She graduated from the Fresno City College Fire Academy, last year.

I have attended many firefighting classes with Nicole, on a Volunteer basis. Although, I am well aware of the dangers involved, I could not imagine how it would feel to lose her in the line of duty. I hope that if that should ever happen, I would take comfort in the knowledge that Nicole was doing exactly what she loved to do, and that she would now be in a better place, because she, too, is a Christian.

I am going to send sympathy cards to each of the other firefighters' families. Unfortunately, those are going to be much harder notes to write, as I don't know if their loved one's were saved or not.

I hope that this letter brings you comfort, somehow. Celebrate Karen's life and her faith, and rest assured that you will be seeing her again.

We will continue to lift you, and your family up in prayer.

Sincerely,

Joy Hamilton

Joy Hamilton

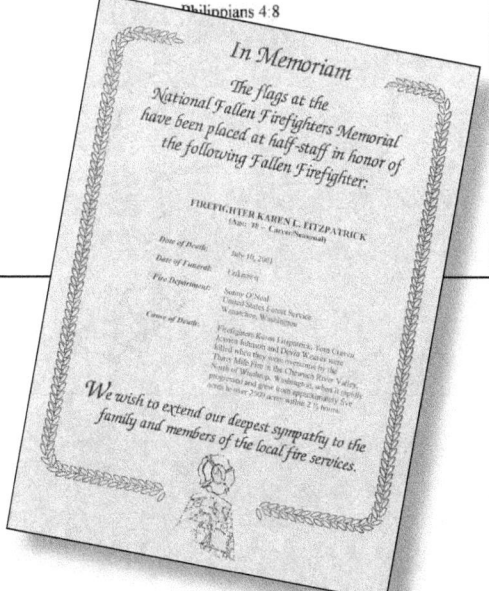

United States Department of the Interior

BUREAU OF LAND MANAGEMENT
Office of Fire and Aviation
3833 South Development Avenue
Boise, Idaho 83705-5354

In Reply Refer To:
1120 (FA-106)

OCT 1 7 2001

Mr. and Mrs. John Fitzpatrick
7903 Poplar View Way
Yakima, Washington 98908

Dear Mr. and Mrs. Fitzpatrick:

The employees of the National Interagency Fire Center want to join with thousands of others in extending our sympathy and support to your family over the loss of Karen. She seemed a remarkable person, one of great faith who was happiest when serving those she cared for. We are certain that she touched many people and influenced them for good. The world is lessened by her absence.

We have a monument at the fire center, dedicated to firefighters everywhere. It is an island of native trees, grasses, flowers and a waterfall in the middle of the our 55-acre complex. When firefighters fall in the line of duty, we place a marker at the monument as a way of honoring and remembering their contributions and their sacrifice. We want you to know that a marker soon will be placed in the monument to honor your daughter. We understand it is a small thing for us to do, but hope that it still brings you a measure of comfort.

When a firefighter dies, it affects people all over the country. We all pause to think of our chosen profession, the risks that are sometimes a part of it, and by whatever way seems appropriate, send our compassion and concern to those who mourn. We hope that in some way, you feel the support and sympathy from people – known and unknown to you – during this time of immeasurable trial.

Sincerely,

Larry Hamilton
Director, Office of Fire and Aviation

Assorted Poems, Letters, and Memories

Karen Lee FitzPatrick

Born: December 27, 1982, died July 10, 2001
Initial Attack Firefighter: Thirtymile Fire:
Winthrop, Washington

A bright shining light was she.
The light within her eyes was
Eternal.
Her life shone forth for all
On earth to see.
Now, Karen Lee…
Her life is not held in a tomb…
But in God's plan
And destiny,
Still gently unfurls
Like the petals of a never-ending
Eternal bloom.
There in heaven, yet here on earth,
Within the many lives of those who
Knew her—and even of those who
Only heard—
Her life goes on.

ANGEL PROMISES

"Last Alarm"

This is the sounding of the Last Alarm for firefighters, Tom Craven, Karen Fitzpatrick, Jessica Johnson and Devin Weaver who gave their young lives in the line of duty. Your Brother and Sister Firefighters salute you for your unselfish dedication and service to the citizens of this Nation in the protection of our lives and property.

Our prayers and condolences go out to your family and friends. Your assignment is complete may you rest in peace.

July 24, 2001

To the family of Karen Fitzpatrick,

I am a Dispatcher for the Yakima Public Safety Communications Center.

I want you to know that even though it was one of the most difficult and heartbreaking things I have ever been asked to do, it was truly an honor to give the "Last Alarm" for our fallen firefighters. It was a tribute that came, not only from my heart and soul, but from the hearts and souls of all of my brother and sister firefighters.

It is impossible for me to express to you the depth of sorrow I feel for your tragic loss. May you take some comfort in knowing that I will always hold a special place in my heart for Karen, Tom, Jessica and Devin and all of you.

With Heartfelt Sympathy,
Carol Guthrie
Dispatcher
Yakima Public Safety Communications

July 28, 2001

To the Family and Friends of
Tom Craven,
Karen Fitzpatrick,
Jessica Johnson,
Devin Weaver,

This memorial was found outside our door the morning of July 12th. We have had it sitting in plain view on our counter at the information desk here in Sedro-Woolley WA. It has been a touching reminder to those of us working in this building as well as our many visitors. We thought you would like to have it.

With Thanksgiving and Sorrow,
The Staff at
North Cascades National Park Headquarters
Mount Baker District Office, Mt Baker/Snoqualmie National Forest

Assorted Poems, Letters, and Memories

This photo of Taps which was sent to us, was especially meaningful as the Washington State Patrol did a 21-gun salute near the end of Karen's graveside service at West Hills Memorial Park in Yakima shortly before the 21 white doves were released into the sky at the end of her service.

ANGEL PROMISES

Hello,

We do not know each other. I saw the item in the paper and wanted to share with you this lovely poem, and others received since, a fine Christian lady sent me after the death December 10, 1971 of my 24 year old daughter from an auto accident six days earlier in Indianapolis, Indiana.

We have a merciful God, for had she lived, Janet not only would have been a vegetable, but violent.

I know! I understand!

My prayers, and God bless you.

(Mrs.) Katy Rector

GOD'S FLOWER GARDEN

It's hard to lose the ones we love,
   To see them pass away,
The sweetest and the kindest gone,
   While others are left to stay.

But if we had a garden,
   With roses fair and bright,
We'd often pick the loveliest,
   And think it to be right.

And so it is with Jesus,
   In His Heavenly garden here,
He often picks the fairest flower,
   The ones we love so dear.

The flowers that are picked by Him,
   Will never fade away,
We know they'll live forever,
   And we'll see them some sweet day.

IN PEACE WITH GOD

No time for a farewell to be spoken
And no time for us to say goodbye
You were gone before we knew it
Only God knows why you were chosen
It broke our hearts to lose you
But dear Karen Lee you are not alone
For part of us all went with you
The day HE called you home
Though your smile is gone forever
Your laughter we cannot hear
And your hand we cannot touch
We will never lose the memory
Of one we loved so very much
So many times we have missed you
And so many times we have cried
If our love could have saved you
You would never have died
But Christ needed your help above
And with love sent for Karen Lee
To share His love and safe haven

– Karen's Family –

My deepest sympathies and my constant prayers are with you. My name is Emily Hinson and I was part of the 21 man crew who were to put out the small fire on July 10. Although I only knew Karen for one short day, as a sister in Christ her face and her every action radiated her love for the Lord. I look forward to spending eternity with her in heaven. Know that my prayers for you will continue as time goes on.

God Bless,

Emily Hinson

...He hath said,
I will never leave thee nor forsake thee. Hebrews 13:5

Emily Hinson of Leavenworth, Washington is a young Christian woman who knew Karen for only one day—July 10, 2001. Emily was one of the firefighters who deployed her fire shelter on the road amidst firestorm winds in excess of 70 mph and lived.

To All Parents

By Edgar A. Guest

"I'll lend you for a little time,
A child of Mine," He said.
"For you to love the while he lives,
and mourn for when he's dead.
It may be six or seven years,
Or twenty two or three,
But you will call him back
Take care of him for me?

He'll bring his charm to gladden you,
And shall his stay be brief,
You've had his lovely memories,
As solace for your grief.
I cannot promise he will stay,
Since all from earth will return
But there are lessons taught down here
I want this child to learn.

I've looked the wide world over,
In my search for teachers true,
And from the throngs that crowd life's land,
I have selected you.
Now will you give him all your love,
Nor think the labor vain,

Nor hate Me when I come to call,
To take him back again?"

I fancied that I heard them say,
"Dear Lord, thy will be done;
for all the joy thy child shall bring,
The risk of grief we'll run,
We'll shelter him with tenderness,
We'll love him while we stay;
But shall the angels call for him,
Much sooner than we planned
We'll have the bitter grief that comes,
And try to understand."

From Karen and Jessica's English Teacher, Dan Peters

*Letter to Students Who are Not Here,
in Memory of Karen and Jessica:*

The hills are green and will be for as long as a month.
Then, as the cheatgrass matures, they will turn red.
By the time you come home,
Fewer than before,
They will have changed to various shades of brown.
Now, though, they are green and some mornings,
When clouds cover the valley, you can squint your eyes
And almost believe you are in another country
Where all year long, hills remain as round and bright
As these ridges are today.
Not quite a year ago, I wrote another letter.

ANGEL PROMISES

I said I don't have anything other than easy answers
That seem tired before I can get them out of my mouth.
Much later, I saw some things were passing through me.
You could call it grief or maybe it was just that so
much had changed.
My friend who was my high school teacher, drove me
Around for more than an hour.
He said, I went to landscape.
He copied down this line: No one loves rock, yet we are here.

Beginning with Murray's letter before Christmas,
Old words have come back to me in new ways.
I didn't know what to do with this one either.
Then it happened five times in five months—
Bales and Hiler and Matson and Lohrasbi and
Two days ago, another friend, a long distance runner,
Brought down what was left of my resistance.

Outside my window the sound of a lawnmower drifts back and
forth. I am not where I was, and you are not here, anymore.
The ridges change as they did before any of this happened—
Before we lost so much.
That's no kind of answer, but I will stand by it.

Across the valley, I can see pillars of smoke where orchards stood
The trees behind your high school empty of blossoms in the wind and rain.
Meanwhile, those beside the river continue to fill with leaves.

Dan Peters—4/18/03 (English teacher
to both Karen and Jessica, WVHS)

Memories and Letters

Excerpts of a letter from J.J. Sandlin, Attorney, 2006

Hello, Kathie:

This is J.J. Sandlin, and I certainly know you very well. I was so devastated by your loss, Kathie, and I want you to know that I thought your daughter was a beautiful, inspirational young Christian lady, and she certainly imprinted on my children while she was my children's babysitter.

Actually, as I am writing this, I realize I have filled my life with activities with my children and my law work, and I wonder if there really is a time for me to have a nice companion, confidante, friend, and/or wife. You are the same age as Star, and I remember you as a very professional, observant, caring, nice young lady. I see that you have also undertaken to place your grief aside and make the best of the terrible tragedy that took your family. You may not be aware of this, but my eldest son, Jeff, died in my arms when he was 21 years old. He was a handsome young man, a good Christian boy, who told me to "tell everyone I was with God when I died." I knew enough about your daughter to be able to tell you that when she faced her death I know she was with God, also, Kathie, and she really did imprint on my children, even my stepchildren."

An excerpt from a letter from J.J. Sandlin, trial attorney, Karen's friend and our former neighbor here in West Valley.

Karen enjoys warm moments with friends on her 18th birthday.

Karen Lee...

From the very lampstand of God,
Like a bright, shining light was she,
Her baby name, "Karilee" meant,
"Refreshing Spirit."
Her name meant "pure."
She was both of these.
She is now walking in the glories of heaven,
But it is we
Here on earth who will miss her most.
She walked in inspiration and light
Sharing of God's truth, love, and might
With all who came her way,
Putting words into motion,
Changing lives.
May the seeds she planted in hearts
Here on earth's lowly shores,
Blossom and flower into souls
Who will one day know the Lord
Both today and forever!

The head and shoulders of a woman in the clouds strongly resembled this outdoor modeling pose of Karen in the winter of 1999, but was a profile. Here, Karen is wearing the long, dark, auburn hairstyle she loved and which typified her the most.

KAREN: IN THE CLOUDS?

Well, all I can say about this story is I'm glad I had someone with me. And that someone saw it first, pointed her out to me, and that someone was a friend who went to West Valley High School with Karen and knew her face well!

In March of 2002, I was driving back with a 23-year-old assistant in Young Lion's Youth Ministry, Isaiah. We were returning to Yakima after some daytime business in Moses Lake. It was about 7:30 P.M. or so, and the sky above us was formulating into an amazing purple sunset with a touch of red on the far left of the sky. I had no sooner made the comment to Isaiah, "This sky really looks like the purple sky behind Karen in so many of my favorite photos of her taken at Laguna Beach right before the fire."

"Kathie, look over there. Look up! Do you see the woman in the sky?"

"What are you talking about?" I said in a deadpan voice.

"Look." Isaiah pointed. "Up there. There's a woman in the sky—in the clouds."

"I don't see it," I said, shaking my head, paying more attention to the road than the sky.

"Look at the red triangle, then go right," he said, pointing up to the sky again through the front car windshield. "Can you just pull over?"

Then I saw it.

Formulated against the backdrop of a purple sky, in wispy, almost hand-painted detail, was the form of the head and shoulders of a woman, a profile. The woman had long hair, which appeared to be blowing in the breeze. She was propelling herself along with her lips as she was blowing a stream of air. She was queenly looking and relaxed, with closed eyelids with lashes. This was outlined in tiny detail in white against purple, as if with a tiny paint brush. The red triangle appeared to be like a tunnel in which she had dropped down into view. A very whimsical and playful form, to say the least.

"I have never seen anything like it!" he marveled, absolutely astonished.

"Isaiah, that's not just a woman. Do you see that long nose, those lips, that jaw line? It looks like Karen!" I said, trying to keep my cool. "Karen, are you playin' around out there?" I laughed.

"I wouldn't be surprised," Isaiah sighed, still a bit dumbstruck. The very playful form might as well have been saying, "Do you see me now? Do you see me now?" Also, I could almost hear Karen's playful voice from the past. "Well, if anyone ever wants to know, my favorite colors are lavender and purple!"

I suppose it might have been just like God to let her tumble out of heaven and delight us for a few moments—about ten minutes I suppose until the form faded with the sunset itself. I looked over my shoulder into the back seat at the camera. I had already known it was there. "That would never have captured the depth and dimension of the cloud formation, probably greater than 50 miles in length," I stated flatly. "I'll just have to paint it some day," I told Isaiah. "I'll just have to paint it." Someday I will.

Karen Street — Her Amazing Room

This is "Karen Street," as her room came to be known as. Her walls bear many wise sayings, Bible verses, and inspirational thoughts. This art table is where she often sat to meditate and read the Bible.

Karen's poster-sized memory photo from the national memorial service for the four young firefighters held at the Sundome in Yakima on 7-24-01 with the flag flown over the Nation's Capitol at half mast the week of July 11, 2001.

Karen Street

Karen's room is an amazing place. Light blue walls are covered with inspirational posters, Scriptures, and wise sayings. Above the entry from the hallway, there is a green street sign, "Karen Street." She loved her white down comforter, her beautiful floral sheets and special blankets and pillows. On her bed was her special bear, "Pooky," that had been drug around since early childhood. Hugged, cherished, and tucked into bed with her for many a bedtime story and evening prayer, he is definitely related to the Velveteen Rabbit, if you know what I mean. Next to him is her favorite Lamb Chop puppet and a Hollie Hobbie doll given to her at birth by a friend. "The Big Three" have sat at the head of her pillow once her bed is made for many years. It is a constant reminder of how much a kid my beautiful young woman Karen really was. That was one of the things everybody really loved about her.

Her worktable and desk was a charming old art table. There she read the Bible, did homework, and talked to friends on the phone—sometimes for hours. Her notebooks from months and years of Bible studies and her favorite old hymnals are still there. The cute puppy calendar on her wall is frozen at July 2001. Her anticipated appointments are still written on it in her handwriting. Her car keys are on the table, and her favorite shoes are out, as if she might suddenly appear at any moment.

Above the computer where she did her homework and wrote her favorite poems and essays, is a large contemporary-looking picture of Jesus. Next to it is written in her handwriting, "Jesus, help me to love you with my life."

This same note is also written on the opposite wall. By the picture of Jesus are intricately drawn blue and white hearts and the painting, "Coming Out...Eternity," that I created when I was 18 years old. The girls have always liked it, and now it has prophetic meaning to us as the girl in the painting looks just like Karen, walking through the woods, transcending from one plane to another plane—heaven. Next to Karen's bed is what we now call, "The Window of Destiny." Karen loved the view from her window and used to remark that she had her "own personal forest" to look at every day. A photo of her in her Wildland firefighter outfit is nearby. The resemblance to the foliage of the Chewuch River canyon foliage and pines, looks just like the view from Karen's window as if that is where she would ultimately go, then to eternity from there. Lining the windowsill are the photos and notes from friends, prom pictures, velvet chocolate gift bag, and numerous dried single roses, each representing an evening or an experience. Under her bed are binders with photos from the high school photography class she loved and another binder filled with precious letters from friends and teachers. On the floor by her bed is what became her blue prayer rug—tearstained to be sure. I still can hear her sobs coming from that spot as she prayed over the rough spots in life, relationships, and all the people she loved and cared about.

On her nightstand by her lamp is her favorite devotional book, *Come Away My Beloved*, the classic by Frances J. Roberts. It was the last thing she read before leaving to report to the fire at midnight on July 10, 2001. Her high school graduation certificate in its red leather case and her baccalaureate program are still sitting out. Phone numbers from friends, photos, and various favorite Scriptures still clutter her old cork bulletin board. Next to it is a favorite magazine cutout of hers, posted on the wall—a bride wearing Karen's favorite white fantasy dress. How she longed to meet her ultimate dream guy and get married and have family, yet she perceived keenly that she never would.

There are two sketches of Karen on her wall. One was done in black and white by a street artist on the sea walk in Victoria, B.C. while we were on family vacation, and another in color by an artist in Seaside, Oregon. Both are beautiful, however they look like two completely different people. Like I say, my sympathy goes to any artist who tried to capture Karen's looks. It's next to impossible, the little chameleon.

Her bookshelf is an amazing collection of books, encyclopedias, photos, and musical instruments in cases. Also, high above, hang some her sports medals, soccer champion photos, and junior Olympic track medals and her most recent, the first place medal in the Women's Lift-a-Thon from West Valley High School. Next to her photos of the senior brunch and a few other senior activities, was a ribbon that said, "Spirit" award. That was a precious one.

And last but not least, something only a few people knew about who ever spent the night in Karen's room—Karen's own little galaxy and star constellation. When the lights go out, the neon white bright stars come on up above on the ceiling. There's the Big Dipper and the Little Dipper and a few other swirling star formations. Then there is a smiley face and a little heart formed in little stars. That was Karen for you. She took "scientific" only so far. A few of the large stars dropped into Sobe's, her red beta fish's, fish bowl. They are still there as well. He has grown accustomed to them. They are parked right next to his little castle, and there they will stay.

Well, I hope you have enjoyed the tour of "Karen Street." When I got the news of her sudden passing, I went straight there at about 4 A.M.

and stood in front of all her Scriptures and wise sayings and beautiful things. The same Holy Spirit that lived so actively in her was there, and it is still good to remember Karen. Her smile and laugh still warm my heart, even now.

Her Walls Speak

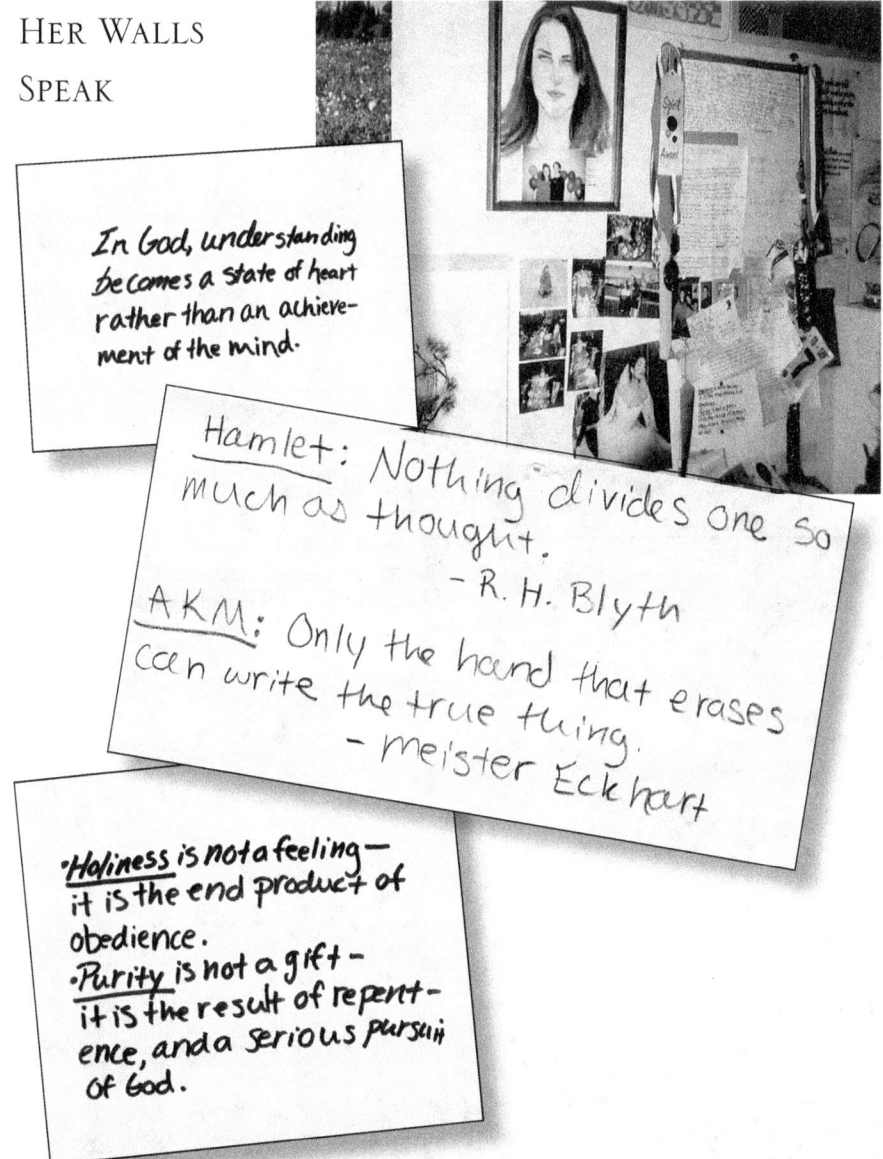

In God, understanding becomes a state of heart rather than an achievement of the mind.

Hamlet: Nothing divides one so much as thought.
— R. H. Blyth

AKM: Only the hand that erases can write the true thing.
— Meister Eckhart

• Holiness is not a feeling — it is the end product of obedience.
• Purity is not a gift — it is the result of repentence, and a serious pursuit of God.

Karen became fascinated with the fact that her name meant "Pure." By her 18th year, she began to do everything she could to live up to her name's meaning.

"The Hot Spot," the art table where Karen sat and read her Bible, wrote journals filled with notes, marked her favorite hymnal, and tossed her car keys.

"The Sobe Corner" where Karen enjoyed her red beta fish whom she trained to be a very animated personality. He responded to her melodic voice, jumped around like a playful little dog when it was time to be fed, and became a somewhat official member of the family. On July 11, 2001, he stood silent and unmoving in his little world, seeming to know his mistress was gone. He was moved upstairs to the kitchen where he could be around people. The happy little fish seemed to die of broken heart a short time after Karen's death. Karen's dog Cici, a red chow, and her tiger cat, Tigger, also passed away shortly after her death. Next to some of her wall writings were some of Karen's athletic medals, and below is a picture of Karen and her first love, Dan, at age 14. This is

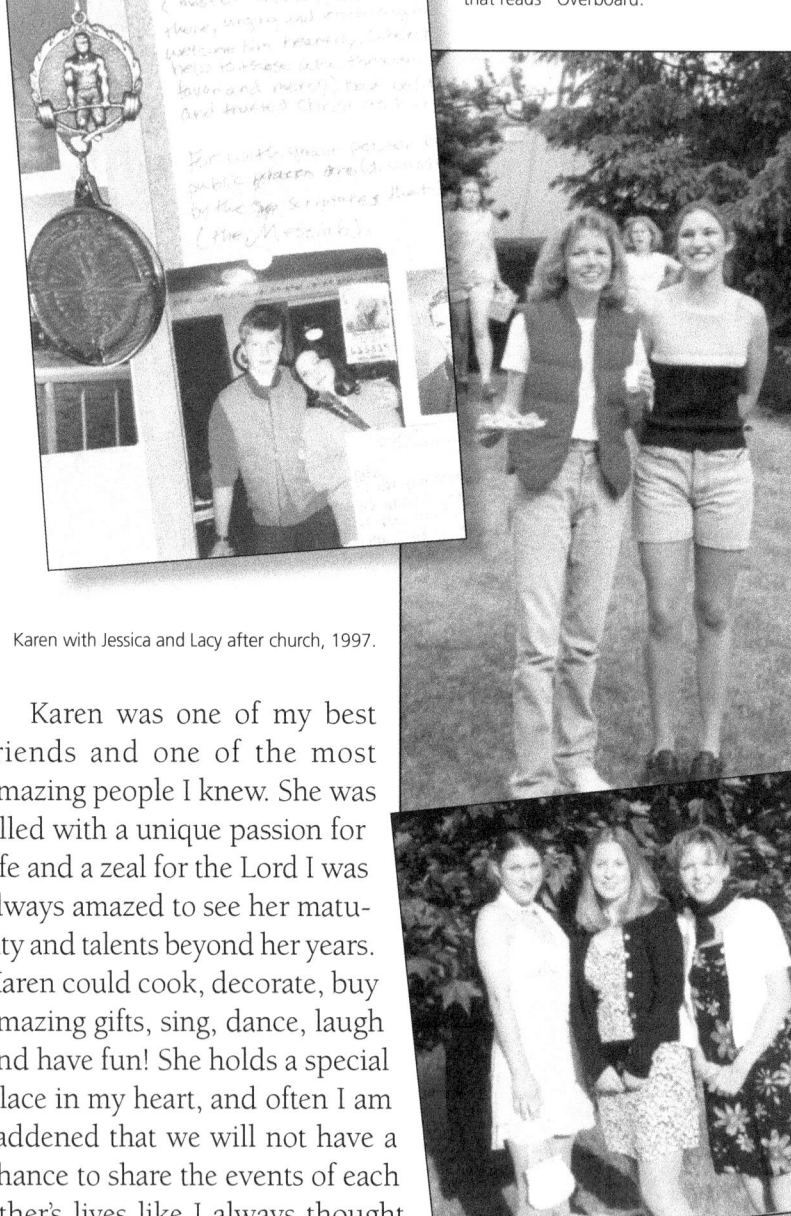

where the single rose idea came from: first love, first date. The dried rose still hangs upside down in her room in the clear wrapping next to the poster that reads "Overboard."

Karen with Jessica and Lacy after church, 1997.

Karen was one of my best friends and one of the most amazing people I knew. She was filled with a unique passion for life and a zeal for the Lord I was always amazed to see her maturity and talents beyond her years. Karen could cook, decorate, buy amazing gifts, sing, dance, laugh and have fun! She holds a special place in my heart, and often I am saddened that we will not have a chance to share the events of each other's lives like I always thought we would. She was instrumental

in my personal walk with the Lord, and I am continually grateful for that. She is unforgettable!

—Lacy Chambers Usry

Lacy and Jessica in a gold rose frame—two friends who were like sisters to Karen. Karen spent countless hours "sowing" into their lives.

A Favorite Poster of Karen's, "Faith Is."

Faith is
Risking for what is
For what is yet to be...
It is taking small steps,
　knowing
They lead to bigger
　steps.
Faith is holding on
　when
You want to let go...it is
　letting go
when you want to hold on.
Faith is saying "yes"
When everything else says "no."
It is believing all things are possible in
Most of the impossibilities.
Faith is looking beyond what is,
And trusting for what will be...
It is the presence of light in darkness,
The presence of God in all—

Ellen Cuomo

Karen's window by the "forest" was lined with pictures of friends and many memories.

Her walls speak of many experiences and much inner reflection.

KAREN STREET — HER AMAZING ROOM

Memories and wise sayings. Karen with her "twin brother" guy-friend, Brent Larsen, at a formal high school event, lower right.

The Big Three: Karen's Lamb Chop puppet, her Hollie Hobbie doll, and her childhood teddy—"Pooky-Bear."

"Crimson was the dress I wore…
Crimson was my lipstick…
Crimson was the break in my heart…"
—*Drops Of Kisses poem collection by KLF*

Karen's favorite devotional book was *Come Away My Beloved*, the classic by Francis J. Roberts. It was found open on her nightstand by her bed, and was the last thing she read the night before reporting to the fire.

WARMLY REMEMBERED

YOU'RE INVITED TO VISIT THE FALLEN FIREFIGHTERS OF AMERICA WEBSITE: WWW.LASTALARM.NET

This site is a permanent archive of comments and tributes to remember our fallen firefighters. You can see tributes to Karen, Tom, Jessica. and Devin by going to the home page, then scroll down and click on 7/2001 NORTH WA CASCADES(4)

Then click on the name you wish to view.

Karen has been most recently listed under "Warmly Remembered" Click on her name, Karen L. FitzPatrick, to open the comments.

June 7, 2001. Karen Lee, far right, with some of her high school gal pals the after the baccalaureate services held at Holy Family Church in Yakima.

Karen, at right, with a couple of school chums at a graduation event in June 2001.

LASTALARM.NET: KAREN L. FITZPATRICK RECENT POSTINGS:

Just wanted to say that it has been years and we still think about you and what you did for all of us. You made us laugh and you made us cry, but one day we will all meet again. **Anonymous, posted April 9, 2006**

It has been years since the death of this dear friend, and I think of her often. She was a person you could always count on no matter what your problem was or where you were. She continually encouraged me in my walk with Christ and left an example of what a passionate believer would be. Her smile and her strength (physically, mentally, and spiritually) will follow me forever, and I thank God I was able to share in a piece of her life." **Barbara Graham, posted August 20, 2004**

Sica, even after three years, it's hard not to cry when I think about you. On the other hand, it's hard not to laugh, as well. As you know, I still struggle at everything I do, but I've finally realized that it's not going to change. We girls floated the river this past summer and, boy, was that a mess! We all agreed it wasn't nearly as fun without you, but that's how most of our outings turn out. I know you're watching over us and having a heck of a time doing it, but it's just not the same. I wish you were here. I wish you could hold Spanks' little ones, visit me in North Carolina, float the river, go to the bar—legally, and be part of all of our lives. I wish you could've gone to Hawaii with us. Greg and I saw a shark, but you know how he's getting old and his eyesight is so bad, he thought it was a whale. We all went snorkeling and Ashley and I got attacked by fish. Course I guess you see it all from above. I want you to know that I think about you every day of my life, and I know that it's true of many others as well. I hope you're safe and having fun, and most of all, I hope you're happy. I can't wait to see you again someday, but until then, watch over all of us as we branch out into the world, get careers, get married, and have children. Well, at least do not send any of the above until I'm 30. Thanks! You touched so many lives while you were here, and you continue to do so from up there. Watch over all our firefighters, especially as the summer fire season picks up. From the bottom of my heart, Sica, I love you and miss you. Please keep me safe and out of trouble, if at all possible, and I'll see you again someday. Love you, your girl Lisa. P.S. Thank you for sending me Jessica. She makes me laugh every day as you did, and I'm grateful to have her as a friend. I see a piece of you in her and that alone brightens my life every day. **Lisa, posted July 10, 2004**

I wanted to say thank you for all you've done for us. I went to the Thirtymile memorial this summer while fighting a new fire, the Farewell Fire. It was the most emotional time I had while doing this job. We used your fire as a break for our fire, keeping a lot of other firefighters safe. I just want to thank you and let you know that you're still remembered and loved in the Wildland Fire community. **Matt, Washington State, DNR**

Yeah, I know it's been too long. I found some peace over time, but that doesn't make it any easier to deal with your absence. I think of you all the time and still miss you like crazy. You are one in a million and will be forever loved. **Mizz Thang aka Chrisa, posted August 27, 2003**

Your sister and your mother and I went to see you today. I love you, my warrior princess. See you soon. P.S. Sarah says hi. **Robert Trevino, posted November 26, 2002**

Karen, I am so proud to read these tributes, many from friends and teachers who knew you. You truly let the light of God shine through you to touch others, and I feel so honored. I miss you so much, but I know you are tucked away in the "treasure box" of heaven, where you'll be safe for eternity. There will no more temptation to be drawn away from the Lord or be knocked off the path or to forsake Him because of the worries and pressures of life. You are there— across the finish line! I must say that you are a bit more of a handful to manage now that you're not here to help me in person. You continue to point more people to the reality of what it means to have a deep walk with God through Jesus Christ than you had in your short lifetime here on earth. Your memory and your vibrant message keep me quite busy. Imagine that! I still like to look at all your Bible verses and inspirational sayings on the wall of your room on "Karen Street." You still lift me up, in that way. Keep shining, my bright morning star—forever! **Kathie FitzPatrick, Mother of Karen Lee, posted November 5, 2002**

It's been almost nine months since we lost you, but it feels like yesterday. I don't know why, but you appear in my dreams night after night, and it makes me miss you even more. I guess it must be a reminder that you are watching over me. I just wanted to say that I miss you so much, and I can't wait until the day we meet again. **(Anonymous) posted March 28, 2002**

Karen, as time passes by, many will forget you. Many will forget the price you paid for us, the fear you experienced minutes before your death, and the joy you possess right now from being with your Savior. But I won't. Your face burns in my mind at least once each day, and I am reminded of the fine Christ-like example you left behind. You were my childhood—freshman semi-formal, Christmas parties with the three of us, band trips, toilet papering. I'm grateful for you and your intense heart. It has made me a stronger person. And had you not died, I may not have learned all that I have since. In the most unshallow way, I thank you for the impact your life and death has made on my life. I have no doubt that this was a work of God's perfect timing, and for that, all of us left behind should be at peace. **(Anonymous) posted October 27, 2001**

Dear Karen: As I shared in the tributes paid to you by your family and loved ones, I felt a deep and hollow sadness for all of us, especially those of us who never had the chance to share in the light of your life. As I try and make sense of the tragic loss of such new and promising lives, I am comforted by the words of your family expressing your devout faith in God. It became clearer to me that He had taken you home because He needed you with Him now. So while your passing is immediately painful, I am certain that the Lord will fill our hearts with the love and faith that you left behind for us. You are an inspiration to me and so many others. I will remember you always. **Kathleen Opliger, Captain, USFS-CA/Honor Guard, posted July 16, 2001**

As I sit and watch this memorial, I remember what makes firefighters so wonderful. The dedications that are signed "friend," "co-worker." Many of these people never knew Karen, but feel a closeness to her. And one by one, the people rise at the memorial, all being united as one, one member of the firefighting family. A family that succeeds together, that fails together, and today grieves together. From my family to yours, our deepest sympathies and condolences go out to the loss of a loved one, the loss of a hero. **Son of a firefighter, posted July 24, 2001**

Dear Karen: Your presence here on earth will be greatly missed by so many. Your smile was contagious and warm and friendly. I'm sorry you had to leave us so soon, but you are truly in the best of all paces. Blessings to you and your family during this season. May all your friends know the Holy Spirit is there to bring comfort to them during this time of loss. I pray that God will use your parting to make His presence known to all who do not know Him. I can't help but think of how in the book of Acts, while Stephen was being stoned, he saw heaven opened up and then the Bible says he fell asleep. Before he could feel the pain of being stoned to death, he fell asleep. Maybe this how God took you as well! I believe it is! Now I know the Lord saves His anointed. **God is a merciful Father. Gloria Frueh, posted July 21, 2001**

Karen Hey, we never really got to know each other, but I remember the first day of school I was really like stressed out and you helped me find my way around. We never really talked after that, just an occasional "hello" in the hallways. My sister is Pamela Walsh, and when she found out you had passed away she was on a cruise to the Bahamas. She was so sad about it and said it was hard to have fun. You guys were pretty good friends, and I remember you guys always laughing at the lunch table. I used to watch to make sure my sister wasn't talking about me. To your family—You raised a wonderful young woman, and it is such a tragedy that her life had to end. I pray that you guys get through this. **Jessica Walsh, posted July 20, 2001**

May God richly bless family and friends with the assurance that Karen is in his care. How thankful you must be for the beautiful memories that you have. These memories will remain always in your hearts. I'm thankful for the hope you have in heaven and the confidence that you have that you will see Karen again. I'm sure that her prayers were heard and answered on behalf of all the firefighters who lost their lives. At that time, she was in the place where God needed her most! May God comfort you. **Anonymous, posted July 21, 2001**

Karen and Lacy preparing for a senior event at the high school, May 2001, At left, Karen was awarded the Spirit award by her peers of the 2001 senior class.

On behalf of our family we extend to you our sincere regret on your tragic loss. We all know the risk we take in our desire to serve the public and communities in which we work or volunteer, never thinking of the consequences and always willing to give more. You can take comfort in knowing that Karen did what she enjoyed and that she went to be with our God. We thank you for Karen and all she brought to this world. **With deepest sympathy, Don Taylor, Benton County Fire Protection District 1 FF/EMT, posted July 18, 2001**

Warmly Remembered

Karen: To you, I say thank you. Thank you for touching my life the ways that you did. Thank you for never failing to make me smile when I was around you. Thank you for helping me with my math in the seventh grade. Thank you for always having an open mind for people. Thank you for sharing your incredible personality with everyone around you. Thank your for attending J.I.V.E. every Thursday. Thank you for every life that you have touched. Thank you for helping to show me the Lord. Thank you for being an incredible friend. And thank you for giving me someone else to look forward to seeing in heaven. To the FitzPatrick family, I extend my deepest condolences. Your daughter was an incredible young woman who touched my life very strongly—along with the many others besides me. Our loss is engulfed by what she has now achieved. Eternal life with our Lord and Savior, Jesus Christ. To both Karen and her family, we will all be together soon, but until then, we love you, and God bless. **Jonas Samuel Barnes, WVHS Grad 2001**

I knew you long ago, and even then your faith in God was strong. I know you are in a better place, looking down right now. You are an inspiration to us all. To your family, you are in my heart and prayers. **Jennifer Frueh, WV Grad '99, posted July 18, 2001**

God bless you and your family, Karen. We are all deeply sorry to have lost such a beautiful girl and hero. You will never be forgotten, even by those who never had the honor of meeting such an outstanding person. **Eric Hill, Northwest Microwave Inc., posted July 18, 2001**

The Yakima Firefighter's Association would like to extend its deepest sympathy and prayers to the family, friends, and fellow brothers and sisters of the firefighting community. Karen will be missed and remembered by all. "Honor thy brothers and sisters as they watch over us, protect us, and keep us in God's hands forever." **Association, posted July 18, 2001, Jeff Pfaff, I.A.F.F. 469 Yakima Firefighters**

Today we lay to rest a beautiful, inspirational young woman. As I sit here, I listen to a song that has helped me deal with the sorrowful tragedy. "It was a test we could all hope to pass, but none of us would want to take. Faced with the choice to deny God to live—for her there was one choice to make. This was her time. This was her dance. She lived every moment, left nothing to chance. She swam the sea; drank of the deep; embraced the mystery of all she could be." Michael W. Smith. This is your time. My heart goes out to her family and everyone else that Karen's life touched. For the last three years since my family has known Karen, she has become part of our family and will always be in our hearts. She will be remembered as a hero. We will truly miss her. **Catherine (Whiteside) Messer, posted July 17, 2001**

Karen, you are incredibly brave. I will never forget how you always laughed at everything I said. I'm glad that I had a chance to make you smile. I know you're smiling down upon us now. You see now all the people who truly cared for you. But we are not going to cry now, simply look up to the sky and smile with you. You're fine, and we're gonna be just fine. You truly were a remarkable person, strong, brave, and talented. We will miss you, and now carry you within our hearts. Your life has come to an end so quickly, but you've managed to do something most people spend their whole lives trying to do. You've made us savor every day and make us believe we can make a difference just as you have! For those who knew you and those who didn't, we think of you and your family. God bless you, Karen, and the wonderful things that you've done while living here with us. We'll carry your memories with us forever. You've made a difference. **Thanks. Nicole C. Ninemire, posted July 17, 2001**

To all my friends and the family of Karen Fitzpatrick: I knew Karen since we started school together. She had the best personality and never cared what people thought. I knew she was into her faith, and you could always see it in her face and the way she carried herself. I knew Karen, but didn't know her as well as I wish I did. When she sang, it was so amazing. The song, "Circle of Friends," made me cry so hard. I will always remember CWP with her. She was so smart. I will always remember her. It's such a tragic thing that happened. I hope all the girls who know and hung out with her are doing okay. I am praying for you guys and am always here for you to talk to. I am in the phonebook. And to the family, I am sorry for your loss and will always be praying for you. Karen really loved her family and was devoted to God, and always listened to her friends. Karen, I wish we got to know each other more than we did. But I will always remember your smile, your strong personality, the way you stood for your faith, and the way you went out and fought that fire. You are a very brave young soul. I am so proud to have known you. You're in my heart forever. **Danielle Pray, posted July 17, 2001**

Firefighter FitzPatrick: You have given your life in the service to a career that was just beginning. All that I know is what I have read about you from those who had the great honor of knowing you. You have placed the ultimate sacrifice upon the altar of service to your fellow man and that of your community. We continue to lose firefighters every year, an expected but never truly accepted reality of the life of a firefighter. You will be remembered by all of us who answer the call to duty many times a day, thousands of times a year. There are only a handful of us who truly understand the unrelenting desire to serve your community. The want to place yourself in harm's way, while others look on without a hint of understanding why we do what we do, and the satisfaction we attain from such a one-of-a-kind career is rarely understood. You were in my thoughts just yesterday while combating another Wildland fire here in California. You were and are a beautiful woman, and an even more wonderful human being. God bless you, Karen. **Eric Brue, Los Angeles Fire Department, posted July 15, 2001**

I had the honor and privilege of knowing Karen FitzPatrick. She had a wonderful spirit and will always be remembered in the halls of WVHS. She touched many lives, and will continue touching them. I know she is in a better place now. Karen will be greatly missed by many people. **Kirstin Irwin, WVHS, posted July 13, 2001**

I am deeply honored and lucky to have met Karen FitzPatrick. This tragedy has left me with great pain and sorrow. My deepest sympathy goes out to her friends and family. Karen was the most remarkable person I have ever had the pleasure of getting to know. Karen, you are greatly missed. Karen, I will keep you in my thoughts and prayers always. **Ryan, posted July 13, 2001**

Karen was one of the strongest people I knew, both emotionally and physically. I always teased her for her terrible eating habits, yet she was able to stay so thin. She loved to get dressed up, but she was not afraid to get dirt under her fingernails. She always had great hair and fashion tips, yet when my problems really got big, she was always there to give insight and support. Sometimes I'd drive up to Valerie's Espresso on a Saturday and we would talk hours on end about nothing at all. We learned how to ski together, though she was better than I, and we shared poetry—poetry about personal events, special people, and our times together. Her eyes were like a creek with a blue-green gleam from a ray of sunlight. I will never forget the nights I spent at her house, the gourmet meals she made, her loud silly laugh, and the decisions she made regarding her faith. She did book reports on the Bible, wrote religious poems, missed my senior piano recital to go to church, and stood by her beliefs when no one else would. She will be most remembered for that. She died doing what she wanted to spend the rest of her life doing—firefighting, and her career ended before I even had a chance for mine to begin. She will not be forgotten. **Jessica Dean, 18, posted July 13, 2001**

Senior Breakfast, June 2001. Karen, on the left, standing with two close friends, Lacy Chambers and Jessica Dean, also two of the originators of the Christmas Tea, usually given on December 23 each year at our house. Karen invested heavily into the lives of these two girlfriends since her early youth with love, friendship, and personal Bible studies. Lacy is now married to a youth pastor, and Jessica is married to a young man who is currently in seminary planning to become a minister. The seeds she sowed live on!

KAT: I'll remember the classes we had, English and band. Remember the "band boys" and all our trips? Skiing at White Pass and Drops of Kisses, Crimson Lips, and Aaron an Inspiration? Your "heart attack" poems that made your neck turn red, but you never wavered. A courage beyond your years. To stand in front of your critical peers and preach the truth takes guts. You always looked so pretty, hair curled and perfect makeup. Even when you did finger push-ups in class, showing us your buff muscles. Your ministry will live on in the hearts of your friends. And we will take comfort in knowing that this fire was only a moment in time, not eternal, and you are shining in the glory of God's love—the Kingdom of Heaven. I look forward to the day we can meet again and rejoice in the love of our Lord.—Jenn "I Am Free" (anonymous) "Don't grieve for me, for now I am free. I am following the path God laid for me. I took His hand when I heard Him call, I turned my back, and left it all. I could not stay another day, to laugh, to love to work or play. Tasks undone must stay that way. I found peace at the close of the day. If my parting has left a void, then fill it with remembered joy. A friendship shared, a laugh, a kiss. Ah, these things I too will miss. Be not burdened with time of sorrow. I wish for you the sunshine of tomorrow. My life's been full, I savored much. Good friends, good times, a loved one touched. Perhaps my time seemed all too brief, don't lengthen it now with undue grief. Lift up your hearts and share with me, God wanted me now, he set me free." **Jennifer Powers, posted July 13, 2001**

Karen with more friends after the baccalaureate service June 7, 2001. These same friends graduated with her the next evening, June 8, walking across the stage of the Yakima Sundome, happily accepting their high school diplomas from West Valley High School.

Senior pool party, June 2001. Karen with some of her gang of friends from school enjoy some time together at a friend's house for a senior swim party. Karen is on the right with the deep tan and swim suit top.

Karen, when I heard the news, my heart had fallen on the ground. You were two years younger than I, but still a great inspiration. I remember the band trip we took to California. You and some of your friends went and made a record. You did not want anyone to hear it, but then on the way back to the hotel, you let us listen to the tape. What a wonderful voice you had. I do not remember the song it was that you sang, but when it was over, the whole bus was blown away with all that talent you had. We were all screaming and going nuts over you. You always had a smile on your face and laughter that stood out from everyone's. You will be greatly missed. May God take you with open arms and help those you knew get through this time in their lives. You will never be forgotten. **Tiffany Lynde, WVHS, "99"**

Karen, you're strong and brave. Honey, watch over us every day! We're gonna miss U!" **Nicole (Nic) posted July 12, 2001**

I had the privilege of having Karen as a Spanish student during her junior year at West Valley. The enthusiasm she brought to my class is the same enthusiasm she brought to everything she undertook. I shall always remember her wonderful smile. As she entered her senior year she shared with me some of her dreams and hopes. In her senior picture she gave to me in June she wrote of her desire to become an EMT and firefighter and to continue her study of Spanish with the hope of some day becoming bilingual to better serve the public. While she was training at the high school in June after school had let out, I ran into her in the halls during a break in one of her training sessions. We chatted a little and then parted with a hug. She was so very happy to be in the Naches Forestry Wildland Firefighter Program—the first steps toward realizing her career dream. Her goal was to serve mankind and God in the best way she knew possible. Karen has certainly done that, and will forever serve as an inspiration to us all. Thank you, Karen, for gracing my life and that of the students and staff at West Valley. You have touched the lives of many, and will continue to do so. You will be sorely missed. In honor and celebration of someone who truly lived life, one final "abrazo" (hug). **Senora Rosemary E. Leiva-Murphy, teacher West Valley HS, posted July 12, 2001**

So young and so brave. May God be with you always." **Justin Bosley FF/EMT (Benton County Fire Dist. #1), posted July 12, 2001**

To all the people who are feeling the loss of this beautiful young woman, my family's thoughts and prayers are with you at this most difficult time. Please take comfort in knowing that she is in the arms of our Savior, and she will be forever, your guardian angel." **(Anonymous) posted July 12, 2001**

Karen was a classmate of mine, and she was always so friendly and sweet. She was inspiring to be around and made you feel good. I am sorry for this tragedy that ended her life. I am happy to have known her and very happy that she knew God and is with Him now. **Tammy Southards, posted July 12, 2001**

To the family of Karen FitzPatrick: I went to school with your daughter. She taught me a lot. She was a very caring and loving person. She touched so many hearts, and even mine. I will always remember the classes we had and the times we talked. I wish you all well and am praying for you and Karen." **(Anonymous) posted July 12, 2001**

"Karen: You will be so greatly missed. God bless you for risking your life in the line of duty. **(Anonymous) posted July 11, 2001**

To the family of Karen FitzPatrick: I offer my deepest condolences. I had the privilege of being one of her teachers here at West Valley High School. The last few years I enjoyed seeing her involved in the music program and in the Tuesday morning student Bible/Prayer group. Though I weep for her loss, I joy in knowing her gain—being with her Lord and Savior, Jesus Christ. Karen used her musical talents at the WV Baccalaureate Service last month as she and two of her friends sang "Circle of Friends" by Point of Grace. May you find strength and comfort in the words, words that Karen lived every day. "We were made to love and be loved. But the price this world demands will cost you far too much. I spent so many years just trying to fit in. Now I've found a place in this circle of friends. In a circle of friends we have one Father. In a circle of friends, we share this prayer. That every orphaned soul will know, and all will enter into the shelter of this circle of friends. If you weep, I will weep with you. If you sing for joy, the rest of us will lift our voices too. But no matter what you feel inside, there's no need to pretend. That's the way it is, in this circle of friends. In a circle of friends, we have one Father. In a circle of friends, we share his prayer—that we'll gather together no matter how the highway bends, I will not lose this circle of friends. Among the nations, tribes and tongues, we have sisters and brothers, and when we meet in heaven, we will recognize each other with joy so deep, and love so sweet. Oh we'll celebrate these friends, and a life that never ends, in a prayer that will not be long before all will enter in to the shelter of the circle of friends. That it will not be long until all will enter in to the shelter of the circle of friends." **Joe Coscarat, WVHS teacher, posted July 12, 2001**

WARMLY REMEMBERED

Karen Lee, Kelly, and Sarah perform the song "Circle of Friends," for the West Valley High School Baccalaureate Services, June 7, 2001.

Dear Karen: I know that you completed the mission that God sent you to us to perform. However, your work and inspiration will continue and never end. As you said in your poem, "The Need Inside," it is communicated from heart to heart without limit to time and space." **Steve Wise, Teacher/Educator/Artist, San Jose, California**

Karen, far right, with her friends after the baccalaureate service. To her immediate left are close friends Jessica Dean and Lacy Chambers.

A happy moment: Karen Lee FitzPatrick, graduation night, June 8, 2001, at the Yakima Sundome, downtown Yakima.

Letters

Karen had a very precious, bulging, three-ring binder full of amazing letters written to her, and, of course, copies of a few she wrote to others. Some were from girlfriends, guy friends, and heartthrobs. Some were from teacher friends and other adults whose lives she influenced. And some, well, (blush!) they were just too personal to publish! Here are just a few.

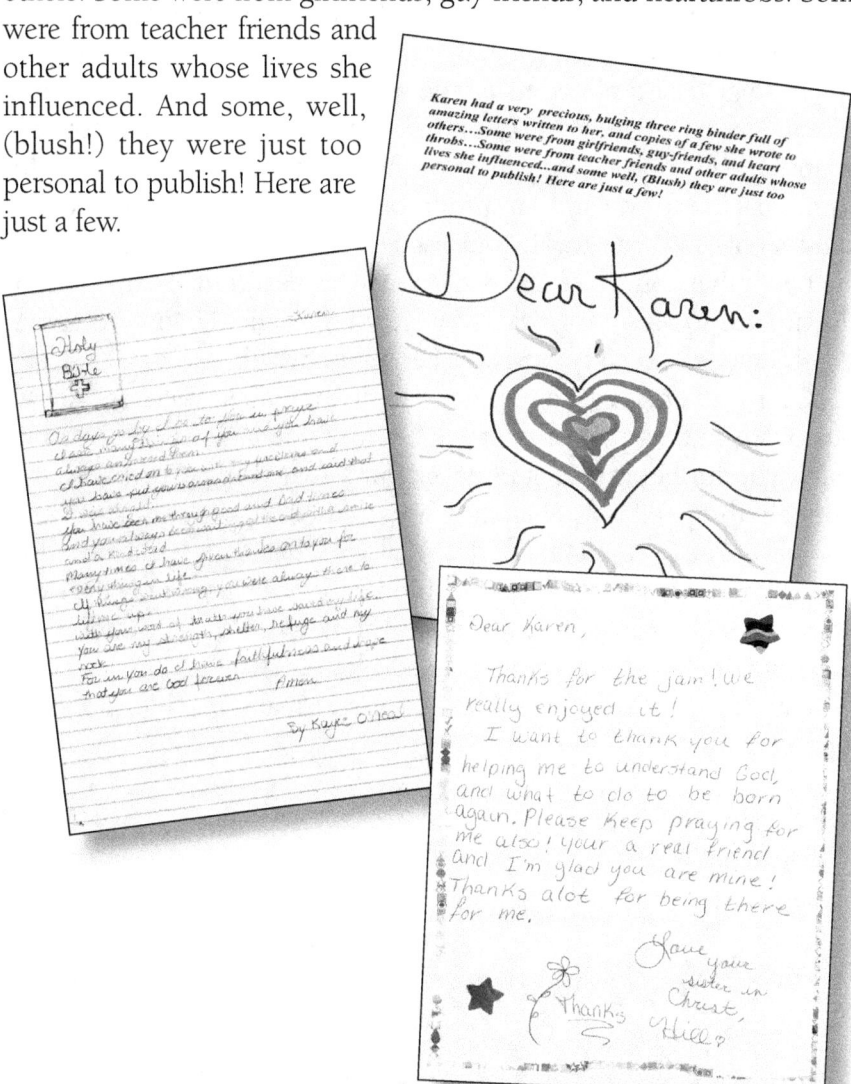

12-11-98

Dear Karen:

You are such a sweet young lady, very dear to me. I have really been blessed by you and how much you have thought of me. All the letters of true encouragement and love while going through the fires. God had used you, sweet Karen, to cause me to have more faith in God. You are truly a blessing to me. I hope I can do the same for you. Please let me know when you are struggling with things so I can help you get through them more easily.

I'm so glad God placed us on the same path with some of the same goals in life so we could help one another. I want to be a part of your life because I really do care for you. I've seen God turn you into a beautiful vessel for Him to use and I'm proud of you. He has blessed you with many talents and I'm sure He is pleased how you have been using them. The poem that you wrote and sent to me was beautiful. Thank you for allowing me to see your work. If I were your teacher I'd give you an A. Which I'm sure you'll get anyway. Let me know, ok?

Karen, if there is ever anything I can do for you please let me know! I just want to be a part of your life because you are so special to me. Thank you for being you, and never think that you can't come to me about anything. I'll try to help any way that I can.

I pray that God grants the desire of your heart for your life. Also, that He guides you into a deeper relationship with Him. I pray the same for myself so we can grow together in the Lord. He is so wonderful! I truly love the Lord! He is worthy to be blessed.

May our dear Lord truly bless you, and make His light to shine upon you always.

Sincerely in Christ,
Love you,
Dee Carter

7-25-46 11:35

Karen,

I told my dad the verse and now he is going to go to church with me and except god in his heart. I am starting a youth group and the youth group gives everyone a Bible. So I will get one soon.

My Dad got the verse but I realy did not get it. I was wondering if you could explain it to me again. Every night I get down on my knees and pray to God. I have JOY in my heart. Jesus, Others, and You. That is what I always say to myself when I am sad. What do you say when you are sad?

love Always
DeAndrea Guzman

P.S. Write Back god be with you!

From Her sister Jaina

1-13-96
Dear Karen:
This letter is to my beautiful sister. You are beautiful in your spirit and also physically. You are beautiful to God when you listen to and obey Him. We will never regret when we make ourselves beautiful to God instead of beautiful for boys. You were chosen by God to be a light in this dark world. That is why He placed you just where you are (in this family and attending West Valley and living in Yakima). God wants you to be His. Don't think you are just "another Christian." God wants your whole heart soooooo much! You are so precious to Him. Give all your problems to God, and all of your heart, and He will bless you so much!

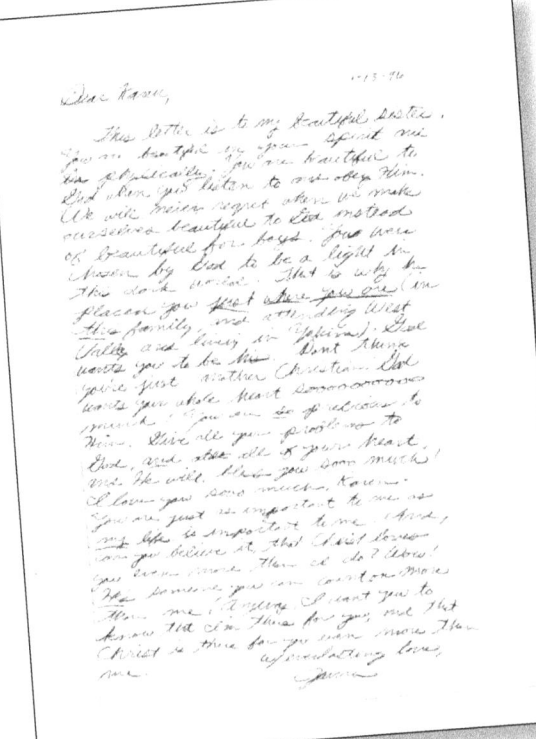

I love you so much Karen. You are just as important to me as my life is important to me. And—can you believe it—that Christ loves you even more than I do? Wow! He's someone you can count on more than me! Anyway, I want you to know that I'm there for you, and that Christ is there for you even more than me.

w/everlasting love,
Jaina

Letters

Karen, *June 6, 01*

Hey Kate, I don't know how to start this letter out without not making it long. I have not known you very well for very long but through art class I have learned so much from you. You have a very awesome personality. You are a great person to talk to about anything. You understand where I am at in life and try to help me with everything I do, or at least try and if you can't then we just say "screw it". I will always remember all the fun times we have had through 3rd period and 4th! We have had a great time. I wish you weren't leaving so we could become better friends. But hey great things always have to end one time or another. It's hard to say good-bye to such a WONDERFUL person. I feel so close to you, and look forward to seeing you every day...! Thanks for always giving me money when I have a craving for food. I hope you always remember me and don't forget my twin Brittany! I will be sending your gift in the mail. I hope you give me your address so I can write to you. I wish I would of met you sooner but hey I'm glad I got to meet you. Remember our talks, remember our smiles + funny moments we have had, and most of all remember our friendship and know that I will always be here to talk.... My # is call anytime! Don't let guys lie to you either Karen, kick them! You are such a great friend and I will miss you.

Always and GOD-BLESS

Stephanie Nicole Wilson xoxo

P.S. You better come see me graduate!

8:00 PM   January 23, 1999

Dear Dee,

I just thought I'd say hi 1:1) I've been going over some of the lesson and I love what is says in 1 John 5 about overcoming if you're bornagain and believe. I've been doing a side study of verses that give inf. on victory over the world, the flesh and Satan. I haven't gotten very far but I'm still searching for stuff. It is very important to believe in the Son's testimony as it says in 1 John 5:10. so we don't make God out to be a liar. This makes Him out as a liar because we have misrepresented and insulted Him.

It's also good that the Holy Spirit witnesses on our behalf. If we have him in us, we will be His witnesses as it says in John 15:26. Another encouraging word is in Colossians 1:23 which says that God is pleased to make known the Gospel to the Gentiles so that Christ can manifest within and among you, the hope of Glory. Our Hope is in Jesus Christ and the Gospel living in us. That comes when we possess the Son of God and have eternal life (1 John 5:11-12).

Prayer is a constant need for the Christian more and more these days in which are perilous. But we must keep of good cheer and of a sound mind lest we be swept away.

Lots of Love Always,

Karen Lee FitzPatrick

ANGEL PROMISES

Dear Dee, September 15, 1998

I'm happy to see you again! Welcome back! Praise God for His excellent promises! I hope you and Steve start reading your Bibles together again and really start spending the quality time needed in the Word.

I'm really happy of how this week has been going. On Mondays now, me and my friend Lacy, are meeting at starbucks on 56th after school to have a treat and look into the Word together. Jessica, my other friend, may be joining us soon also. It was very encouraging to meet with her last yesterday. God was showing me on Sunday that meeting for Bible study with my friends will help me to grow better. It also helps you live more accountably and encourages you to do it.

A verse that really stood out to me lately was Ephesians 5:11 - Take no part in and have no fellowship with the fruitless deeds and enterprises of darkness, but instead [let your lives be so in contrast as to] convict them. This verse is important in everyday life to remember. I picked up this verse when I was finishing Ephesians, which is loaded with great stuff!

Keep reading the Word and spend time putting God first. Have a great week! :)

Lots of Love Always Your Sister in Christ,

Dear Gabriel, June 2001

I've just recently gotten to know you a little better in speech class. Before that, I didn't really know you too well, (I still don't) But I really think you have a lot of potential you don't give yourself credit for. Just remember, God has plans for your life just like He does for me, and we will never really be happy unless we fulfill those plans He has. It's simple, really. Give me a call some time 966-7965.

Lots of Love Always,

338

More About Karen

Notes from J.I.V.E — "Jesus Is Very Important in Everything!"

Karen attended a weekly Bible study group held on her high school campus. If you were a student who was attending, you had to be cut from a strong cloth of dedication, as it was held early in the morning before school started.

I rescued these notes on "Relationships" that were in some of Karen's assorted papers. To me, these short notes stood out in neon letters because, as an individual who heads up ministry teams that go into Yakima County Youth Detention, I knew this was one of the hardest areas for teenagers to properly master. I have spoken to and led groups countless times, involving both boys and girls, in which there had been serious failings in the area of relationships. Some were in jail because of their bad associations with others. I've sat with teen girls who were incar-

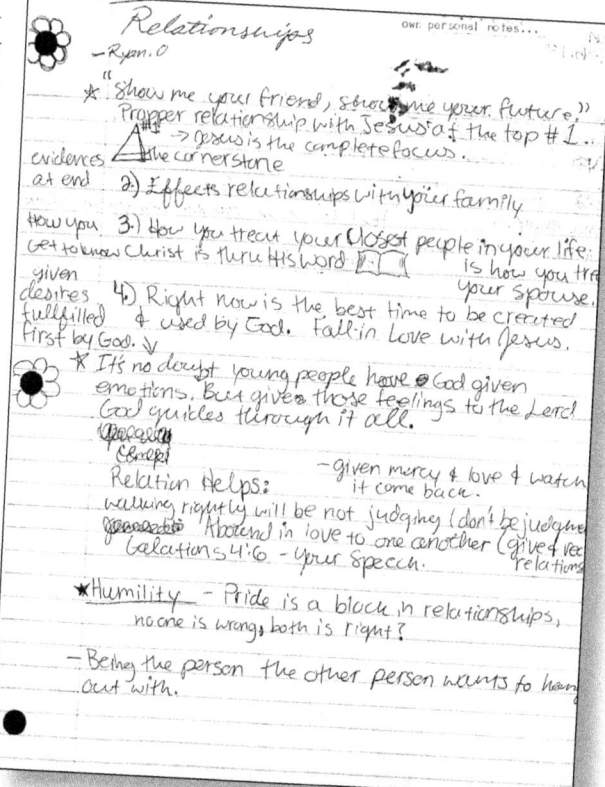

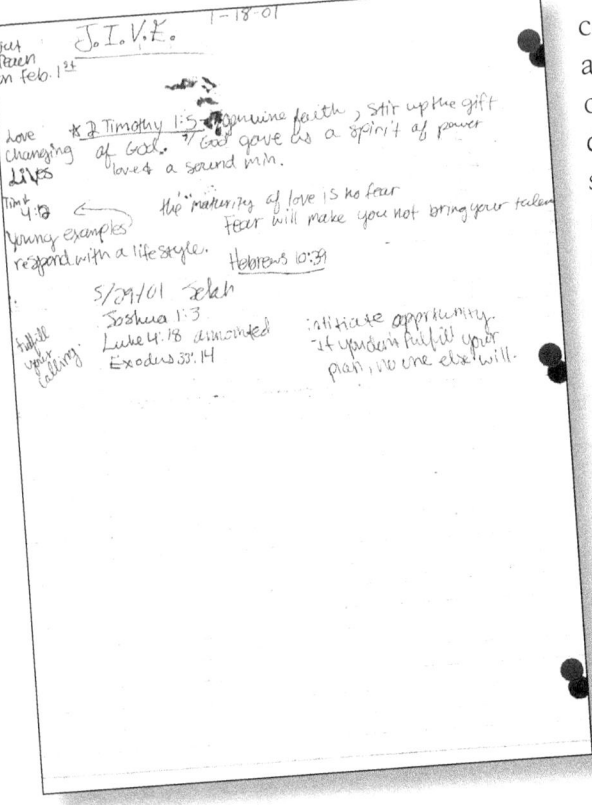

cerated and pregnant and 14 and 15 years of age because they did not consider basic standards in how they conducted their personal relationships. Their lives and emotions will never again be the same. Now there is a life of a new baby involved.

These notes have also visited these small groups many times as I pass out copies to the teens, particularly the girls. I tell them about who Karen was. She struggled with having strong moral standards in her relationships with guys just like anybody else. "We are going to take a little visit to J.I.V.E. with some notes out of Karen's own Bible," I tell them. The young man, Ryan, who led the group at the time, was our senior pastor's son, who is now a pastor himself. He lived what he preached and has a marriage with a wonderful Christian girl with whom he is currently planning a family and a future. Interesting, out of this small group of dedicated young people who met early in the morning before school for Bible study arose spiritual giants, teachers, and evangelists who still continue to this day.

More About Karen

Is The Worst Thing that Can Happen to You to Die?

Is the worst thing that can happen to you to die? Or is the worst thing that can happen to you to die and not be ready?

Some day we all have an appointment we can't break. On that day, your heart will stop beating, you will stop breathing. Your eyes will close, and your Spirit—the real you—will leave your body and spend eternity somewhere. The question is, where?

While we are still alive and walking on the planet, we can make and cultivate that choice. We prepare, kind of like making both a reservation and a relationship. We learn how to do that in God's roadmap for life, death, and the hereafter—the Bible. Now, if you don't think the Bible is relevant for today, well, I guess you didn't know Karen or someone like her—a real Christian. Like anything in this life that is genuine or phony, there is a difference.

I bring this up because many people who learn of the story of the Thirtymile Fire and read this book and are focused a little more on Karen's life, will have the same classic question: "Why didn't God save her—or all of them?" Well, actually God did save Karen many times in her lifetime. There were many close calls, the most recent of which was a loud, shattering car wreck December 8, 2000, in which her car was totaled by a teenage boy who hit her from behind while she was on the way to pick up her friend Rosie at the Glenwood Shopping Center for a sleepover at our house. The rescue workers at the scene of the crash couldn't figure out why this girl did not seem to have a scratch on her. Karen was a little sore for two days and figured she'd better go give the family chiropractor a call to be checked over, but it was nothing serious.

God does see ahead. He has eternal values and often makes decisions that have the best eternal outcome. How different that is from the way we think in our puny little earthly minds. Yes, it was painful to loose her. Yes, we miss her. Yes, the circumstances were terrible and unjust. Yet somehow, in God's mind, there is a much bigger picture. As time goes on, I see it more clearly too.

Second Corinthians 5 reminds us that this earthly body that we so dearly love is but a "temporary tent." If our lives are right with Him—the God who made heaven and earth and every cell in our bodies, when we one day die, will then award us an eternal home in heaven! The Bible says we will rule and reign with God forever. What an exciting future! Sadly, if we're not prepared, Satan, the adversary of our souls, has the battle over us won, and we will spend eternity burning in hell, the garbage heap of the universe. It was really only meant for Satan and his fallen angels—not for humankind.

Karen's mind and determination was set fast like flint to warn those in her world of those eternal choices set before them while there was yet time. She even died on her knees praying with those close around her facing the point of eternity. Karen did not fear disapproval or persecution. Since she was so well connected to the "heavenly zone" and made God's love so real to others, I really cannot recall when there was any!

More About Karen

After 9/11, there was even more tragedy than that which was obvious. Many news features on radio and television and major magazine stories about the Thirtymile Fire and the four young firefighters who were lost in the blaze were cancelled. That made our job of keeping the story and the cause for greater safety alive next to impossible. The following was one of those casualties. "The Last Prom, The Last Flame," scheduled to appear in one of the very large youth magazine publications in America, never appeared. So here it is for you now.

The Last Prom, the Last Flame.

By Kathie FitzPatrick

The story of the passing of Karen Lee FitzPatrick, 18 year old firefighter—Thirtymile Fire, July 10, 2001.

It was mid-May, 2001. The warm breeze was filled with the faint smell of spring flowers as the flower beds and hills brimmed with blooms in the Yakima Valley. It was early evening. A car drove up into the gravel driveway of the towering three story house with-large view windows on Poplarview Way.

"Karen, Matt is here!" Her mother, Kathie, called out, down the hallway. Behind the heavy antique door with frosted blue glass, Karen was still finishing the last touches of her makeup and carefully crafted "prom look."

Whether attending with a "guy friend" or romantic date, Karen hardly ever missed a high school homecoming or prom event. She had a collection of evening gowns that were the envy of her girlfriends.

The "newly transformed" Karen emerged in her long, white, shimmering, beaded gown. She had white roses intertwined in her hair, which was swept up majestically with invisible hair pins. Her makeup was perfect. Her high cheekbones shone with Mother-of-Pearl shimmer, and her crimson lips smiled brightly. Karen's happy blue eyes shone with rare radiance. This was a night that she had been anticipating with much longing and meticulous planning. Her tan was striking against the long, white, sleeveless formal. Karen had those perfect, muscular arms. One might have guessed she was athletic, but probably would not have guessed she was a weightlifter who had just broken a women's record for bench press in the Spring Lift-a-Thon held at West Valley High School in Yakima, Washington. Karen was five foot eight, and a slight size six. She was a former soccer champion whose youth team had won the State Championship in 1994, and was known for her unusual strength and speed. She had been the classic tom-boy in earlier days. But now, when she stepped into glass-slipper mode and into one of her long evening gowns, she was the proverbial princess and the fabled Cinderella, all in one.

"Karen, Matt's gonna think you look like you're wearing a wedding dress!" Kathie commented as she saw her moving down the hall to the White Room, where Karen customarily met her dates for formal events. Her beautiful gown rustled softly as she moved gracefully toward the formal receiving area for her dates.

"Oh, Mom! It's just that I've worn just about every color, especially red. It was time for a white dress. Doesn't it look great with my tan?"

"Yes, darling, it does!"

She opened the door to the room, where the crystal chandelier hung brightly. Soon the doorbell rang. "I'll let Matt in. Wait 'til he gets a look at you. The poor boy may faint!" her mom kidded her. Karen readied herself to meet Matt and pose for photos. Soon, Matt's footsteps could be heard softly treading the carpet on the stairs of the spiral staircase from the lower level. The full moon shone brightly through the skylights in the high ceiling. The stage was set.

Matt appeared at the doorway. His bright brown eyes and young boyish look were a contrast to his dark sophisticated tux. Matt looked both stunned and delighted when he saw her. Karen's face glistened softly with the evening cheekbone glitter she loved to wear. It certainly enhanced the glow she already possessed. In moments, they were out the door to an unforgettable evening.

The dinner and dance held at the Yakima Convention Center was certainly grand! Through it all, Karen was discovering that her high school "buddy" who had lived down the street for years, and sometimes worked with her on class projects, was becoming more of a heartthrob than she had anticipated. After the prom events were over, Karen had an unusual request.

More About Karen

"Matt, let's go ice skating."

"What? Are you kidding?" he laughed. Karen was known for last minute, capricious ideas. After the shock of the initial idea, Matt decided it was a delightful suggestion. They drove to the ice arena on the east side of town situated by the Sundome arena and the fairgrounds.

"You're crazy, you know that? He laughed, as they emerged from the car.

"Aw, come on, you know it will be fun!" Karen laughed, with a sparkle in her eye.

Soon they were gliding across the ice—Matt in his black tux and Karen in her long dress as it whirled majestically around her. Apparently, that same evening some professional skaters were getting in practice sessions as well.

"Wow, you two look great!" one of the women skaters commented to them as they rested on the side of the skating rink for a moment. "Let me show you some great moves," she offered, shoving off energetically back to the center of the ice. "Watch this!"

"Come on Matt, let's go!" Karen said, pulling Matt by the hand. The young professional skater showed Matt and Karen some simple but elegant moves. Soon they were gliding across the ice like a fairy tale prince and princess.

Karen's crimson lips smiled brightly, as she gazed into the eyes of her "prince." She wondered what the future held. Would it be different between them after this special evening?

The next morning, the early light of Saturday morning sunbeams filtered into Karen's room. The sign above her door read, "Karen Street." The long, white, beaded gown was on a hanger on the door, and the white ice skates were resting on the floor at the foot of her bed. One of the cats, Muff, was curled up on the comforter at the end of her bed, purring softly. Her sister Jaina, who was almost four years older, was asleep in the adjoining bedroom. Karen pulled the covers up over her head to shut out the light. It seemed like the morning sun had risen a little too early after prom night, as the sharp, unfriendly sun rays began to filter brightly into the room. Karen rolled over to try to get in a few extra winks, but she could faintly hear sounds of someone rustling around in the laundry room down the hall.

"Mom, is that you?" Karen asked softly and sleepily, her tasseled head peeking up.

"I came downstairs to pick up the laundry basket," Kathie said, poking her head curiously in the door. Karen turned over and gave her mom a mischievous little grin. "You're lyin' now," Karen responded playfully. "I always know when you're makin' things up!" Karen laughed, with the sudden hearty laugh she was lovingly known for.

"Well, it's hardly ever! You know that! How did things go last night?"

"I knew that's why you came down here!" Karen kidded her mom. "It was a Cinderella dream!" she smiled, as she stretched a bit in her white satin pajamas. "Upon arriving at the ice arena…" Karen began, sounding very proper, "We met some professional skaters. They were really nice to show Matt and me some new, really great moves. So we danced around the ice better than I ever have! It was the first time Matt and I ever tried it. We went gliding across the ice like magic. Matt looked so handsome in his black tuxedo. It was so romantic, like a movie," she sighed. Karen had those bright neon stars on the ceiling in her bedroom. It almost seemed as if some of them had just fallen into her eyes.

"Mom, I really like him a lot."

"Do you?"

"Yeah. But he's talking about joining the Navy, and moving back east. If I was to get serious with him, in a few months, I could be a Navy wife living on the other side of the country. I don't feel comfortable with that. I think it's too soon to jump into something like that. It's too big. Too different."

"You'd like to take things a little slower?"

"Yeah. But it seems like Matt is really going to do this Navy thing. I don't think I can talk him out of it. I'm not sure right now how it will all work out," she said, rolling over and sitting up. "I'm not too sure it would be what God would have for me. I just don't know right now." Karen was a strong Christian who made God a part of her everyday life and tried not to make big life decisions without "asking God about it."

"I'd better get up!" she yawned.

In talking further with her, her mom sensed Karen's struggle. She appreciated her not jumping into anything too sudden. That demonstrated at least a shred of healthy maturity. She wondered if Matt had the same interest in Karen. At least she was letting someone else get a glimpse into her world before any really big decisions were being made. Karen and her mom walked down the hallway together, talking. Her sister Jaina was still asleep.

"I just can't picture me all of a sudden moving away from this valley and all the people I love." They had breakfast and talked about it further. Soon afterwards, Jaina joined them, appearing at the top of the stairs, still in her pajamas. She was already catching the drift of the conversation.

"Don't let some guy talk you into something that will be all wrong for your life!" Jaina offered, sounding like a protective big sister.

"It's just he will be going away soon—sometime in July—into the Navy. He'll be gone for three years," Karen said sadly, hardly touching the food on her plate.

"So? You're young. You can wait," said Jaina, taking another bite of her French toast.

"Yeah, but he won't. He'll find some girl over there on the East Coast and go and get married." There were no easy answers. Matt's commitment to Karen could be the key. Or maybe she just needed to let it go. Her mom and sister sensed it must be hard for her. Kathie and her daughters continued their girl talk for another half hour.

"You're just going to have to pray about it, Karen. God will show you the whole picture. Soon it will be clear," said Kathie, pouring her the last bit of coffee. "I hate to cut this short, but I have to show my listing on Ahtanum Road in about one hour." Karen knew her mom's career in real estate often cut into the weekends but was understanding about it. It was especially true during the early youth soccer days.

"That's OK. Thanks, Mom."

Karen's family didn't see much of Karen over the next few days due to her involvements in her small church as music director and working at Valerie's Espresso after school. She came and went with little conversation. It was also time to work on last minute details of the year-end senior events such as the senior awards brunch and the graduation ceremony itself. Kathie went down to Karen's room to put some clean jeans away from the laundry room and set some mail on her desk when she noticed a job application laying out with a ballpoint pen beside it. It was for the U.S. Forest Service.

"It must be the summer job she's been talking about," her mom remarked softly, talking to herself. "I wonder what she'll be doing for them."

As her Kathie later sat in her home office looking at real estate listings on the computer, she suddenly had a thought. She knew they were not going to make it to Hawaii that year for summer vacation. Her husband, John, had waited too late to give her a workable date, so the opportunity for that season had gone by. But what about that special airline pass? She looked in the file in the lower right drawer where the airline information was kept. She was thinking about the trip Karen took last summer with her dad on business and then on to see cousins in New York and Chicago. They had gotten flight information wrong, and Karen and her Dad wound up in Atlanta! Poor Karen was also sick as a dog from air sickness to boot! Her mom had heard her say, "I was so sick, I just lay down on the carpet on the airport floor, I thought I was going to die! Dad had to pull me up and practically carry me on to the next plane!" After the fiasco, the airlines sent both of them a free ticket, but it had to be used before August of the following year. Kathie opened up the New York file from the lower desk drawer. There it was.

Karen was working her usual three to six shift at Valerie's Espresso downtown, when she saw her mom drive up to the takeout window in her sporty Subaru sedan.

"Hey, Karen," her Mom smiled, when she caught the first glimpse of her.

"Hey, Mom! What'cha up to? Are you here for the usual?" referring to the iced rum mocha she usually ordered.

"Yes, but I'm also here for something else."

"Something else?"

"Yes. Remember the trip back to New York last August when the airlines messed you two up and put you on the wrong plane?"

"How could I forget! I got so sick! Wow, was I a cute shade of green!" Karen laughed, mixing her mom's coffee drink.

"I'm sure you'll work out the air sickness thing next time," Kathie winked.

"The next time?" Karen asked, stopping her stirring for a moment.

"You're going to Laguna Beach for one week after graduation! I've got it all set up with your Aunt Suzanne!"

"Wow! Really? That's great! Thanks!" Karen was overwhelmed with the surprising news. Kathie's sister Suzanne had a fabulous home just two short blocks from the oceanfront in Laguna Beach. It was the favorite family vacation spot.

It's not Hawaii, but it's the next best thing." Kathie laughed, taking her drink and handing Karen the $2.50.

About a week later, Karen picked up the mail as she drove by the mailbox in front of the house. Moments later, Karen bounded up the stairs from the lower level. She had already excitedly ripped open a brown envelope with a letter in it from the U.S. Forest Service.

"Mom! I got the job! I'm supposed to report for training next week," she beamed, still holding the letter of acceptance in her hand.

"Great honey. I'm happy for you," Kathie could feel her daughter's excitement. She knew it was the news Karen was waiting for. "Where will you train?"

"Right here at West Valley High School. They are going to set up camp right here at our local high school. Lucky for me. I've heard some trainees are coming from far distances." Karen explained the timing, as the graduation ceremony was planned for June 8 at the local Sundome arena. "I have a week off in between, I think." The trip to Laguna Beach fit in perfectly!

That evening at dinner Karen discussed the new developments with her family. "I'd much rather have you working with me this summer," her dad said, as he poured Karen another glass of juice. "How will we ever get the house painted or the fence fixed?"

"Sorry, Dad, but it's time for me to think about the future, you know. Besides, Mom thinks it's about time for you to have a few things hired done around the house and yard," she winked.

"Yes, here, here. I vote for that one! We're getting too far behind to catch up through family project time, Kathie reminded him. "And it seems like you are traveling more than ever."

"My back and neck always get knocked out of alignment when I do that kind of work," Karen's older sister Jaina reminded him. "Then you have to pay the chiropractor, so you might as well pay for help."

"Your chiropractor doesn't cost that much!" retorted John. "But it looks like I'm outvoted!" Jaina got up and started carrying dishes to the sink. "Did you pray about this? And what does Tom think?" Jaina asked, referring to their friend who led the weekly Bible study Karen and her father attended.

"Yes, I prayed about it. I think it's a good way to earn college money. Tom thinks it's OK, if that's what I want to do," Karen answered.

"You should have seen Karen's final speech paper she gave last month. It was all about why she wanted to be a firefighter," Jaina said, rinsing off the dishes.

"Does this decision have anything to do with the fire that happened right here on the field by the house about three years ago on the 4th of July?" moaned John.

"You'll have to admit, she was a real champ! The fire would have gotten our house for sure if it hadn't been for Karen jumping the fence with those hoses," Jaina pointed out. "The fire truck was just not positioned at the right angle to get at the fire.

"Well, that might have been part of it," Karen admitted. "I want to use my strength and speed to help people. Firefighting is a noble profession!" Karen smiled with a rare glow—the glow she was known for as a lighthouse of strength and peace to her friends.

"Besides Mom, my college counselor says that there is a good chance I can get into the EMT program sometime after I'm a cadet with the Fire Science Program at the college. The Yakima City Fire Department sponsored six last year!"

"I see," Karen's mom replied. "Well, it sounds like you have your career path all mapped out. For a girl who didn't think she had much of a future as an adult, you're doing pretty well at getting started!"

Kathie FitzPatrick was referring to all the times her Karen had come home from school, plopped down in a chair and stated flatly, "Mom, it's so hard to talk to the school counselors about my future. What future? They all want me to go to college. I keep having these feelings that I will never really grow up to be an adult. I don't think I'll live long enough to be a full grown adult who will have a marriage and a family. I don't know what to do about these feelings," she would say, looking dark and troubled. Kathie, helped her cope with these unusual premonitions as well as she could, advising her to "Make plans anyway. God knows our appointed time."

Just after midnight, July 10, 2001, Karen was called out from the Naches Ranger Station to join her fire crew in what later came to known as, The Thirtymile Fire. It became one of the most controversial, fatal forest fires in recent history, second only possibly to the Storm King Fire in Colorado that took the lives of 14 young firefighters in 1994.

On July 10, 2001, at approximately 5:20 P.M., in a thin and flimsy aluminum fire shelter, deployed on a rock scree, amidst screams, horror, and chaos, Karen knelt and prayed with her three trapped comrades, Jessica, Devin, and Tom, as they faced the point of entry to eternity. In her last breaths, she also prayed for the safety of those on the road below them who did survive. Their crew was entrapped by a mega crown fire that had advanced into an explosion and firestorm that suddenly raged upon them in the narrow Chewuch River Canyon near Winthrop, Washington, in the North Cascades. This time, four were killed. Eight firefighters and two campers survived. Who knows how or why God makes these eternal decisions? According to the coroner's report, at approximately 5:30 P.M. that day, as Karen and her entrapped comrades huddled together in their protective aluminum fire shelters, they succumbed to smoke inhalation and breathing products of superheated combustion, and died. A witness from the creek below, peeking up from under his fire shelter saw a fireball roll around then hit the rocks where they were like a torpedo. The fireball then flared up and rolled over them, like a "three pronged claw out of hell," he described later in a phone conversation to Karen's mom, Kathie.

The forces of good and evil at war again? It would seem so. But who was ultimately the real winner in this battle? At six o'clock on July 10, a mysterious cumulous cloud formed above them. At the top of the cloud were four linear steps. Since then, the dramatic photo of this cloud has come to be known as the Stairway to Heaven Picture, and has been placed at many of the memorials remembering the four young firefighters.

In the last hour before the explosion, as they were cut off in the USFS van by the fire and could not cross the road, the van in which Karen was a passenger turned around, parking near the entrapment site. "We're going to die," Karen had announced shortly before. Within twenty minutes before the explosion that sent the Thirtymile Fire totally out of control, she lifted her camera above her head and, with a huge smile and perfect joy, took a photo of her own face, as if to say to her Father in heaven, "I'll see you soon." She did.

Karen Lee FitzPatrick was believed, at that time, to be the youngest professional female career firefighter to die in the line of duty in America. She was 18 years old, slightly more than three weeks out of high school. (USFS records, and Fallen Firefighter of Emmitsburg, Maryland) You can read more about Karen at the www.lastalarm.net website. Look for Karen L. FitzPatrick, "Warmly Remembered." Additional references on the Thirtymile Fire story: Medal of Valor Firefighters by Michael Middleton, MacGraw Hill Books; The Thirtymile Fire, Chronicles of Bravery and Betrayal, by John Norman Maclean, Henry Holt Publishers, New York.

Graduation Night, June 8, 2001

There are few things I remember as vividly as snapping this picture. The ceremony was over and everyone was milling around down below on the main floor below the platform where all the young grads had just marched across to receive their diplomas.

Matt and Karen stopped briefly to hug, laugh, and pose for the photo. In a short while they and the others from the senior class of West Valley High School would change into casual party attire and board chartered buses that would transport them to the big graduation party about an hour's drive away.

Matt had been a really great and treasured friend of Karen's. He had been the "boy next door," or I should say down the street, who helped her with her homework and science projects and was also her last prom date in May 2001. After the last prom, Karen agonized with Matt over relationship issues, but ultimately freely released him to whatever he would decide about the future. Shortly after that, Matt did join the Navy and moved away from the area.

Only about four weeks later, while in training for the service in New Mexico, he heard the tragic news of the loss of four young firefighters near the Canadian border near the small mountain town of Winthrop, Washington. One of them was the glowing, loving Karen FitzPatrick. Heartbroken over such horrible news, he got permission for a short leave to rush back to Yakima. Matt arrived in town on July 17, just in time to join the procession to West Hills Memorial Park for the graveside service. Matt deposited into our hands these original poems he wrote about Karen. To me, they are such precious gems. Yes, Matt, we all wondered, Why did God have to take her? As time goes on, we can only guess. Thank you, Matt, for these wonderful poems.

> "Questions of Pain" 7-12-01
> By
> Matthew Lee Williams
>
> I sheed my tears
>   to releve the pain
> I wheap for her
>   to sooth the wound.
> I pray for her
>   to keep us strong
> I morn for her loved ones
>   to mind the hurt
> I never got to say goodbye
>   or
> tell her thank you for
> all she's done.
> I didn't get to give her
> one last hug
>   or
> see the smile that she
> never lost
> I miss her warm embrace
> I miss her guidance + laughter
> I ask "why did you have to
>   take her?"
> I ond get "she's done her job
>   here and its time for her
>   to be beside you."
>
> dedicated to: Karen Lee Fitzpatrick

"In your Hands"
By:
Matthew Williams

7-12-01

You took her from this
earth and placed her in
your hands.
Her devotion to you was
very strong.
She ~~was~~ a special person.
She gave me guidance by your
words.
She lived by your word, not
caring what others thought.
There was never hate in her,
just love and capation for
everything.
She had a life filled with
memories.
I wish she was still her.
I miss her so much.
But I know she is being taken
care of better than we could.
Take care of her and
"Keep her in your hands and
never let her go."
dedicated to Karen Lee Fitzpatrick, my best freind.

Senior Wills

I Karen Lee FitzPatrick, will Lacy Ann Chambers, all my love and God's blessing upon her bright future in ministry. Jessica Lynn Dean, all the pianos in the world to last those fingers a lifetime of success. Kathy Murry, a hot Ellensburg born wrestler at Gonzega to marry someday. Mr. Peters, a child to help create his own family and pass on his stories. They're all we have. Mr. Altshuler, a single personality. And my photography classmates, better subjects to talk about. Kelly West, a good singing voice at 7 A.M. and a bright future with her Evan, honey. Simone, an extra set of my car keys. Eva Lohrasbi, a giant stamp instead of all those stipple pens. Kelsey Volker, a Notting Hill experience with the handsome Prince William Charming. Kyle Obermiller, unlimited strength and a silent gaze through the weightlifting room's mirrors. Aaron Jameson, a promised future with Cheryl Purcell. Stephanie, my change purse. Last, but never least, Matthew Lee Williams, a yellow daisy, a hug every day, and a pair of ice skates from the best prom ever!

More About Karen

Getting Smacked Hard with a Strong Sense of Destiny

I sat in my brother's office in Charlotte, North Carolina. It was October of 2002, and we had just returned from the National Fallen Firefighter's Commemoration that was held in Washington, D.C. My brother, Dr. Joe Horacek, his wife, Debbie, and their children, Karen's first cousins, had experienced the honor of the events held over a four day period the week prior, to remember firefighters who perished in the year 2001, including the 9/11 firefighters and the Thirtymile Fire firefighters. The music, the processions, and the services were grand beyond all comprehension and description.

When Karen's picture came up—her high school senior picture in which she wore a demure blue top, sporting her bright eyes and dazzling white smile—on three large screens hanging down from the ceiling of the MCI center, the crowd of thousands gasped. There was a hush. "She is so young!" a voice in the crowd commented. As her family, we stood up briefly, then sat down again. It was near the end of that program. The four young firefighters from the Thirtymile Fire in Washington State were being recognized. We had just sat through three hundred and some odd number photos of the 9/11 firefighters in which friends of the New York City fire and police departments and their friends and families stood to remember them as well. It was starting to feel like being with family as we had just spent the last four days with the 9/11 firefighter families living in Marriott Hotels, eating meals together, sharing tears, photos, and stories of our lost loved ones. My brother's family had taken off early to head back home, and we were following a few days behind to join them for a visit there in Charlotte before returning home to Washington State.

His soft, brown leather couch felt comfortable to me as I watched him maneuver around the computer on his desk nearby. Joe had become somewhat the family historian, checking into names, relatives, and links going back into our Czech heritage.

"I'm having trouble figuring out which relative that Hapsburg connection is through," he commented in puzzled tones. "I'm sure it's through our grandmother's side." We talked more about it, fine-tuning some of the history and names we knew best through our father, Henry, and looking through some old childhood pictures of some of the family taken in Prague, Czechoslovakia, and Vienna, Austria.

"Look at this," he commented, as he prepared to show me something on his desktop computer. "Do you know what Horacek means in Czech?" Now the name, by the way, is pronounced "Hor-a-check."

"No, what does it mean?" I asked, with rising curiosity.

"It means, 'fire on a small mountain.'"

This hit me hard. Go figure. "Really!"

"It also refers to the refining fire." Joe brought up a long flame that covered the length of the screen. This was amazing. It had been a personal spiritual matter with both Karen and me—and any serious Christian, for that matter. The "Refiner's Fire" spoken of in the Bible is a symbol of the Holy Spirit's ongoing work in our lives.

"In Czechoslovakia, they often use it to make those clear glass beads with the little flowers in them." He said as he showed me some on his key ring and pulled a few out from his drawer. Only recently he had visited Czechoslovakia and had done a medical missionary trip to Romania, as well.

I said, "Now, of course, other people do have that name as well."

"Yep."

I was waiting for some divinely inspired, very deep explanation, but did not get any.

"Well, it's a sign to us, isn't it?"

"Yep."

How my life had been hit—marked, and will never again be the same—by a "fire on a small mountain," which was also my birth name.

More About Karen

I Wish I Had Known Karen Better

"I kinda knew Karen, but I wish I had known her better." We often hear this from some of her former high school peers in the community now that she's passed on. Well, for all those that say that to us, we say, "You really can know her better!," By reading some of her writings, you crawl right next to her very soul. In this collection, you'll hear some of the same words and same oral reports she gave live and in person in high school English and speech class. So read on and enjoy.

A Few More Comments from Karen

Karen FitzPatrick
3-15-01
Speech Period 3

SELF-CONFIDENCE

I bet that many of you could remember the first time you had to stand in front of a group of people to speak, either giving a report or simply helping the class figure out an assignment. It's very common to feel intimidated in those moments, especially if you don't do it much. The more you practice speaking in front of others, the more self confidence you will gain from those experiences.

One very good example of having self-confidence positively effective public speaking would be the poetry and drama class I took in the middle of last year. Writing good poetry was one challenging thing, yet reading it well in front of the class every Monday, was another thing. Most of the poetry written in the class was encouraged to be free style, and to mainly get us in the flow of opening us up to begin to write real poetry. As beginning poetry writers, most of us found that the best poetry we wrote was almost a little too personal to share with everyone. You could imagine this made it all the more difficult to read in front of the class. You were extra nervous and shaky.

Having the guts, or just pretending to, when each one went up to read their poetry, was all part of achieving more self confidence. How did it help one gain more self confidence? Perhaps it was to feel more free to express yourself in front of others. But in this class, that may have been an understatement of expression. Those students read to us their heart and soul; not just a speech to promote or educate others. This for some was almost next to impossible. Writing deeply about a parent or a close friend that died, however long ago, brought tears to the speaker's eyes as they would struggle to finish the remainder of the poem. Did they cry in part because of their lack of self confidence? It's hard to tell. Emotion can certainly affect the way a speech, public or poetic, can be presented.

After having that class all trimester, and up to the last day that I read one of my last poems, I almost still felt the way I did as I stood to read my first poem, in a class where I was alone. Everyone stood in my shoes when Monday's reading came. Being confident in the poem that I chose to write and perfect, somewhat helped my performing ability. When I knew my poem made sense and portrayed the subject well, I felt more proud to read my poem to the class. Your poetry does reflect your views and experiences in life. And, in turn, how self-confident you are will definitely come out in your poetry; your beliefs in death, love, hate, joy, and peace, will all be exposed in the light of poetry. This may cause some people to think twice before they will stand up to read their poetry, which remember, is a personal part of you.

Overall, self confidence is not only needed to make it through speaking about sensitive personal issues, but also to complete the image of what you are saying to your listeners. Even for a report, visual aids are nice to have when presenting information to a group. It is then true that the visual representation that you give when making a speech can just as well add or take away from what you are saying. Having a good level of self confidence will help you boldly have the strength to present your information well. Perhaps ways you can gain more self confidence would be to have your speech well rehearsed before the presentation and to know that your information is correct. If you ask me, I still need pointers on achieving more of this strength when speaking to groups of people at any time. But, as I'm sure, that's what we're all here to learn—how to build up our self confidence when speaking to others.

Karen's Thoughts on the Death Penalty: A High School Assignment.

Karen FitzPatrick
(CON) Death Penalty
Facts and Statistics

Introduction: The Death Penalty is the result in believing, "An eye for an eye and a tooth for a tooth." If anyone should produce death by murdering another, they themselves should die as referred by capital punishment. Our constitution clearly permits the death penalty practice and therefore is not unconstitutional. (Read highlighted part, then the Fifth Amendment. Note:) The Due Process Clause of the Fifth and Fourteenth Amendments says that no person shall be deprived of life without due process of law.

They are clearly treated as fairly as possible in the process of refuting justice.

- DNA and other high-tech methods are used to find who's truly guilty or innocent for the most part. The ones who are found to be guilty should be put to death. The RJA, Racial Justice Act, will enable a condemned inmate to challenge his death sentence, but not the underlying conviction. The RJA's goal is to eliminate race as a factor in the death penalty determinations. The RJA was included in the 1994 anticrime bill.
- The method of life extinguishment used with carrying out the death penalty is a lot more kind compared to the death they gave their victims. What would be inhuman and cruel would be if the murderers received the death they gave their victims.
- For Example: An eleven-year-old girl was raped by four men, then killed when they suffocated her by stuffing her panties down her throat. Did that little girl deserve that painful and horrible death? No! Those four men should die for what they did.
- Some may find this hard to believe, but back in January 17, 1977, Gary Mark Gilmore had a death sentence by a firing squad in Utah.

The way he approached his executioners was to encourage them to "Let's do it!" He was eager to face his death. Why is it that some inmates have such a strong death wish? It has been proven that some would rather be executed than be sentenced to life imprisonment. They answer "The state says that we're guilty and deserve death. Why prolong it? I don't want to spend the rest of my life in prison waiting for it to happen. They said it, and we'll be glad to do it."

- The death penalty should remain the same so that it will be feared by criminals to perhaps think twice when killing someone and getting caught. And those who do murder even say themselves that they're guilty and deserve death. Anyone who murders should themselves be murdered. Even if they are mentally retarded. They are still capable to kill, and therefore reap the consequences of their actions.

Rebuttal: (Show U.S. overhead) Thirty-eight of the fifty states in America practice some method of the death penalty in their states. We have been practicing it for so long as part of our law enforcement, why reverse it now?

(Show overhead of Chronology) This is our history in using the death penalty in different cases throughout our history, and it still remains a prevalent way to bring justice and vengeance to whom it's deserved.

- 73% of Americans already support the death penalty and only 38% say that only the most brutal murderers should be executed.
- If there are innocent people who don't deserve death, DNA testing will prove that. DNA testing from rape cases have led to the release of mainstream suspects in 26% of the cases sent for FBI analysis.

Notes Vs. Pro For Rebuttal:

This assignment was never finished. Karen had a sudden interruption in her thinking:

(Notes from Kathie, Karen's mom) Karen was working on this assignment for her high school world events class. The only time I saw her waiver from this principle was when Karen walked into our living room and caught me reviewing a video, "The Choice Is Yours," for use in my juvenile detention ministry with teenagers. Within the body of the video was the life testimony of David Berkowitz, formerly "The Son of Sam" serial killer.

As a young adult, David fell into a circle and ultimately a trap of Satanist friends who promoted a creed of murder and violence. Through association with them, the dark urges grew deeper. He ultimately wound up being convicted of six murders and given six life sentences in a state penitentiary in New York. After being in prison for 10 years, he came to the Lord through the testimony of an inmate friend, Rick, and a Gideon's New Testament, experiencing as genuine a conversion as anyone could. In time, he matured as a believer. For years now, David Berkowitz has written journal notes that are posted on the Internet by various ministries that bless many worldwide, and he is active in leading men's ministry in the prison. There are two websites: www.forgivenforlife.com and www.ariseandshine.org

Back to the testimony video: When Karen saw the light in his face and passion for Christ as he spoke, "I've been a Christian for 10 years now. I used to be called the 'Son of Sam,' but my new name is 'Son of Hope!'" he smiled in the 1998 edition of this video. Karen was bug-eyed.

"Wow, look at that!" Karen marveled. "Now, if they had killed him with capital punishment, he wouldn't be blessing all those people! I gotta really think about this now!" she said, rolling her eyes and leaving the room to go on to her next task. We talked about David's testimony from time to time, and she was truly impressed he was genuinely converted. So was I. Matter of fact, we have exchanged letters from March 2001 until the present, and David Berkowitz has inspired the teen felon boys I talk to in youth detention through both letters and video not to go down the same road he did, but to put God first in their lives for all the real answers in this present life. They listen. Believe me, they do.

By the way she talked, I thought Karen was going to write David B. at least once, but with the heavy schedule of that last senior year and with readying herself for graduation, it just never seemed to happen. I don't know where all her letters are, and I would love to find one sometime, but I'm sure not going to make anything up. She has a signature that no one can fake anyway! David was aware of Karen before she passed away, and it was a big shock when he heard her name on the news that broadcast the story on the radio in his prison cell. At first he could not believe his hears. He wrote to me immediately.

"Yes," I replied sadly. "You did have it right the first time."

David mentioned Karen and the fire episode a few times in his journal, but then dedicated his entire journal notes entry July 10, 2004, the third year anniversary of the Thirtymile Fire, to remember the life of Karen. It included pictures of her and "Karen Street" and ran about 10 pages long. In a new book out in 2006, "Son of Hope," (through Morning Star Publications) publishing his journal notes for all to see in book form, he placed a tribute to Karen on the Dedication Page. He wrote me about it earlier in 2006. "If they followed my instructions correctly, I placed a tribute to Karen on the dedication page of the new book." I was pleased to hear it. And, yes David, it is there!

Karen's Comments on Health:
A Homework Assignment

What an active summer I just finished! With the weather as hot as it was, drinking enough water is important to keep hydrated. At least 64 ounces a day is required for good health. Drinking more is required if one is active. For the past two weeks (Sept. 1–Sept. 14), I've kept a total for each day, how many ounces I drank and what kind of liquid it was. Then, I told how I felt from drinking enough water and how my health improved.

Part of a healthy diet is to drink enough water to keep you hydrated. Keeping lots of fluids flowing through the body will help you from getting sicknesses easier, like catching a cold or flu. Also, drinking the sufficient amount of water will make you feel better and more alert. Just like eating helps your brain to think better, from the promotion "Eat breakfast, think better in school." Just coming out of summer and into school, the weather was still hot, so it was easy to drink more water anyhow. But as the weather grew colder, and I was also busier with sitting at my desk to do homework, drinking a lot of water was not what I felt like doing when I was not so active. But if I keep track of my water intake, I can make sure to drink at least 64 ounces a day to keep a healthy feeling.

I drink more water than anything. If you refer to my intake report, you'll find that I drink more water than espresso, a little amount of soda pop, not too much juice, and not much milk as well. The variety of what I drink is almost just as important as how much I drink. No, I'm not addicted to caffeine. I've worked at Valerie's Espresso for almost two years, and I have a drink every time I work because it's free. What a deal, huh? Well, I don't drink as much pop because it's loaded with sugar, dehydrates you, and is bad for muscle tone. I could always look to increase my intake of fruit juice and milk for calcium and strong bones. Recently, I have been drinking a lot more juice because my family happens to have a bunch of apples that my sister likes to juice every day. So I drink a fair share of all that good stuff. But I will have to increase on my vegetable juice intake as well.

The report of benefit that I got back from my body was good in a few ways. I haven't been sick this year because of the inflow and outflow of fluids that kept me healthy and cleaned out so I wouldn't get rundown as easy. My dad always told me to drink a lot of fluids when I am sick to flush my body of the sickness. Getting your rest along with a healthy diet also contributes to this benefit. Benefits could very well depend on the kind of liquid you're drinking. Like caffeine being a drawback to the hydration process as well as soda pop drinks. So far, water is the healthiest liquid to keep flowing through your body.

Overall, it's interesting to look at the benefits and improvements in my health when taking record of my water intake. This will help me keep aware of the importance of drinking enough of the right fluids. Whether or not I've kept physically active, keeping hydrated is still important. I plan on continuing the intake record to an extent of keeping a keen awareness as part of my physical health. With hot or cold weather, eight cups a day will keep the doctor far away.

Mr. Dan Peters
West Valley High School
9206 Zier Road
Yakima, WA 98908-9298

Dear Mr. Peters:

The final portfolio that I have handed in to you presents the most improvements my writing has ever undertaken. A whole lot of work, time, and effort went into improving my writing when constructing the final drafts. As a senior in high school, I expect my writing level to be improving and expanding with creative ways of expression. The essays we read and referred to when writing our three essays helped open our understanding to new ways of arguing and creating a central point around a certain issue. Trying to maintain a clear point of view, when being a writer, is important yet hard to accomplish. I feel as though my writing searches for clarity rather than displaying it. Learning this helps explain why writers must write from a reader's point of view. Peer editing helped work this asset into our writing. Having good writers give suggestions about our essays is very helpful when in search for clarifying and correcting our own essays. This was a challenging task given us to know the best method of editing and revising our essays for the final drafts.

The first essay I revised for the portfolio was my second paper, "Lilies Grow in Difficult Places." This was my favorite, most organized and clear piece of writing I may have ever written. In this essay, I wasn't just arguing a point about an issue as in any other paper containing a normal thesis. But instead, this essay was about a personal experience I had when God changed my life around. The testimony of a changed life is a miracle and contains the powerful message of salvation. The friends that I had read the essay really liked the story and how the verses and parables fit in so well to act as metaphors. The comments you made most often on my writing was to be more clear. Then, as I would work on clarifying my experience, you would write on the bottom of the page or after a verse, "I see." At first, I thought my writing wasn't unclear, but instead, the experience itself. I found it hard to write about such feelings I've rarely experienced and almost didn't expect others to fully understand what I could not quite put into words. Even if this is the case, I feel pretty confident about the accuracy I portrayed in this essay when writing of my conversion. It's almost like poetry (writing inspired by passion).

The second essay I decided to revise for my portfolio was my last paper written, "Separated, Yet Connected." This essay also had some personal religious experience involved in it as well. In this paper, I related the Amish and Indian communities to each other, and the importance of why each society was separated from the modern dominant American culture. I referred to Mary Louise Pratt's essay, "The Arts of the Contact Zone" to describe the views she represented of the contact zones between different cultures. Then I took the idea of changing the original (culture) by and through reproduction from John Berger's essay, "Ways of Seeing," though he speaks of reproducing historical art. I've done the most revising to this essay. Adding research to this essay was one of the improvements made. My peers helped me present a counterargument of some kind showing how the Amish isolation could be detrimental to Amish communities as well. The others I had read my paper also liked the originality of the topic between the Amish and the Indians. You commented on most of my writing as being good, but my research and evidence as weak. I found it hard to clearly make connections to metaphoric insertions that I tried using. Trying to make these connections was the weakness of this paper. I had trouble constructing a thesis clearly in this essay, but by the third page I was able to insert one to help clarify the relation to the contact zones and the metaphor of a salad bowl American society. There were a lot of things I needed to "slow down and explain." Maybe the tone of my writing does this to me when I try to hit a main point. Sometimes I clearly describe a detail and other times I run over information that could be more important if I dug down deeper. Evening out this tone will be what is fair to all my writing. This essay exposes the flaw in mostly the third and fourth pages. The particular strength of this essay was the conclusion. "If you have a good intro and conclusion, your paper is made," I remembered hearing. Doing this was a big help to the essay following through when making that tie between the introduction and conclusion. Just one of the many tips I've picked up in this English class.

I decided not to insert my first essay, "Narcissism as Suppression," because my writing had simply not improved by then. For this first assignment, I didn't quite know how to be original with my ideas. I took a lot of Susan Douglas' ideas and even half of the title of her essay. Therefore, I was not confident about this essay in that way. You told me in your comments that it was a good first essay, and I do believe it contained good writing, but not my best. I didn't appear to have much trouble with being clear because I restated a lot of facts in slightly different ways-you can't go wrong there. Constructing our own argument and thesis is the hardest. Referring back to my first essay, my peers editing was mostly mechanical errors or cutting down my tendency for wordiness. You and they seem to agree with my presented argument with the facts and evidence given in Douglas' essay, "Narcissism as Liberation." This essay was no doubt a strong essay with a relative point about our modern trend society. Not everyone may be acquainted with the word narcissism, but they're sure forced to experience what it means when referring to fashion. But again, I expected my better work later in the trimester.

All three essays from the assignment sequences were a pleasure to write when learning so many new ways to express an argument. The metaphoric transitions we as a class learned to use really helped our essays become original and conscious of many other relative points worth mentioning. Using metaphors in our writing helps organize the structure of an essay and helps our readers expand their level of understanding, hopefully. I always found out if this was true or not when others would read my essays and try to make perfect sense of them. Working to make the corrections on my essays was where my writing developed most, making sense in the midst of all the confusion. These are just a few of the many contributions to my writing that I've picked up in another wonderful trimester in Mr. Peter's class.

"Thanks for direction, Peters."

—Karen Lee FitzPatrick

More About Karen

Karen FitzPatrick
5-22-01
Speech per. 3

Three Things in a Brown Bag Speech

Now, if I were to live on one of Hawaii's islands, that in itself would be a dream come true. But, of course, I haven't got to visit Hawaii yet. But I will.

First of all, living on a Hawaiian island would force you to live a more simple life. Fewer things are better, right? Personally, I'm not a very materialistic or vain person. And I believe I've been raised to not be. The first thing, as I was taught, was not to store up riches on earth, but in heaven where no one can steal or destroy it. For where your treasure is, there will your heart be also. My Heavenly Father cares more for my needs. So He tells me not to worry. You've probably already guessed where these sayings are found. The Bible would be the foremost possession I would take to this island, because man shall not live or be sustained by bread alone, but by every word that proceeds from the mouth of the Living God. Jesus gave His reply to Satan when He was in the wilderness. So I guess this reply is sufficient for me as well.

The vitality of the Bible itself is one thing, and its importance in my life is another. I just don't leave home in the morning without having looked into it for direction and pray to God for strength to help me walk in it. I could always use more devotion to studying this book so that it will come alive for me. But when I read it, I always look for something I can do or obey. Reading the Bible is useless unless you act upon what it says.

Second of all, I would bring my trusty old hymnal along to lift my spirits by singing a song or two. This hymnal has direct correlations with the Bible as well. As you may know, I love to sing. And another thing you may know is that some of these songs may date to over three hundred years old. A little old-fashioned for you? No, just when sung by old people, maybe. The words to these songs are what really matters. The words tend to uproot you out of your nonproductive, complacent life and help establish you in the true and narrow way. In my church, our hymnals came from churches who were throwing them away to revert to singing more comfortable choruses instead, I guess. But as for me, being the song leader my church, it is my job to pick and lead the songs for each Sunday. So far, these first two books play a huge part in my life. Yet I couldn't separate one from the other.

Third of all, since I love to cook—and bake especially, that's when I have time, of course, I would bring one of my favorite cookbooks along. You don't always find me in the kitchen. But when you find me there, some of my favorite desserts to bake are lemon meringue, apple, or cherry pies, strawberry meringue tortes, chocolate mouse layered cake, German chocolate cake, maple syrup frosted carrot cake. And don't worry, lunch is within the hour yet, in case you are getting hungry! I do like to experiment on new recipes I find and not just make the same things all the time.

The reasons I bake are for birthdays, special occasions around the holidays, for church potlucks, and sometimes just for my family. My dad loves berry pies. But on this island, whichever in Hawaii will do, I'm sure I'll learn to cook Hawaiian style and perhaps even open up my own restaurant someday.

Karen FitzPatrick: "Why I Want to Be a Firefighter"

5-31-01
Speech Final

For some people, deciding on a future career is easier for some than for others. How do you choose just one talent from the number you're given? In my case, I could be a singer, an artist, a musician, a beautician, a physical trainer, or a gourmet chef like Martha Stewart, who's all in one. Then what about my strength? I may not be a big bodybuilder, but I have endurance that I'd like to keep my whole lifetime. What career would best fit my image? Firefighters have an image of having superhuman strength that makes them heroes of the day, while, on the other hand, policemen who fight crime don't get nearly the image over giving out unreasonable speeding tickets and liking jelly donuts too much. Firefighters are also good cooks. Since they live at the station for half the week, they get the chance to wine and dine in their own fabulous kitchen.

When I began thinking about what job would use the most of my talents, I began drawing conclusions from a personal experience that I had on the 4th of July almost three years ago. At ten o'clock Friday night, a fire was started next to my house by some illegal fireworks. The fire moved quickly toward my house as it burned the brush on the hill just over our fence. My family woke me up to come and help put it out with garden hoses. So in my flannel shorty pajamas and thongs, I grabbed a hose to squirt up over the fence. Within minutes, our dry cedar fence would be on fire. So I jumped the fence into the fire and stomped it out away from the fence and watered the base of the fire out. Soon, the firefighters came and had trouble getting their equipment down the hill from the road above our house, so they used our garden hoses for a while. Later, they came looking for me to thank me and told me I did a good job "saving my own bacon." I guess that meant my fence.

In turn, this experience led me to choose my required job shadow to be at the fire station. Since I was doing this as a requirement, I didn't really know if I would be interested in it or not. So when I went last October, Friday the 13th, I remember, I went out on one of the twelve-hour shifts from 9 A.M. to 9 P.M. It was really cool talking to most of the firefighters who were giving me a tour of the station. I acquired some pretty good advice on how to get started as a firefighter as they told me about their own experiences through the years. Just by observing them, I could tell how much they loved their jobs.

Two of the women firefighters I spoke to told me that they started out in the forestry wildfire fighting seasonal jobs and also volunteering. So that's what I'm planning on doing this summer. This job is mostly forestry with fighting occasional fires. I can get experience without having a lot of prior college training. Then, after getting some experience, some of the schooling needed to apply to be a firefighter would be your EMT. (Emergency Medical Technician) fire science course from YVCC, or get a "firefighter one" which is an out of town course that includes all prerequisites needed. Or you could go into the Army reserves for eighteen weeks and be paid five thousand dollars along with acquiring your "firefighter two." I was just called last night about that, and that may save me a lot of time and even making money. Isn't that what the Army's there for?

But anyhow, a lot of firefighters may not even make their first year of probation before getting hired on because the probation year is a testing period of when firefighters can be fired at any time due to poor training habits. As you can imagine, this may be the most stressful year of a firefighter's life. One of the most difficult things to accomplish when on your first year training on probation is memorizing the map of the city then having to draw it with all the streets and landmarks freehand. They do this because they all share the responsibility of driving. A lot of the training is done at the station. They are always updating drills and learning how to use newer and better equipment. But besides all these wonderful things you must learn down to an instinct, a firefighter must be in top physical shape.

More About Karen

With a combination of weightlifting, aerobics, and yoga, firefighters mostly work on muscle toning and cardiovascular fitness. Without this training, you could die. The reason why yoga is important is to keep flexibility and to regulate metabolism. A good thing to remember when working out is that if you get too big, you might not fit through a window. A good example of physical training class would be the Eric Torre's New York Fire Department Combat Challenge Real-Life-fitness obstacle course. He tailored his crunch after actual firefighter techniques. This way you have a chance to work your training into fitness and second nature instinct.

Along with keeping fit and having a good diet, keeping hydrated is essential. When it gets hotter outside, don't you want to drink more water? Well, of course. Try being in an 800 degree environment. Firefighter's bunker gear is hot even without being in a fire. But when you step into a fire, there's a two minute rule in and out, to break for water. This, among many other factors, are just some of the dangers to worry about. But there are so many benefits to this job, and they outweigh the disadvantages by far. Helping people solve emergencies, possibly saving lives, and helping people in any way to keep them safe, are all concerns I would have as a firefighter.

So far, firefighting will keep me actively helping others and staying in shape. Also, I can occasionally cook my favorite foods for everyone while living at the station, and you never know when singing may come in handy! They sure can get bored around there sometimes! I think firefighting will make use of all the talents I have inside me! It takes a certain kind of person to be a firefighter, and I think I am one of them.

As graduation nears and I make plans for the future, I consult my Master for all directions, because ultimately, as you know, I've given my life to be used by God. Sure, He could be glorified in my helping others by firefighting, but what about doing what He wants? This consideration is one every follower of Christ has to make. I am not my own. I was bought with a price when He forgave my sin. I've always prayed to God to lead me in the way my future is to go and go work His plans into my plans. Yet that is how I've taken firefighting recently. I've never had the childhood dream of firefighting, maybe like Kelsey who's done ballet all her life and has that dream. Yet I have built-in characteristics I never knew that God would lead me in this direction to perform. So I will take each day He gives me as an opportunity to further His purposes when always keeping in mind Jude 1:23, which says to "Strive to save others, snatching them out of the fire and destruction." This application I take as literal, physically and spiritually. God has given me this command, among many others, which I will use to guide me in my future pursuits.

—Karen Lee FitzPatrick

Karen's Journal Notes

Jude 1:23; Strive to save others, snatching them out of the fire; on others take mercy

Karen's journal, an amazing collection of writings: a combination of Bible verses, spiritual revelation, and personal experiences written down in ordinary spiral notebooks. Some entries were notes from her Bible studies, some were her own personal views, daily trials, victories, and, hopefully, lessons learned. Her last entry was July 6, 2001.

Karen used to love to write things down that impressed her and make record of her feelings and personal experiences. She also used to collect wise sayings, proverbs and Bible verses. Some were posted on her walls as constant reminders. Some were tucked away in diaries and journals, and some sayings she created herself. She was also very interested in what the Bible had to say about fire. She became fascinated with the verse in Jude 1:23 that states we should make every effort to "snatch them from the fire," meaning we should share the gospel with everyone while there was yet time and help save them from hell, and Psalms 66:10, "You have purified us with fire, O Lord like silver in a crucible." Karen prioritized sharing the reality of heaven and hell, and how to not go to hell often. People listened as she spoke out of great authority and love for others. Seeds that she planted in people's hearts about eternity and the need for salvation grew and are still flourishing today. This is another way she lives on.

Preluding her last few weeks before going to the fire, Karen was caught up in a whirlwind of romantic dilemmas and decisions about relationships. She was extremely fond of Matt, who was the neighbor boy, the guy who helped her with science projects and was her high school prom date in May of 2001. After the prom, Matt delivered heartbreaking news to Karen that he was in love with a girl from a family where he was renting a room in their house. Matt also revealed that he anticipated joining the Navy and moving far away out of state. Such is life sometimes, in the volatile and ever changing, budding new lives of youth Karen's age, just branching out into the new beginnings of adult life.

While in training, then later working for the U.S. Forest Service, Karen met a new friend, Aaron R., who she thought seemed to have a huge resemblance to her childhood sweetheart Dan, thought to be out of the picture forever. Dan and Karen's forced breakup by Karen's dad when Karen was about 14 had left a broken-hearted trail of both memories and emotion that did not seem to be easily mended. Plus, Dan was afraid of Karen's dad—and for good reasons.

Then, at the age of 18, as Karen began to spend more time near the Naches Ranger Station in Naches for the USFS, near Dan's family home, Dan started coming back around. Already a little jealous because his younger brother Matt C. had donned a tux and taken Karen to the romantic "Bed Of Roses" homecoming event, in the fall of 2000, by June of 2001, Dan had reemerged as a young adult of 20, ready to try to win Karen back. In her last journal entry of July 6, 2001, Karen describes the possible reuniting of her and her early teen sweetheart.

Since Dan's family lived up in the mountains not far from the Naches Ranger Station, it gave them a chance to spend more time together, romping and playing on the 4 x 4 vehicles in the mountains and walking in the woods, just talking and dreaming together about many things. Sometimes Karen wondered if she would ever be allowed to reunite with Dan. There were volatile feelings and opinions among both their friends and families on the prospect. By this time, Dan had another girlfriend in the background as well. Such drama! Who knows how all this would have eventually played out? It is only written on the wind.

Karen's Journal Notes

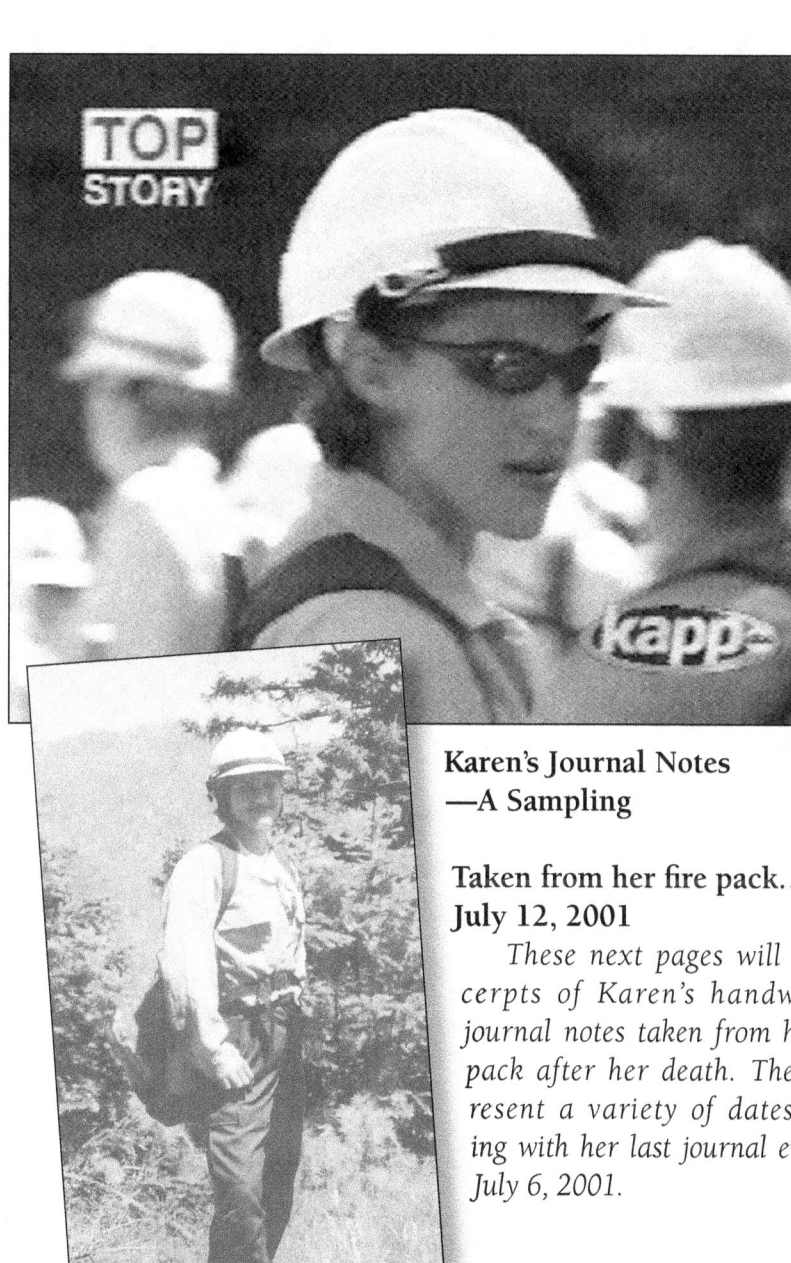

**Karen's Journal Notes
—A Sampling**

**Taken from her fire pack...
July 12, 2001**

These next pages will be excerpts of Karen's handwritten journal notes taken from her fire pack after her death. They represent a variety of dates, ending with her last journal entry of July 6, 2001.

March 3, 2000
When the heart speaks,
The mind turns to peanut-butter

Enjoy who you are.
Don't hate yourself
for what you aren't.

— Heather Graham

✶

Confidence and belief in one's self are almost essential to one's success, but conceit is the one certain poison to kill all chance of it.

Take your victories and defeats in your stride, and keep your feet on the ground and your head a triffle smaller than your hat.
— Bill Tilden (SCP)

March 3, 2000

A man who wants to lead the orchestra must turn his back on the crowd.

Before you say anything about anyone, let your words pass through three gates: Is it true? Is it kind? Is it necessary?

Kind words can be easy to speak but their echos are truely endless.

— Mother Teresa

Love your life poor as it is.

March 3, 2000   4

A friend can tell you things you don't want to tell yourself.

— Frances Ward Weller

Worry is the misuse of imagination.

Blessed are the flexible for they shall not be bent out of shape.

Trouble is a part of your life, and if you don't share it, you don't give the person who loves you enough chance to love you enough.

— Dinah Shore

It takes a women a long time to learn that flirtation is attention without intention

Anything that angers you conquers you.

You can't be brave if you've only had wonderful things happen to you.

The most handicaped person in the world, is a negative thinker.   SCP

Andy.S
Persistence is the key. Determination, hard work and good intentions are all brought together with persistence. Ignore the pessimists who want to bring you down, and stand in the way of your dreams

April 19, 2000

'Most of today's Christians are their own worst enemy and are blind to that fact.'
— Karen Fitzpatrick

Jai-D's Salon & Gifts
Hair • Nails • Massage • Tanning • Facials • Pedicures

Mary Ahmady
Hair Stylist

7200 West Nob Hill
Yakima, WA 98908   509-966-3528

April 18, 2000
'The cutest hair cut around.'

Sometimes, settling for less than you hoped for can be just as satisfying, even for others.
   — Ms. Stylish 2000 K

May 12, 2000   Our Town.
— A second of reflect: (what I don't want to leave behind)
Aaron — I will attempt to put into words how I feel: You're are so beautiful, to me no better words can express this, but trying can't hurt. Everything about you is so magical, & inquisitive. Nothing more has ever amazed me more than to listen to you speak and to watch your way of living. But It's like your sailing on cloud 9, and I'm so far behind to even catch a glimps of your eye, just a second of your time, to tell you; that I love you.

you mean so much to me...

July 31, 2000

Today I write in relating to 6-20-00 back when I received Christ as my Lord and Saviour. But the quote at the beginning of this journal reminds me of how my perspective has been after I received Christ. Looking back will surely not help me unto victory. But sometimes the past isn't easily forgotten. Like when Mark still calls me at times or past feelings arise as I forget what misery they caused me, & the sin looks sweeter than I once discovered but forgot like Jesus' dicsiples. Lord help me to hate the things you hate in my life. I went to fall in Love with the Lord as my Husband, but how do I grow into that Love when I need it now?

Karen's Journal Notes

August 9, 2000

Today was a great day! (No bad Luck involved!) I cleaned rooms at Gameridge Motel with Dee, then worked Espresso. I had a great opportunity to talk with Leslie about the things I've been learning (true faith, apostasy, and my daily reading John 10). I was encouraged to share, warn & admonish the best I know how, & then also just listened. I mostly prayed that God would lead her into all truth if she was truley willing to find & receive it. I sang hymns as well, There is A Fountain, There's room at the Cross, What A Friend we have in Jesus and Come Holy Spirit, Heavenly Dove –

Yesterday's Bible study lesson mostly encouraged us to want to confess Jesus freely and openly so He will freely confess us before the Father for forgiveness of sin and intersecion prayers. [Luke 12:8]. I need to be more devoted each day to Jesus changing me & me giving of myself to Him. I'm going back to school for my Senior Year! Pretty soon and I need to get established in a regular patern of studying, praying, and confessing Jesus. I pray for wisdom when I am to make him known. I don't want to misrepresent Him. So I'll just stick to my testimony and that Jesus is the only way to salvation. Praise His Holy Name for All His blessings on those who are His!

Karen's Journal Notes

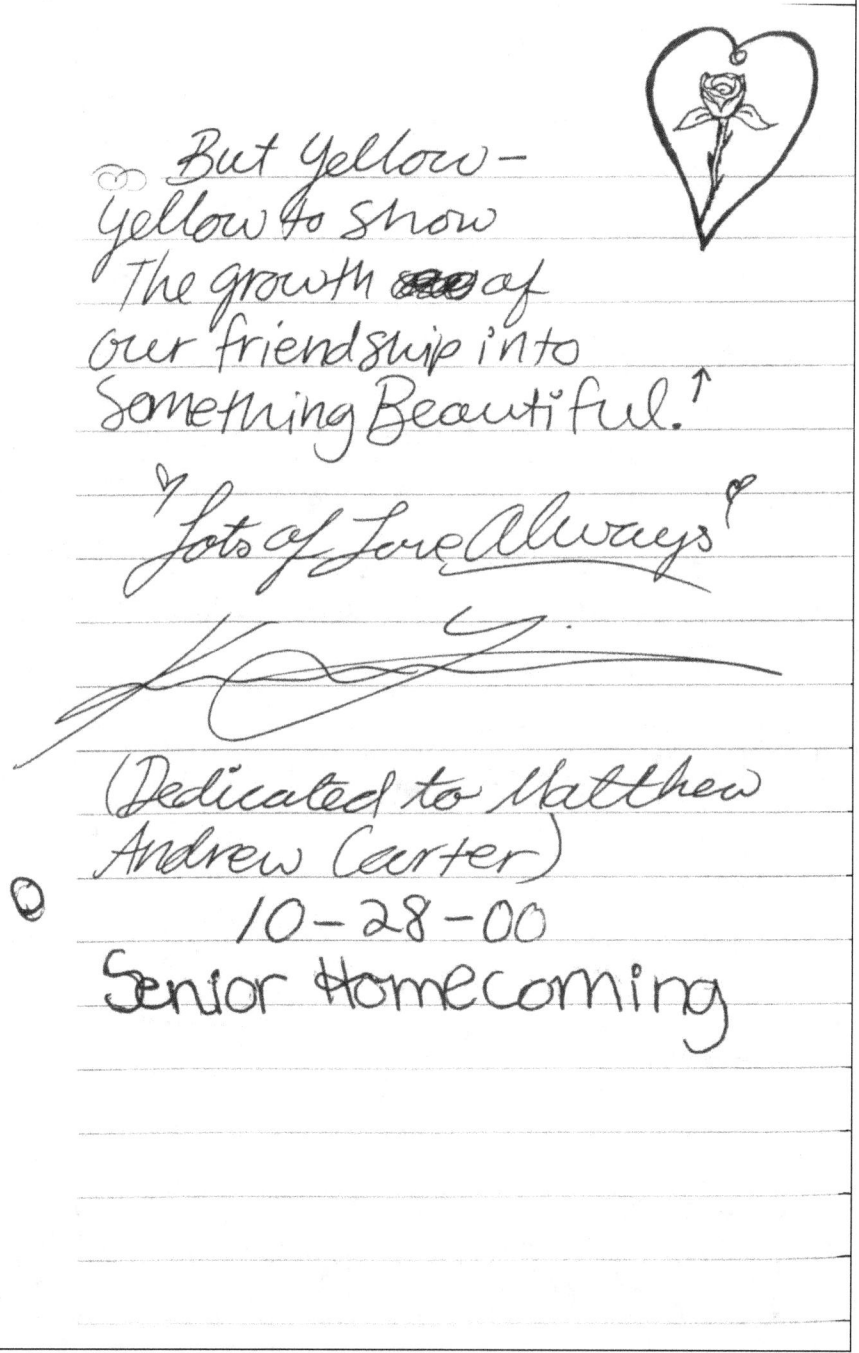

But Yellow—
Yellow to show
The growth ~~and~~ of
our friendship into
something Beautiful.

"Lots of Love Always"

(Dedicated to Matthew
Andrew Carter)
10-28-00
Senior Homecoming

(A NEW YEAR, A NEW Start!)
February 6, 2001   I AM 18
                   12-27-01

Sooo, much as happened to me since I last recorded any thing in this book of thoughts. But this isn't a journal. If I started writing about it, I don't think it would stop. A brief soon summery is: Mark Bachteller came in into my life and showed me how much I needed Jesus Christ in my life. On ~~father~~ June 20, 2000 at 2 PM I received the Lord and became born again. WOW! Simply great! 5 months later I was back in the pig pen with my first love's little brother after Homecoming. one month I got into an car accident months after that, I realized that I attract 45 yr-old men, — one of my best friends and a guardian of my soul — yeah, you know who. But I can faithfully say, God surely protects me through all the crap that come my way. It's always

Karen's Journal Notes

Last night, I dremt that I put my love life past Behind me, never again to affect my future. I dremt that Dan had died and layed in a coffin. To let him go, I stood beside him lying there, took off my necklace w/ ring and put it on him saying, "Take the past with you, it will never live again." I must not look back, I will never be fit for the Kingdom if I don't steadfastly put my hands to the plow and strive on

I will never quit trying —

K

There is too much for me to lose, yet everything to GAIN

for my good!

March 6, 2001

The close of this very difficult Trimester is very near and finals are just around the corner.

AP English &
AP Government

          C
Wilson 680. +
1984 245. +
crucible & 200. +
Lasser
Hamlet 500. +
All Kings Men 180. =
       2,105.
Pages
Read this
Trimester.

Poetry is disscribed in meeny different ways:

- The spontaneous overflow of ~~the~~ powerful feelings
  — William Wordsworth

- A Revelation n words by means of words.
  — Wallace Stevens

- The clear expression of mixed feeling.
  — W. H. Auden

~~Seniorities~~ Senioritis is kicking In.

DOWN WITH OVERLOAD!

March 9, 2001 (replaced left head light)

Dear Mr. Peters,

    I'm sure you're used to only hearing the best from your former senior students after they take your classes, & I can see why. You do have one of the most rewarding careers that exist. I'm even kind of sad I don't have a class 3rd trimester with you, but still, the end isn't until June.

    Thank you for being you. A Good teacher makes school what it ought to be; a place to learn and project our stories. Life would be a mess without people who teach, guide and care enough to impact others lives for the better.

Sometimes I wonder where'd I be without looking to my Savior to change me inside out. Jesus teaches me by His example and His message. Both is needful when effectively teaching others. I pray that someday you will fully <u>rest</u> in understanding the simplicity life in Christ holds only if <u>you will let</u> your trust lie in Him for <u>ALL</u>. <u>Nothing</u> is more sweeter...

"Lots of Love Always" ♡

Karen Lee Fitzpatrick

— Tomorrow we enter the end. —
3rd Trimester begins 3-14-01

July 6, 2001

Senior pictures, prom (Matt), Graduation, Fire fighting & Aaron Micheal Rowe (Dan). A list of things I already know and would be needless to write about $ now. I'm on my first fire mop-up down on the Dalles of the Columbia River. It beautiful & fun yet my feet are just killing me! My new cell phone works well & I want to use it more than I should because I miss everyone. & I've only been gone a couple of days after only getting a couple hours of sleep because Dan & I stayed up late 4xing & talking about our promised future together. It's so out of the normal but it's happening between us again. It never

Karen's Journal Notes

stopped & if God truly allows it, He will give Dan a new life and me to be his wife. He & I truly do fit to make one, eventually.
　　Lord, please help me to abstain until I can be ~~eomep~~ committed to Dan in marriage. My promise & chasity ring will keep its meaning with God's help (Aaron). I need to show the world how it works.
— "Make me Salty Lord."

"Lots of Love Always"

LETTERS FROM AND TO AMBER...

Karen Lee FitzPatrick, age 18

Karen participated in Young Lion's Youth Ministry Program by writing letters of encouragement to teenaged girls who were incarcerated.

Karen was too young to join me personally in the Young Lion's Youth Ministry Program in Youth Detention, but she took interest in the teen girls I worked with who were incarcerated. Here is a sampling of her letters from and to Amber:

March, 1999

Dear Karen,

Thanks for writing to me. It was really sweet. It has been three weeks since someone wrote to me. Anyway, my name is Amber Lee Mc———. I'm 17, almost 18. I'll be 18 in July. Yeah!

Well, I met your mom almost a year ago. I was going down the drain, big time. Your mom helped me find myself and the Lord. And it worked! I found Him hiding in my heart deep down inside. Well, to make a long story short, He is with me 24/7. I pray every night, and I'm reading the Bible right now. I started from the beginning to the end. Right now, I'm in Matthew chapter 6. I have been doing a lot of studying and prayer—so much that I feel like I'm going crazy. So anyway, you're 16, huh? A year younger than me. I have a question. Would you mind us becoming something like a pen pal? Cause right now I need a friend more than anything else. So would you mind?

Is your church school—is that like "home schooled?" Cause I used to be home schooled, but it didn't work. I had to be with others! So you're probably wondering why I'm in here and for how long. It's okay. I made a mistake, and now I'm dealing with it. I'm in Echo Glen for a theft charge. I got 15 to 36 weeks. I leave here in November '99, or maybe sooner. I have already been in here for about a month, and it feels like I just got here!

Thanks for the picture of you. You are very pretty! You look a lot older! On the back it says WVHS. Does that stand for West Valley High School? Well, I used to go to East Valley Central a long time ago, but not now!

Well, I don't really know what to say, but thanks! Ask me some questions—anything. I'm not embarrassed to answer anything. Hope we can become very close friends. Tell your mom to write to me, and that I said "Hi."

P.S. It was nice meeting you! Oh yeah, my favorite song is, "There's Power in the Blood."
Ever hear of it?
Bye,
Sincerely, your friend,
Amber Mc———.

March 5, 1999; 8 P.M.

Dear Amber:

Hello, I am Kathie's 16-year-old-daughter Karen, and I would like to do what I can to help you with your spiritual needs. Jesus is my Lord and Savior, and He has set me free from my sin! I go to an all-day home church on Sundays that teaches me many things in the Bible that I wouldn't normally hear in church. My mom doesn't go because she is involved in Stone Church. But anyway, I would like to share some things that should encourage you.

1.) Read in the Gospels where you can really learn about Jesus.

2.) Don't go by your feelings. We Christians live by faith!

3.) Philippians 4:6 "Do not fret or have anxiety about anything, but in every circumstance and in everything, by prayer and petition (definite requests), with thanksgiving, continue to make your wants known to God."

I love the Word of God! And certainly we need to love it, because it's alive and full of power (Hebrews 4:12) and has the power to save our souls! (James 1:21). Yes, there are lonely times in the Christian walk, but God says in Proverbs 18:24 that many friends will prove themselves a bad friend but there is one who sticks closer than a brother. We aren't alone with Jesus by our side. Since we certainly won't always be popular telling people what you learned in your Bible reading, as it may convict them of sin and disgrace them, but God will be surely honored, and that's what counts!

I personally will admit to you that being my age and living by this brings loneliness and trouble sometimes, but this is actually supposed to encourage us. In the letters of the apostle Paul, he describes sometimes how his life is going. And he would even get beaten and walk away rejoicing! But anyhow, you must grow up in these things. Don't worry too much about it now where you're at. I'm just sharing some things in the Word.

The most encouraging thing I find in the Gospels, has to do with how much Jesus loves us. How He teaches the disciples valuable lessons, heals people, and gives parables with priceless meanings. Even in John 3:3 when Jesus tells Nicodemus that "you must be born again to even see the kingdom of heaven. Some are like in Matthew 7:24-29 about how if you act on (obeying) the Word, you hear you will be building your house upon the Rock and have a firm foundation. If you hear the Word, and don't act on it, you are like the unwise man building his house on the sands, and when the storm came, great was the fall of it. Now stop and think about this. If you hear (faith comes by hearing what is preached from the Word of God, Romans 10:17) the Word of God and really take it to heart and act upon obeying it, doing this will make you strong in the Lord, and stand firm in the storms of life. But if when you hear and do nothing about it, you will be building on the sand and will fall in calamity when trouble comes. Remember: you are always building on one of these two grounds.

Matthew 6 is so good! Read it. It is so practical and easy to grasp and relieves the stress of everyday life. Not having to always worry about making ends meet, and just simply getting the hang of trusting Jesus to have more of your commitment. Jesus is so good Through my experiences in reading and praying there is a quiet time I can spend afterwards by shutting everything else out and just thinking of Jesus and what good I just read about Him. There is such blessed peace and confident trust that comes with doing this. Jesus has said many things encouraging such practices. Like in Luke 10:41-42 when Martha was troubled about many things, as many are today, and told her sister to help her, but she was listening to Jesus, at his feet. So He replied to Martha there is need of only one, or but a few things. Mary has chosen the good portion, which shall not be taken away from her.

You can count on Jesus to be there for you. In Hebrews 13:5, the Word says that God will not forsake you nor let you down. Be encouraged, Amber! Hebrews says that we have a High Priest (Jesus Christ) who understands everything we go through, even temptations, as He did experience when He was human. So for this, let us boldly draw near to the throne of grace to receive mercy for our failures, and to find help coming just when we need it!

Lots of Love Always,
Your Sister in Christ,
Karen Lee FitzPatrick

Nearing the Time of the Fire...

Karen wrote a very meaningful note inside her graduation picture jacket bearing the favorite black and white photo she used to send to friends and family in a formal black photo jacket with a silver lining. She wrote in silver pen to her grandparents these words:

Dear Grandparents:

June 2, 2001

I'm finally graduating! It actually came a lot sooner than I expected (I still don't feel like I'm graduating). I thought to send you a senior portrait of myself that I developed in my photography class. Neat, huh? I sure like that class.

For the summer I've been hired on by the Ranger Station up at the Pass to do forestry and wildfire fighting. This way I'll get some experience in time for the bad fire season ahead. But overall, I plan on living out God's will and plans for my life and not mine. So pray that I'll always follow His directions! I miss all of you down there!

XOXOXOXO!

Lot's of Love Always,

Karen Lee

Karen's Journal Notes

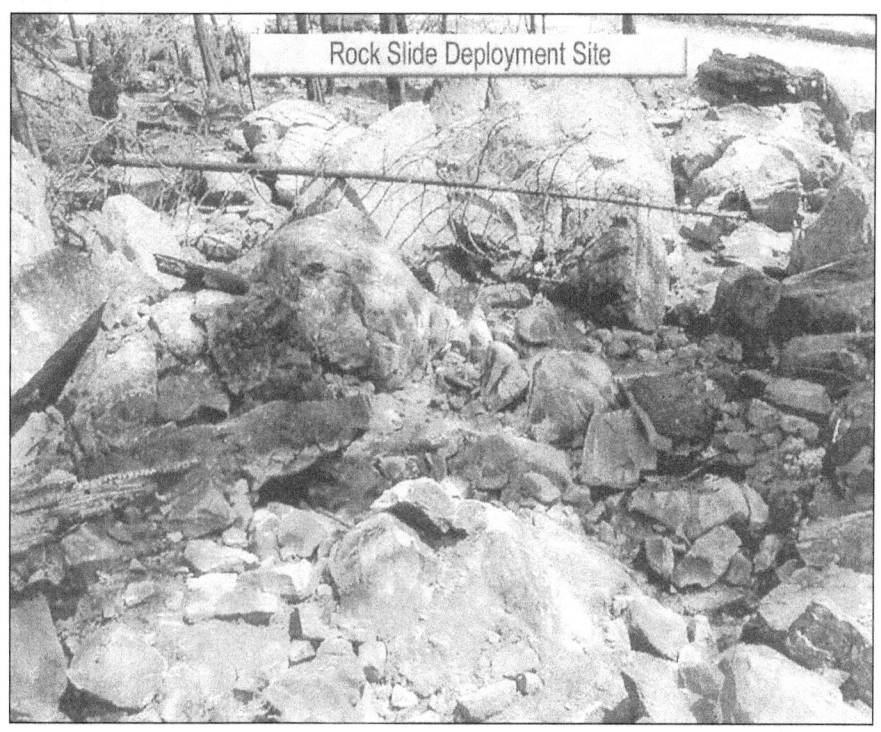

7/10/01

"In God, understanding becomes a state of heart, rather than an achievement of the mind."

—Karen Lee FitzPatrick, from the Wall Writings of Karen Street

About the Author

A native of the San Francisco Bay Area, Kathie FitzPatrick was born in Berkeley, California, and raised primarily in the Walnut Creek-Danville area of the east bay region. Kathie excelled as a young person in high school in the areas of advanced art, advanced drama, public speaking, musical performance, and writing. As an adult, Kathie spent the major portion of her professional career life in the creative areas such as writing and television producing. She also attended Solano College in Suisun City, California, for television production.

In 1990, the family moved from Benicia, California, to the Pacific Northwest. Kathie continued in the field of television producing for a season, but then took a big career leap into real estate in 1994. Kathie currently works actively in real estate and is also an income property owner and investment specialist. Her other strong interest lies in the area of heading up a youth services nonprofit organization specializing in youth detention, antiviolence, and teen rehabilitation. Young Lion's Youth Ministry Program, based in Yakima, Washington, has been in existence since 1997. See www.younglions.org "Extreme Teen Rescue," by Kathie FitzPatrick, is a program/manual that helps others successfully spearhead Young Lion's Youth Ministry Program groups in youth detention centers in their local communities. Currently, groups exist around the USA, Canada, and overseas. Karen was too young to come in with the local Young Lion's group founded and headed by her mom, Kathie, but sometimes wrote letters to the teen girls who were incarcerated. One of those letters, "To Amber," is included in Angel Promises.

Kathie currently lives in a large, three floor home adorned with antique stained glass windows in the Yakima Valley region overlooking the West Valley, which was the original family home since 1990. She shares the house with her young adult daughter Jaina FitzPatrick, two male cats, Kirby and Mufferd, and Karen's fish, Sobe, (third generation clone) a real character for a beta fish. The house, nestled up in the hills of West Yakima, is affectionately called "The Pink Castle." It is.

Kathie FitzPatrick desires to continue to further the story of the Thirtymile Fire in the effort and hope to eventually see greater strides made in the area of firefighter safety for all firefighters in the future.

Kathie enjoying the butterfly conservatory in Niagra Falls, Canada.

In the apple orchard. Yakima is world famous for apple production.

Kathie FitzPatrick as the Director/Founder of Young Lions Youth Ministry Program

www.ingramcontent.com/pod-product-compliance
Lightning Source LLC
Chambersburg PA
CBHW052007070526
44584CB00016B/1656